TROPICAL RAIN-FOREST

THE LEEDS SYMPOSIUM

Other publications of the Leeds Philosophical and Literary Society

Proceedings of the Leeds Philosophical and Literary Society: **Literary and Historical Section**
Vol. xix, Part V, 1984: *Philosophers, Iosis and Water of Life* by C. Anne Wilson

Proceedings of the Leeds Philosophical and Literary Society: **Scientific Section**
Vol. xi, Part III, 1983: *Biomass, Chlorophyll Concentration and Calorific Content Dynamics of Epiphytes on Larch Trees in Southern England* by B. D. Turner

TROPICAL RAIN-FOREST

THE LEEDS SYMPOSIUM

EDITED BY

A. C. CHADWICK AND S. L. SUTTON

Department of Pure and Applied Zoology
University of Leeds
Leeds LS2 9JT, U.K.

SPECIAL PUBLICATION OF THE

LEEDS PHILOSOPHICAL AND LITERARY SOCIETY

CENTRAL MUSEUM
CALVERLEY STREET
LEEDS LS1 3AA, U.K.
1984

British Library
Cataloguing in Publication Data

Tropical Rain-Forest: The Leeds Symposium — (Special publication of the Leeds
    Philosophical and Literary Society)
    1. Jungle ecology
    I. Chadwick, A. C.   II. Sutton, S. L.   III. Series
    574.5'2642'0913   QH541.5.J8

ISBN 0-950-19213-9

Printed in Great Britain by W. S. Maney & Son Ltd, Hudson Road, Leeds

EDITOR'S PREFACE

It is hardly surprising that research work done on the ecology of the tropical rain-forest should be so diverse in character, given the extraordinary diversity of the tropical forest habitat. The enormous variety of plant and animal forms present, together with the ever expanding range of techniques and methodology for study, not to mention the unique contributions of individuals in the discipline, militate against a ready cohesion in any compilation of current studies. Nevertheless, what binds together any group of tropical ecologists is a consuming interest in the richness of the flora and fauna and the interactions of these and also a concern for the future of the tropical rain-forests, increasingly threatened as they are by pressures of development and exploitation. The Symposium 'The Tropical Rain Forest: Ecology and Resource Management', held at Leeds University in April 1982 exemplified these points admirably. Whilst the richness of the information presented by the more than 300 participants who assembled from all around the globe was of a high order, its variety and scope of interest was even more striking. It was gratifying to the organizing committee of the symposium that it proved possible to assemble and publish manuscripts based on the oral communications (Sutton, Whitmore & Chadwick 1983) so that all can take advantage of the expertise and breadth of knowledge represented. It was also evident at the Symposium that there was a great deal of valuable and interesting information to be found in the work presented at the poster sessions. The present volume is formed from manuscripts based on some of these posters and once again the aim is to allow this work to reach a wider audience. All presenters were invited to submit manuscripts. Some no doubt had already found alternative avenues for the publication of their results. The editors are grateful to the authors represented here for their co-operation and forebearance during the negotiations preceding the finalization of plans for the volume. They also express their gratitude to the various referees who assisted in our endeavours to maintain a high standard in the contributions.

The Editors wish to thank the sponsors who helped to make the Leeds Symposium a success, first and foremost the British Ecological Society and the Leeds Philosophical and Literary Society, publishers of the present volume. Financial support came from the Royal Society, the Scientific Exploration Society, the World Wildlife Fund, the British Council and UNEP. The organizers thank them heartily. The University of Leeds and in particular the Department of Pure and Applied Zoology helped in staging the symposium and the production of this volume and we record here our grateful thanks.

A. C. CHADWICK

S. L. SUTTON

REFERENCE

Sutton, S.L., Whitmore, T.C. & Chadwick, A.C. (1983). *Tropical Rain Forest: Ecology and Management Special Publication No. 2.* British Ecological Society. Blackwell Scientific Publications. London.

Readers might like to know of two further publications:

(i) *Reaching the Rain Forest Roof.* Mitchell, A. W. (1982) A booklet on techniques of access and study in the canopy. 36 pp. £2.50 or £4.50 airmail from B. H. Blackwell Ltd, Broad Street, Oxford or Leeds Philosophical and Literary Society, Central Museum, Calverley Street, Leeds LS1 3AA, UK.

(ii) *The Preservation of Tropical Moist Forest.* Chadwick, A. C. & Sutton, S. L. (1983) International Relations 7, 2304–2322.

An activity within the
Global Environment Monitoring System
of the
United Nations Environment Programme

CONTENTS

INTRODUCTION

A. C. CHADWICK

University of Leeds, Department of Pure and Applied Zoology

Tropical moist forest research has a long and distinguished history in the annals of the study of the natural environment and more recently in the proper discipline of Ecology. The Tropical Group of the British Ecological Society was the first to be formed, in 1961, of the specialist study groups of that Society. It is perhaps inevitable given the nature of scientific research funding in this century that most tropical ecological research has been utilitarian, with predominant emphasis on exploitation for the benefit of mankind of the vast resources offered by the tropical forests. Increasingly, however, scientists working in the field, scientific administrators and others, are coming to the realization that exploitation programmes are running out of control, with profound consequences for the future of the world's tropical rain-forests and even, possibly for the world environment (Poore 1976; Chadwick & Sutton 1983). Furthermore it is emerging that despite this looming crisis research on tropical forest subjects seems to be on the decline. A progressive reduction in research effort over recent years has been identified by comparing tropical entries with total entries in the ecological literature, from about 3% of the total in 1979 to about 1% in 1983 (Cole 1983). Various factors may be suggested to account for this, including perhaps, an expansion of non-tropical ecological research programmes at the expense of tropical research. What cannot be denied however is that a greater concern for and support for research on the tropical environment is called for, rather than a seeming withdrawal of interest. The tropical rain-forest environment is one of the richest in plant and animal diverity in existence and it is distressing to report that in many places its very existence is under threat if it has not actually disappeared (Global 2000, 1980). Species are being lost for ever at an ever increasing rate as the forest area diminishes and the opportunity to investigate these species and their adaptations and interactions is disappearing. If nothing else, man's self-interest should alert him to the need to investigate living organisms, plant and animal, threatened by extinction, some of which must surely be useful to him (Myers 1984).

The present volume hopes in some way to redress the balance in the decline of tropical rain-forest ecology publications. It was obvious to all the participants at the Leeds Tropical Rain Forest Symposium that in addition to the outstanding verbal presentations there was a mass of exciting and valuable information offered in poster form. It was feared that some of this work might not be subsequently made available in published form, as so often happens at such meetings, if such an opportunity were not presented to poster authors. Council of the Leeds Philosophical and Literary Society generously agreed to fund the publication of a volume to be based on the posters and the present volume is the result. The Leeds Philosophical and Literary Society is a local 'improving' society dating back to 1820 which has published Proceedings in a Literary and Historical Section and a Scientific Section for many years. It was decided to include in this Special Publication manuscripts based on twenty-two of the abstracts and it has also proved

4 Developed countries have as great an economic stake in the long-term survival of tropical rain-forests as do the countries in which the forests grow. Developed nations should therefore consider assuming a much larger share of the costs of conserving this habitat. For example, market prices of tropical forest wood must rise to reflect the real value of those products. Developed nations should provide increased training programmes in tropical ecology and management.

The Symposium delegates felt that the fate of tropical rain-forests has become of vital interest to people everywhere. Conservation of the forests should illustrate the concept of one world, indivisible in its interactions and responsibilities.

SECTION I
COMMUNITY STRUCTURE

The application of system analysis and modelling as tools in tropical forest ecosystem research

E. F. BRUNIG, J. KREYSA, N. SANDER AND T. W. SCHNEIDER

Institute and Chair for World Forestry,
Federal Research Centre for Forestry and
Forest Products and Hamburg University, Hamburg

SUMMARY

1 Ecological and physio-ecological research in Borneo and Amazonia gives clues to the nature of interdependency between structure, function, dynamics and site at plant and forest stand ecosystem levels.

2 Natural ecosystems interact with man-made economic and social ecosystems. Ecosystems interact in an integrated hierarchic order from basic biological to high-order social systems. The structure and functioning of a corresponding hierarchy of ecosystem models is briefly described.

3 Within and between the real systems matter, energy and information are exchanged. Analogously, information is exchanged within and between the hierarchically ordered models. As in reality, selection and aggregation happen during transfer between model levels.

4 Information from higher-levels can guide practical management and basic research at lower levels and *vice versa*. Sensitivity analyses indicate critical factors, processes and elements. The research programme contributes to the UNESCO-programme 'MAB', the bio-chemical cycling project of SCOPE of ICSU, and the forest sector model project of IIASA.

THE DEVELOPMENT OF THE CONCEPT

The senior author studied vegetation structure, soil features and land form along ecological gradients at different sites in Kerangas and Kerapah forests in Sarawak and Brunei (Borneo) between 1950 and 1963. The study included transects in Mulu and Bako National Park and on the Merurong Plateau. Analysis of the data produced evidence of a consistent coincidence of sclerophyllic and xeromorphic morphological and biochemical features of leaves, trees and stand canopies with xeric and oligotrophic properties of soil and site (Brunig 1961, 1965, 1966, 1969, 1971, 1974).

Analysis of within- and between-stand variation of floristic and geometric structure of 57 sample plots and two 20 ha plots, including stratification by means of ordination and classification techniques, showed that:

species distribution patterns are strongly correlated with patterns of variation of edaphic factors;

species richness and diversity, assessed according to various indices are primarily controlled by soil and physiographic factors;

population dynamics, vicarious occurrence of species, exclusion of species as a result of 'biochemical warfare' and the effects of external destructive impacts (lightning, storm, pests) superimpose an independent pattern of variation (Brunig 1964, 1970, 1973; Brunig & Sander, 1983).

This apparently simple network of interrelationships is complicated by variation of scale from single-tree small-gap size to uniform large-gap size of up to several hundred hectares, such as some of the uniform even-aged 'ulat bulu' areas (Anderson 1961) in *Shorea albida* forest in Sarawak. This complicated interaction of many dependent and independent variables at different scales of variation and different sequences in time has contributed to the many misinterpretations of pattern, dynamics and site-influences in tropical moist forest.

Corroborating evidence has been produced more recently by the study of similar forests in the International Amazon Ecosystem Research area at San Carlos de Rio Negro (Brunig *et al.* 1979a). This supported the hypothesis that the variation of vegetation structure at medium scale *sensu* Ashton & Brunig (1975), as well as the concurrent changes of tree physiognomy, are adaptations of the plant species and of the vegetation communities to the physical and chemical conditions of the site. These physiognomical features seem to be linked to physiological adaptations. Both contribute to the control of essential processes in the plants and corresponding flows of matter and energy betweeen individual plants and between vegetation canopies and the environment. Ultimately, these assumed adaptations determine the survivability of the plant and vegetation systems. These processes include transpiration, heating, cooling, nutrient cycling and preservation, biomass formation and decomposition.

Site-related variation has superimposed upon it variation at small gap-size scale which is largely determined by stand dynamics due to factors controlling regeneration and mortality. The 3-dimensional histogram representing the living above-ground tree phytomass stock at the natural forest observation area in the International Amazon Ecosystem MAB-project area at San Carlos de Rio Negro (Fig. 1) reflects both variation at medium and small scales of space and time. The pattern of variation of leaf area is practically identical, but the range is more compressed, very large above-ground tree phytomass carries relatively less and very small above-ground tree phytomass carries relatively more leaf area. This may possibly be linked partly with variation of amounts and of rates of activity of the root phytomass. Root mass seems to be relatively large in association group P and Q (Klinge & Herrera 1978) with very low above-ground tree phytomass and low leaf area index.

Both variation patterns closely agree with the patterns of forest association groups (Fig. 2) and of soil types (Brunig *et al.* 1979b) in this area. At the same time, leaf morphology and orientation exhibit sclerophyllic, xeromorphic gradients in the same manner as in Bornean kerangas along two gradients. One proceeds from more mesic and favourable soils (association groups H, I, J) to extremely unfavourable soils (P and Q). The other proceeds from the ground layer to the top canopy within stands in each association group. This coincidence of the patterns of spatial distribution of phytomass, leaf area, floristic associations, soil types and leaf characteristics repeats so closely the

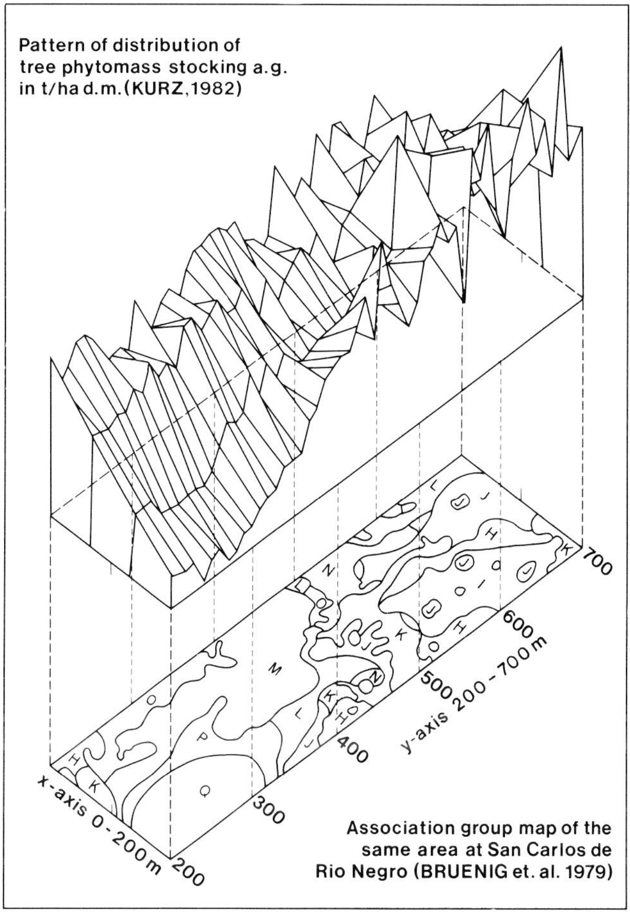

FIG. 1. (a) *Top*: Pattern of distribution of the dry weight of trees over 1 cm diameter above ground in 50 (X-axis) by 10 (Y-axis) m rectangles. Values are in *t*/ha dry weight above ground. Each 10 × 200 m transect is divided into 4 rectangles which gives 4 values in each transect. The print-out of the X and Y scales has been slightly modified for clarity.

The lowest weight value is 2·5 *t*/ha (rectangle X = 150–200; Y = 230–240 in association group Q), the highest value is 485·9 *t*/ha (rectangle X = 150–200; Y = 670–680 in association groups I and K).

(b) *Bottom*: Vegetation map of the association groups (names are termed in vernacular tree names)

H Yevaro-Cunuri-Jigua-Seje complex forest
I Yevaro-Jigua-Congrio complex forest
J Jevaro-Macure-Cunuri complex forest
K Cunuri-Yevaro-Yaguacana complex–simple forest transition
L Cunuri-Yucito-Piapoco simple forest
M Cunuri-Yucito-Yaguacana simple forest
N Piapoco-Yaguacana-Macure simple forest
O Mixed Cunuri-Yaguacana-Tamacuari complex–simple forest transition
P Cunuri-Yucito-Arepillo-Medla luna (simple closed bana woodland)
Q Yucito-Concha amarillo-Lengua vacca-Cupi (simple open bana scrub)

maintain operationality. They are not only practical and rational, but also realistic. Each system level also has it's own level of resolution. Required information detail at the plant or forest stand level would merely be insignificant and disturbing background noise at the central model level, where its effect should work only through highly aggregated information.

Proceeding downward in the hierarchy, the process is reversed and disaggregation of information gained by simulation at a higher level provides data which can be applied in testing the feed-back reactions between levels and which can give valuable guidance to research and management at the natural ecosystem levels.

REFERENCES

Alder, D., Synnott, T.J. & Smith, J.P. (1978). GROPE: A standardized growth projection method for tropical rainforest. In Brunig, E.F. (ed.). *Transactions of the International MAB-IUFRO Workshop on Tropical Rainforest Ecosystems Research.* Chair for World Forestry, Hamburg–Reinbek, Special Report No. 1.

Alder, D. & Schneider, T.W. (1979). A stand growth model as a tool in studying management options for MAB-rainforest ecosystem projects and for temperate forests. In: Adiosoemarto, S. & Brunig, E.F. (eds). *Transactions of the Second International MAB-IUFRO Workshop on Tropical Rainforest Ecosystems Research.* Chair for World Forestry, Hamburg–Reinbek, Special Report No. 2.

Anderson, J.A.R. (1961). The destruction of *Shorea albida* forest by an unidentified insect. *Empire Forest Rev.*, **40** (103), 19–28.

Ashton, P.S. & Brunig, E.F. (1975). The variation of tropical moist forest in relation to environmental factors and its relevance to land-use planning. Paper submitted to the FAO Conference on Moist Tropical Forest. Published in: *Mitt. Bundesforsch. andst. Forst-Holzwirtschaft*, **109**, 59–86.

Brunig, E.F. (1961). *An introduction to the vegetation of Bako National Park.* Report of the Trustees of National Parks, 1959–1960. Government Printer, Kuching.

Brunig, E.F. (1964). A study of damage attributed to lightning in two areas of *Shorea albida* forest in Sarawak. *Commonwealth Forestry Review*, **43** (2), 134–144.

Brunig, E.F. (1965). Guide and introduction to the vegetation of the kerangas forests and the padangs of the Bako National Park. In: *Unesco Symposium on Ecological Research in Humid Tropical Vegetation.* Kuching, 1963. Unesco Regional Office, Tokyo.

Brunig, E.F. (1966). Der Heidewald von Sarawak and Brunei — eine Studie seiner Vegetation und Ökologie. Habil. Thesis, University of Hamburg, pp. iv + 117, published as *Mitt. Bundesforsch. anst. Forst-Holzwirtschaft*, **68**, 1968.

Brunig, E.F. (1969). On the seasonality of droughts in the lowlands of Sarawak (Borneo). Erdkunde, 23 (2), 127–133.

Brunig, E.F. (1970). Stand structure, physiognomy and environmental factors in some lowland forests in Sarawak. *Tropical Ecology*, **11** (1), 26–43.

Brunig, E.F. (1971). On the ecological significance of drought in the equatorial wet evergreen (rain) forest of Sarawak (Borneo). *Transact. First Aberdeen–Hull Symposium on Malesian Ecology.* University Hull, Department of Geography, Miscellaneous Series, **11**, 66–97.

Brunig, E.F. (1973). Some further evidence on the amount of damage attributed to the lightning and wind-throw in *Shorea albida* forest in Sarawak. *Commonwealth Forestry Review*, London, **52** (153), 260–265.

Brunig, E.F. (1974). Ecological studies in kerangas forests of Sarawak and Brunei. *Borneo Literature Bureau for Sarawak Forest Department*, Kuching, 250 pp.

Brunig, E.F. (1976). Classifying for mapping of kerangas and peatswamp forest as examples of primary forest types in Sarawak (Borneo). In: Ashton, P.S. (ed.): *The classification and mapping of Southeast Asian ecosystems.* Department of Geography, University of Hull, Hull, 1976, Miscellaneous Series, **17**, 57–75.

Brunig, E.F. (1982). (ed.). *Transactions of the Third International MAB-IUFRO Workshop on Ecosystems Research.* Deutsches MAB-Nationalkomitee, MAB Mitteilungen, **10**, Bonn, 138 pp.

Brunig, E.F. (in press). Oligotrophic forested wetlands in Borneo. In: *Wetland Forest Ecosystems.* Ecosystems of the World. Elsevier Scientific Publishing Company, Amsterdam.

Brunig, E.F., Alder, D. & Smith, J.P. (1979b). The International MAB Amazon Rainforest Ecosystem Pilotproject at San Carlos de Rio Negro: Vegetation Classification and Structure. In S. Adisoemarto & E.F. Brunig (eds). *Transactions of the Second International MAB-IUFRU Workshop on Tropical Rainforest Ecosystems Research,* Chair for World Forestry, Hamburg–Reinbek, Special Report, **2**, 67–100.

Brunig, E.F., Heuveldop, J., Smith, J. & Alder, D. (1979a). Struktur und Funktionen im Regenwald des internationalen Amazonökosystemprojektes: vorläufige Mitteilung über Klassifikation der Bestände, Variation der Bestandesstruktur und Niederschlagsmerkmale. IX. Symposium über biogeographische und landschaftsökologische Probleme Südamerikas: Wald und Wasser. Max-Planck Inst. für Limnologie, Ploen, 1978. *Amazoniana,* VI (4), 423–444.

Brunig, E.F., Grossmann, W.D., Kreysa, J., Sander, N. & Schneider, T.W. (1981). The testing and integration of dynamic system models by information exchange and simulation. *MAB Mitteilungen,* **10**, Bonn, 44–68.

Brunig, E.F. & Sander, N. (1983). Ecosystem structure and functioning: some interactions of relevance to agroforestry. In: Huxley, P. A. (ed.): Plant research and agroforestry. Proceedings of a consultative meeting held in Nairobi, Kenya, 8 to 15 April 1981, 221–247.

Grossmann, W.D. (in press). The problem of global renewable biological resources: A hierarchy of models for evaluation of the consequences of increasing intensity and scale of use of the forest resource. *Wood Power,* **80**, Pergamon Press.

Klinge, H. & Herrera, R. (1978). Biomass studies in Amazon Caating a forest in southern Venezuela. 1. Standing crop of composite root mass in selected stands. *Tropical Ecology,* **19**, 93–100.

Kurz, W. (1982). *Biomasse eines amazonischen immergrünen Feuchtwaldes: Entwicklung einer allgemeinen Biomasse-regression* (Biomass of an Amazonian evergreen moist forest: development of a general biomass regression). Diploma Thesis, University of Hamburg, 115 + 14 pp.

Sander, N. (1982). Reaction of tree species from Amazonian and Bornean kerangas to stress. *Research Report, Institute for World Forestry,* Hamburg, Manuscript.

Schneider, T.W. & Kreysa, J. (1981). Das Douglasien-Wachstumssimulationsmodell Dousim. In: Schneider, T.W. & Kreysa, J.: Dynamische Wachstums- und Ertragsmodelle für die Douglasie und die Kiefer. *Mitt. Bundesforsch. anst. Forst-Holzwirtschaft,* **135**, 1–75.

Tint, K. & Schneider, T.W. (1980). Dynamic growth and yield models for Burma teak, *Mitt. Bundesforsch. anst. Forst-Holzwirtsch.,* **129**, 1–93.

Strata in tropical rain-forest at Taï (Ivory Coast)

D. Y. ALEXANDRE

*ORSTOM BPV, 51 Abidjan Ivory Coast**

SUMMARY

1   In the course of a study of the light regime of the undergrowth of the Taï-forest in the Ivory Coast a set of fish-eye photographs has been taken and analysed. The photographs reveal that the cover presents a higher mid-elevation hole-density than expected. This is discussed and a model is suggested to account for the observations.

2   It is proposed that forest layering is explained by the existence of a densely shaded 'exclusion volume' for other trees beneath each existing tree crown.

INTRODUCTION

Since the publication of 'The tropical rain forest' by P. W. Richards in 1952 the question of tropical rain-forest stratification is certainly one which has greatly occupied tropical ecologists.

The reason of this interest is, of course, that whilst the structure of the forest cover has important bearings on every aspect of the forest ecology, the forest strata are very difficult to distinguish.

No doubt, secondary forests and some almost monospecific forests have obvious strata. For most mature tropical rain-forests, however, this is not the case.

After Richards, Newman (1954) made an important contribution to the understanding of TRF stratification: he pointed out that young trees still growing quickly have to be considered separately from adult trees which show almost no growth in height. This author states also that the height of the lower branches is one of the most distinctive features of stratification. This distinction between young and adult trees has been further developed by Oldeman (1974) who introduced a new concept: the 'surface d'inversion'. The inversion surface may be of two kinds: structural or ecological; in a young forest the morphological inversion starting at the lowest living branch is at the same height as the ecological inversion which empirically may be at or about half the total height of each tree, but the author gives no further justification of that particular height. When the forest gets older the inversion surface continues to ascend whilst the ecological surface does not and both get further and further apart. Later on Hallé *et al.* (1978, p. 333) wrote: 'Strata (and inversion surfaces) should not be confused. Our opinion is that there are no strata in the forest as subdivisions of the total population but in certain plots there are demonstrable horizontal "sets" composed of trees of the present.' Following personal communications from Horn, Hallé *et al.* (1978) explained why trees of the present should form horizontal sets. They describe (p. 338) a model where tree crowns separated by gaps are opaque, globular and form a single layer. They write: 'Through the gaps between two

**Present address: ORSTOM BP 165, 97305 Cayenne France*

trees light enters and illuminates zones below. Immediately under each crown there is dense shade . . . At some distance from the crowns there are atmospheric cells receiving light from one gap, two gaps and three gaps . . .'. The point here is: why should this apply to the trees of the present and not to those of the future? This is not obvious, as trees of the future can be as old and as large as those of the present. Trees of the future keep to the basic models described by Hallé & Oldeman (1970) and have a narrow crown ('lollipop trees'). The trees of the present are those that profit from an increased amount of energy by the process of the 'reitération' and have a wide crown.

Kahn has developed Oldeman's concepts and has introduced the concept of volumes defined by homogenous content; these volumes are called 'hoplexols' (Guillaumet & Kahn 1979). In Kahn's terminology a volume usually filled with leaves of mature trees of the present is called 'palyphyse'. In this system there are words for any volume with respect to its content. A volume containing mainly leaves of submature trees (trees of the future) is called 'prophyse'.

All these views concern the same fact, i.e. the difficulty of defining real strata in the sense of particular tree height classes, whether these concern total tree heights or heights of parts of trees. For example, in the Ivory Coast Huttel (1967) and more recently van Doorn (1973) have studied tree height in 'The Banco' forest near Abidjan in an attempt to define strata. Neither found any particular height frequency for their 0·25 ha sample plots. At Pasoh forest Kato *et al.* (in Kira 1978) measured leaf biomass and leaf area on a clear-felled plot 20 × 100 m. Their results clearly show two strata: a tree stratum, with a bell-shaped distribution having a mean height around 30 m and a ground layer with an L-shaped distribution having an abundant occurrence of seedlings and Monocotyledons, mainly Palmaceae.

Except for the ground stratum, which may be present and well defined, we may now conclude that the tropical rain-forest is not, in general, layered. However, it may well be structured. Is it structured and if so, how?

For structurally-simple stands, like corn fields, the simplest way to predict the light intensity profile inside the vegetation may be to study the cover structure but conversely light intensity profile studies may give insight into cover structure and this may be particularly useful in the case of a high forest, the structure of which is difficult to observe directly.

METHODS

Fish-eye photographs offer a tool which permit an indirect access both to light intensity profile and to stand structure. This technique has given good results within certain limits: even with the best available film the negative area of a 35 mm camera is very small and one cannot completely record the multitude of tiny holes in a dense forest cover.

In 1979 we tried to take fish-eye photographs, in a regular sample pattern, from a station of Taï forest we were studying (Alexandre 1982).

The film was developed and high-contrast positives prepared on 18 cm wide paper. The pictures were divided in 9 concentric coronae and the gap area in each corona was evaluated and expressed as a proportion of the total corona area. (Fig. 1)

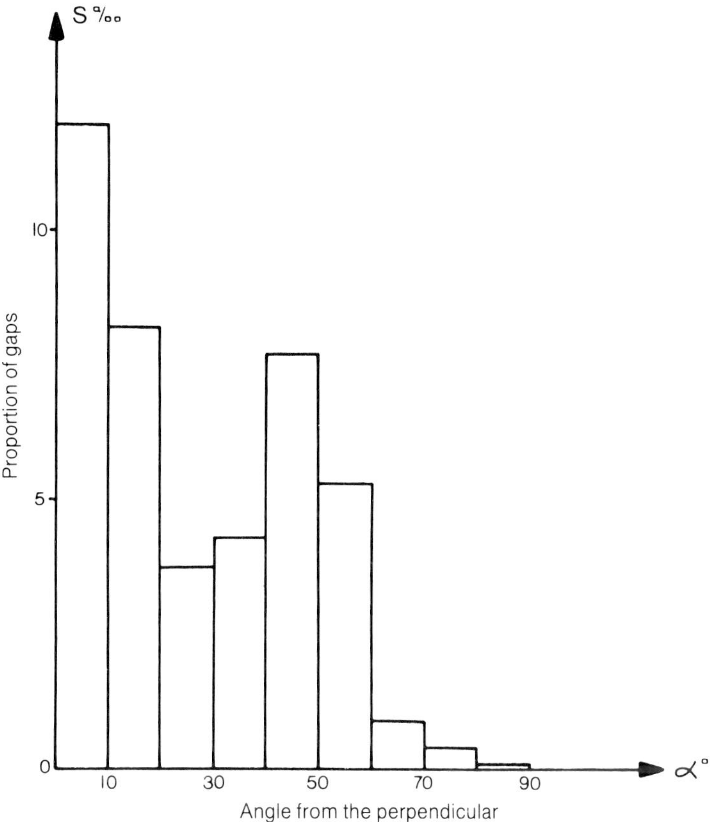

FIG. 1. Mean angular densities of the gaps in the cover of the Taï forest, computed from 12 fish-eye photographs expressed as ‰ of surface occupied by gaps in each of 9 concentric coronae.

Owing to technical limitations, this gives a rather crude estimate of the angular gap-density. It is, however, sufficiently precise to serve as a basis for a discussion about the forest structure.

RESULTS AND DISCUSSION

With regard to angular gap-density, the photographs allow the sampling points to be ordered in two sets. In the first set we have those which show a high density of holes in the central corona, corresponding to vertical or near-vertical light beams. The second set, on the other hand, show densities at high elevations which are low or zero. However, it is important to note that both sets of sampling points show a high gap-density at mid-elevations when photographed from the ground.

If the leaves were arranged at random, whichever direction or inclination they had, the angular gap-density would appear to decrease smoothly from high elevations to low elevations.

transparency of the whole cover are hypothetic and chosen empirically in accordance with our experience in the Ivory Coast. Here $r1 = 5$, $r2 = 6.2$ and $r3 = 15$ m; the transparency of the whole cover is taken as 0.18.

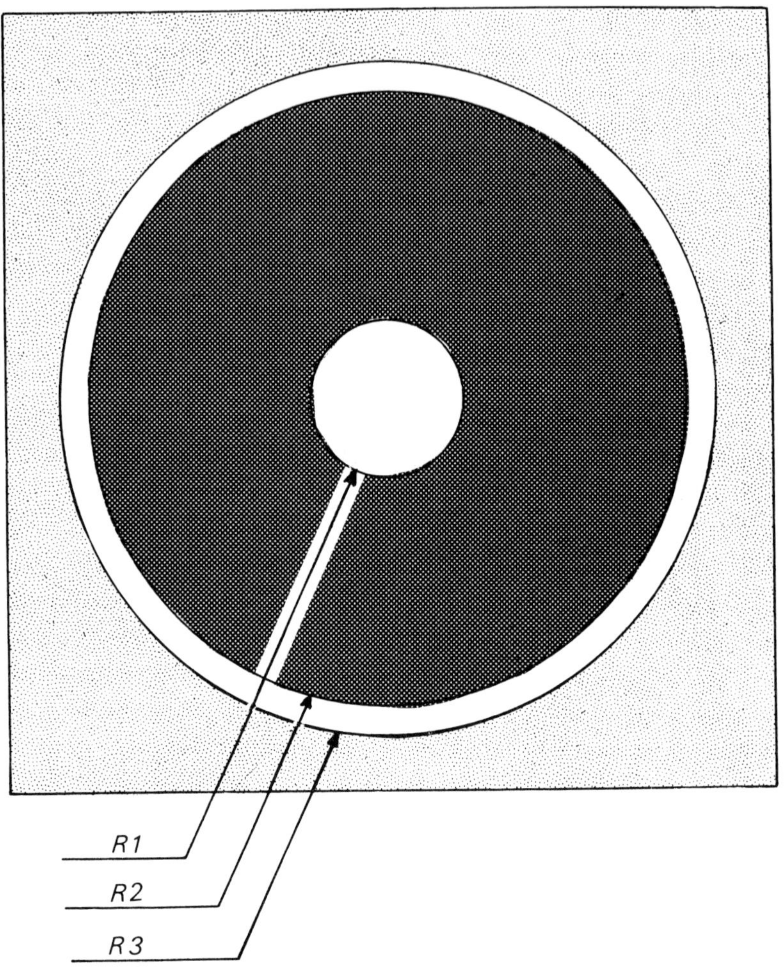

FIG. 3a. Light, dense shade and diffuse illumination under a canopy hole

In order to simulate the conditions below the middle of a hole we take a hole surrounded by a black corona, then a transparent corona, lastly the grey zone (Fig. 3a). Here the hole diameter has great importance, which is why we have taken three empirically observed combinations of diameters (see legend to Fig. 3).

We see from Figs 2b and 3b that at a distance of the crown equal to its radius (here 5 m) the light conditions become uniform. Immediately underneath the crown there is deep shade and it is likely that no tree could live under such conditions. Downwards from the centre of a hole the light diminishes rapidly. In some cases, when the hole is small, light intensity reaches a minimum then can grow again as one passes downwards owing to the increased lateral light. This supports Horn's theory quoted before. If a hole in the canopy is large enough a sapling in its middle will grow slowly for a long time, till it reaches the height where light increases rapidly. At that point the sapling may grow quickly and have a chance to reach the adult stage. If the hole is smaller the same sapling will never reach the height where the light starts to increase for it would have to overcome a zone of very dense shade first.

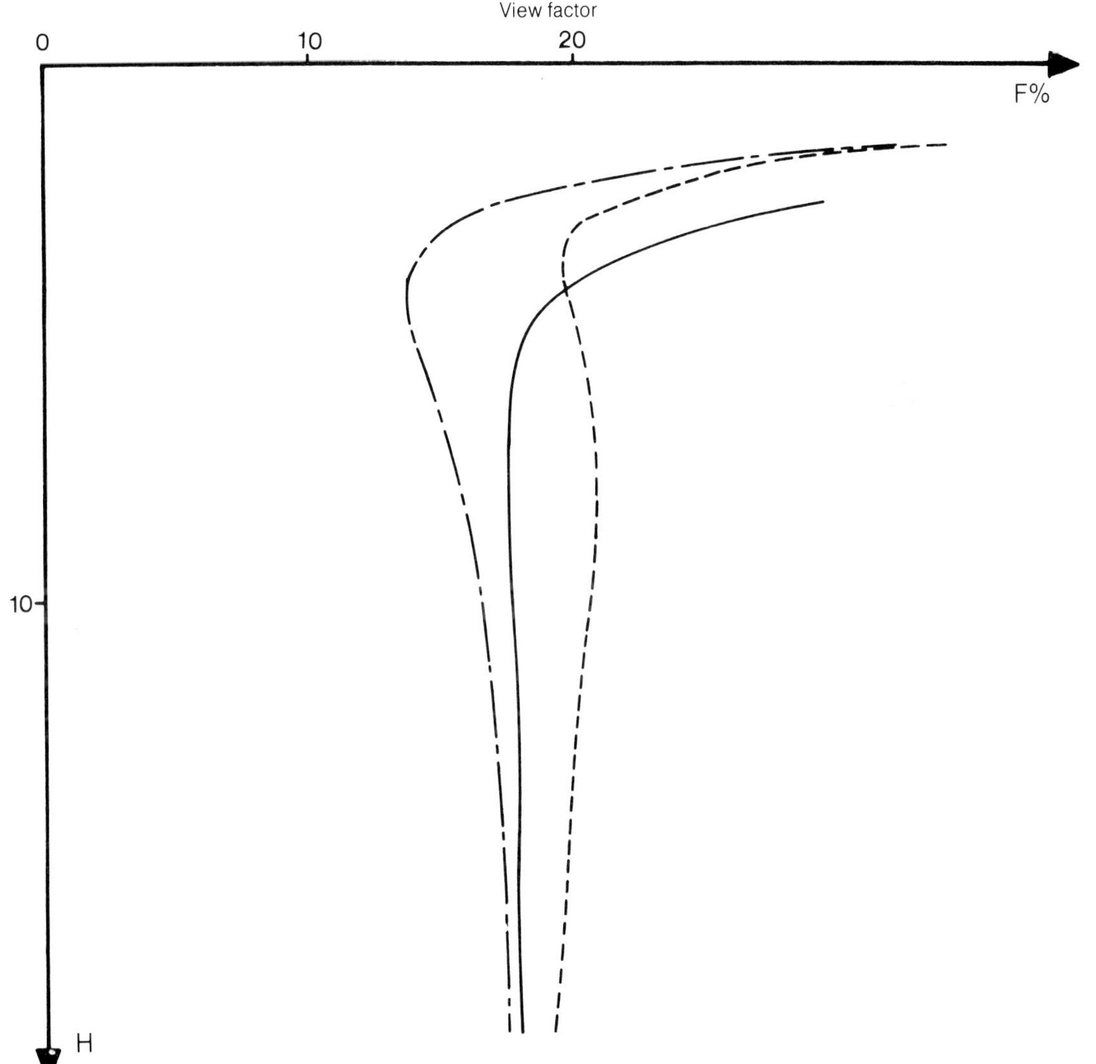

FIG. 3b. Computation of the light profile at the plumb of a canopy hole.
$$F = \sin^2 \text{arc tan.} \, (r1/H) - \sin^2 \text{arc tan.} \, (r2/H) + (1 - T) \cdot (\sin^2 \text{arc tan.} \, (r3/H)) + T$$
$r1$ is the radius of the hole, $r2$ the radius to the next holes and $r3$ to the rest of the cover.

———————	$r = 1.5$	$r2 = 6.2$	$r3 = 6.7$
— ‒ —	$r1 = 1$	$r2 = 6.2$	$r3 = 6.7$
‒ ‒ ‒ ‒ ‒	$r1 = 1$	$r2 = 5$	$r3 = 6$

In the case where a stable storey of canopy trees is found, another storey of small trees must exist below. The distance between the two should be approximately equal to half the mean diameter of the upper tree crowns.

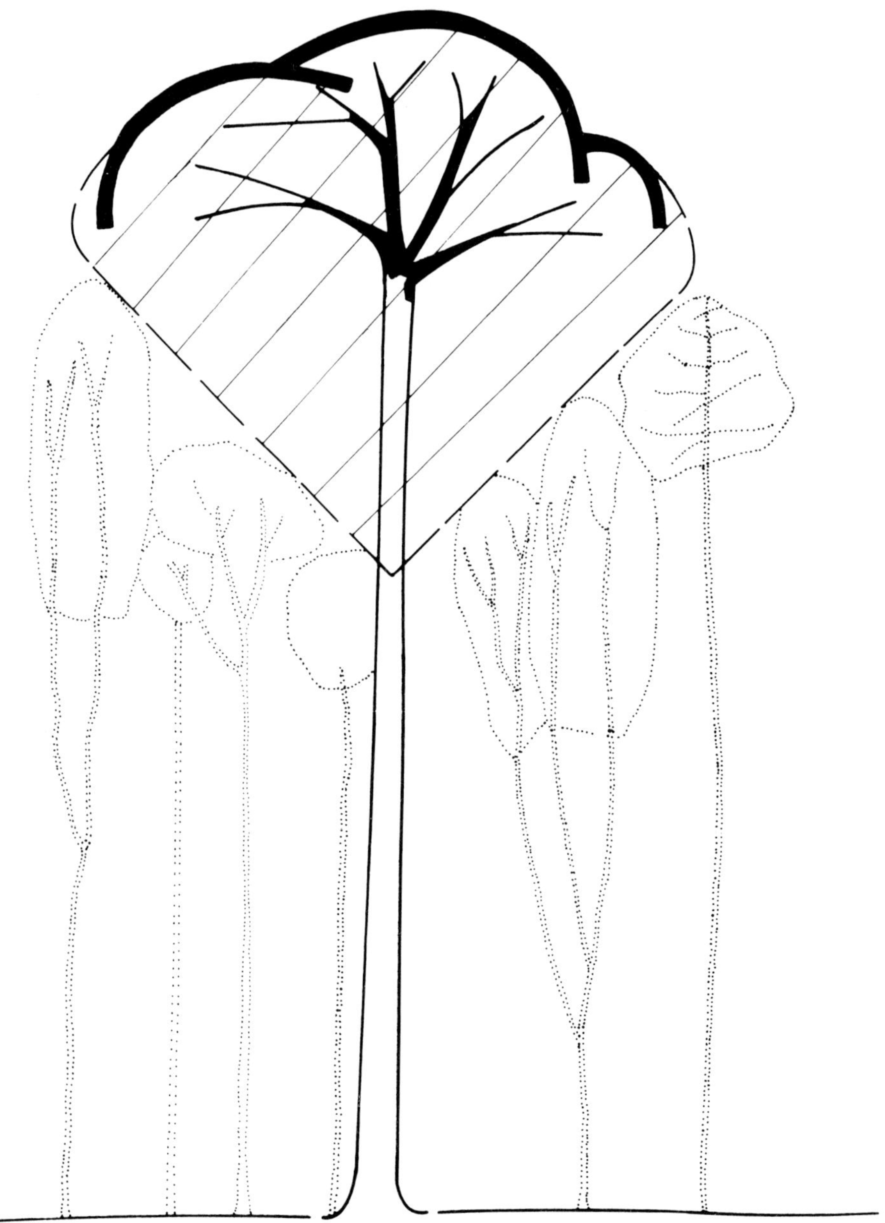

FIG. 4. Schema of the exclusion volume created by a dense crown. In the hatched zone the light is dim enough to preclude the presence of another crown.

This is not normally the rule, however. Let us assume that under each tree, with a dark enough crown, there is a pear-shaped volume where no other tree can find enough energy to survive (Fig. 4). This volume is here called the 'exclusion volume'. It is postulated that a salient feature of the exclusion volume is that it must be slightly wider than the crown that produces it, in order to explain the observed gap-angle maximum frequency. When the crown of a growing tree reaches the exclusion volume either its growth must stop or its crown must bend. Thus, by virtue of their location, the upper trees control the location of the lower ones and these in turn control the location of those still lower. Of course, as long as a tree grows upwards, the trees underneath can grow also, unless the upper crown also widens. It is in this sense that the trees of the present control the layering of the forest and, in my opinion, all the lower trees must be affected by the upper ones.

Fish-eye photography produces proof that Taï forest, although not layered, is definitely structured.

This particular structure results in a very high frequency of gaps under 45° in the undergrowth. It is possible, even probable, that dicotyledonous plants utilize completely the dominant vertical component of the penetrant illumination below the forest canopy. The remaining oblique component may then be used by monocotyledonous plants with tilted leaves (A. de Rouw, pers. comm.).

Observed facts of forest tree growth have been explained here by postulating the existence of an exclusion volume under each crown. This hypothesis must now be tested in various forests by appropriate measurements of structure and light-intensity profiles.

REFERENCES

Alexandre, D.Y. (1982). Etude de l'éclairement du sous-bois d'une forêt dense humide sempervirente (Taï, Côte-d'Ivoire). *Oecologia generalis*; in press.

Anderson, M.C. (1966). Stand structure and light penetration, II — A theoretical analysis. *Journal of applied Ecology*, **3**, 41–54.

Guillaumet, J.-L. & Kahn, F. (1979). Description des végétations forestières tropicales: approche morphologique et structurale. *Candollea*, **34**, 109–131.

Hallé, F. & Oldeman, R.A.A. (1970). *Essai sur l'architecture et la dynamique de croissance des arbres tropicaux*. Masson (Paris).

Hallé, F., Oldeman, R.A.A. & Tomlinson, P.M. (1978). *Tropical trees and forests — an architectural analysis*. Springer Verlag (Berlin).

Horn, H.S. (1971). *The adaptative geometry of trees*. Monographs in population biology no. 3. Princeton University Press, 144 pp.

Huttel, C. (1967). *Ecologie forestière en Basse-Côte-d'Ivoire*. Rapport de stage ORSTOM (Adiopodoumé) Multigr.

Kira, T. (1978). Community architecture and organic matter dynamics in tropical lowland rain forests of Southeast Asia with special reference to Pasoh Forest, West Malaysia. In *Tropical trees as living systems*. Tomlinson & Zimmermann (eds). Cambridge University Press, pp. 561–590.

Newman, I.V. (1954). Locating strata in tropical rain forest. *Journal of Ecology*, **42** (1), 218–219.

Oldeman, R.A.A. (1974). *L'architecture de la forêt guyanaise*. Mém. ORSTOM 73, Paris.

Richards, P.W. (1952). *The tropical rain forest*. Cambridge University Press.

van Doorn, J. (1973). *Etude de la structure et de la floristique de stades de succession secondaire après défrichement de la forêt sur sables tertiaires* (région d'Adiopodoumé). Rapport de stage ORSTOM (Adiopodoumé) Multigr.

Tamai, S. (1976). Studies on the stand structure and light climate. II Methods of investigating the sunfleck on the forest floor. *Bulletin of the Kyoto University Forests*, 48, 69–79.

Tropical Rain-Forest: The Leeds Symposium, pp. 25–52

The forest vegetation of Silent Valley, India

J. S. SINGH, S. P. SINGH, A. K. SAXENA AND Y. S. RAWAT
Department of Botany, Kumaun University, Naini Tal — 263 002, India

SUMMARY

1 The present study deals with the structure, composition, regeneration status and plant diversity of Silent Valley Forest in the Western Ghats, Kerala State.

2 The total tree basal cover ranged from 29 to 103 m^2/ha and the density from 620 to 709 plants/ha. A total of six tree strata in the mesic upland forest, five in the less mesic upland forest and four in riparian forest were recognizable. Two other strata, one represented mainly by shrubs (treelets) and the other by herbs were also present. The trees are typically slender exhibiting flying buttresses at the base and the vegetation is rich in epiphytes and stranglers. The riparian forest had a larger shrub population as compared with the other forests and the herb layer in all the forests was poorly developed. Leaf size was predominantly mesophyll. The bark of the trees was remarkably thin.

3 On the basis of data on population structure, a total of five patterns were recognized in the present forests, and in general, proportion of species with expanding population was low. The tree layer diversity (Shannon–Wiener index) ranged from 3·52 to 4·15. Diversity tended to decrease with increasing girth class of tree. A high value for beta diversity in riparian forest indicates a rapid micro-habitat change. Dominance-diversity curves for the forest exhibited log-normal distribution and limited dominance in resource partitioning by two to three species.

INTRODUCTION

The proposed construction of a reservoir in Silent Valley of Kerala, India, has raised several controversies including whether or not the forest lying within the confines of Valley represents a typical tropical rain-forest. The present paper reports on the results of a short-term (April 1981) vegetational study of the Silent Valley forest on four easily distinguishable habitats, viz., river bank, moist upland, less moist upland and dry ridge top. The likely impact of the proposed reservoir is discussed in Singh *et al.* (1984).

STUDY AREA AND METHODS

Location

The Silent Valley is located on the lower side of the Nilgiri plateau (11° 5′ 33″ N and 76° 27′ 15″ E) at an altitude of about 800 m with peaks rising above 2000 m. The Valley runs from north to south along a perennial river Kunthi Puzha. After a reconnaissance of the entire Valley, four easily distinguishable sites were selected (Table 1).

On both sides of the river, the riparian vegetation comprises stunted trees with tall shrubs. On some ridge tops and slopes where burning is frequent, the vegetation consisted of grassland with a few scattered fire-resistant trees. On the upland along the hill slopes the vegetation is dominated by tall slender trees. The differentiation of the upland forests into mesic and less mesic was based on the visual condition of the forest floor at the time of observation. The mesic upland forests are located on the hill slopes facing the river while the less mesic upland forests are on hills on outer side of the valley proper.

TABLE 1. Location of the study site

Locality	Habitat type with respect to moisture	Dominant life form	Altitude (m)	Aspect	Slope angle (0)	Type of Human influence
Veliaparathod area and near Kummatanthod	Riparian	Tall shrubs	1050	South-west	20	Negligible
Near Kummatanthod on the Veliaparathod road	Mesic upland	Tall trees	1120	South-east	40	Negligible
Panthanthod area	Less mesic upland	Tall trees	1100	North-east	30	Substantial in recent years
Veliparathod area	Dry ridge top	Grasses with few scattered trees	—	—	—	Recurring fire

Silent Valley has apparently been devoid of human settlements during recorded history. Recent felling operations were, however, evident. Man-induced fire appears to be an important factor in some localities. Burning of grassland and grassland/forest borders was noted every day during our stay. Near the proposed dam site some buildings and roads have been constructed, which have led to clearance of vegetation in strips. Between the two upland forests, signs of past biotic operations were more visible in the less mesic forest site. The riparian forest was not subjected to substantial felling, but herds of elephants often passed through.

Climate

Formal climatic data for the Silent Valley are not available. However, some generalizations can be made from recent climatic field research in southern India (von Lengerke 1977). The area in which the Valley is located, receives over 5000 mm rainfall annually. The prolonged dry season (March–May) observed in adjoining regions of Silent Valley (Champion & Seth 1968, von Lengerke 1980) seemingly is not representative of the Silent Valley proper. Average minimum temperature ranges from 8°C to 14°C and the average maximum from 23°C to 29°C.

Vegetational Analysis

The tree layer was analysed through 10 × 10 m quadrats; 10 for less mesic upland forest, 8 for mesic upland forest and 5 each on two locations in riparian forest. Vegetation which has emerged during about 10 years following clearance in strips along the roads was sampled by 10 quadrats of 5 × 5 m. In grasslands only a list of plants was prepared. Girth at breast height (gbh at 1·37 m from the ground) of all the trees and saplings in each quadrat was measured and recorded individually by species. Arbitrarily, an individual with ≥31·5 cm gbh was categorized as a tree, with 10·5–31·4 cm gbh as sapling and with ≤10 cm gbh as seedling. Within each of these quadrats, a sub-quadrat of 5 × 5 m was used for sampling the shrubs, seedlings, climbers and herbs. Other measurements included tree height, height to first branch and canopy width for each species. Height of tree and canopy depth were measured using a Haga altimeter.

The vegetational data were quantitatively analysed for abundance, density, frequency (Curtis & McIntosh 1950); A/F ratio (Whitford 1949); relative frequency, relative density and relative dominance (Phillips 1959). The sum of relative frequency, relative density and relative dominance represented Importance value index (IVI) for the various species (Curtis 1959).

Profile diagrams were prepared following Knight (1963). To include maximum number of species in the profile diagrams, an area equivalent to 40 × 10 m was chosen. Numbers of trees, saplings, shrubs and climbers included in the diagram were based on their density. Trees were selected for inclusion from among all trees of each species actually measured in the field by using a random number table (Campbell 1974).

Mature leaves from 100 species were collected at random from the mesic and less mesic upland forests and Raunkiaer's (1934) leaf size spectrum was constructed.

Bark thickness of all trees occurring in each quadrat was also measured.

The trees were categorized into seven 34 cm gbh classes, starting with 31·5–65·5 cm, and a 273+ cm class, for the analysis of population structure. The individuals <31·5 cm but >10 cm gbh were categorized as saplings and those ≤10 cm as seedlings. The total number of individuals belonging to these classes was calculated for each species. The relative density of each species in each class was calculated following Knight (1975):

$$\text{Relative density} = \frac{\text{Total number of individuals in a girth class of a species}}{\text{Total number of individuals of all girth classes of all species on a site.}} \times 100$$

Diversity index (Shannon & Wiener 1963) and concentration of dominance (Simpson 1949) for different layers and for different girth classes in each forest were calculated from density data. Beta-diversity for riparian forest at one location near Kummatanthod was calculated for total tree species and for all ligneous species, separately, following Whittaker (1975).

RESULTS AND DISCUSSION

Phytosociology

Tree layer

In the riparian forest, *Elaeocarpus tuberculatus* was the most dominant followed by *Eugenia* sp. and *Poeciloneuron indicum* (Table 2). *Palaquium ellipticum*, the most dominant species of the mesic upland forest was absent in the tree layer of this forest.

TABLE 2. Analysis of riparian, mesic and less mesic upland forest vegetation

Species	Riparian forest				Mesic upland forest				Less mesic upland forest			
	Frequency (%)	Density (plants/ 100 m^2)	Total basal cover (cm^2/ 100 m^2)	IVI	Frequency (%)	Density (plants/ 100 m^2)	Total basal cover (cm^2/ 100 m^2)	IVI	Frequency (%)	Density (plants/ 100 m^2)	Total basal cover (cm^2/ 100 m^2)	IVI
TREE LAYER												
Elaeocarpus tuberculatus	40	0·4	1210	40								
Eugenia sp.	60	0·6	269	28	38	0·9	196	22				
Poeciloneuron indicum	40	0·6	348	25								
Olea dioica	20	0·2	770	24								
Toona ciliata	20	0·6	306	20								
Clerodendrum viscosum	20	0·6	176	18								
Unidentified sp. D	20	0·4	230	15	13	0·1	66	5	10	0·1	51	5
Cinnamomum macrocarpum	20	0·2	312	14								
Litsea wightii	20	0·4	124	13								
Ficus sp.	20	0·2	229	12	13	0·1	2586	30				
Unidentified sp. C	20	0·2	193	11	13	0·1	44	5	10	0·1	45	5
Alseodaphne sp.	20	0·2	129	10					40	0·9	478	38
Unidentified sp. A	20	0·2	115	10	13	0·1	18	5				
Gordonia obtusa	20	0·2	102	10								
Unidentified sp. B	20	0·2	61	9	13	0·1	233	7	10	0·1	41	5
Holigarna nigra	20	0·2	57	9					20	0·2	193	14
Calophyllum elatum	20	0·2	57	9					10	0·1	258	12
Helicia sp.	20	0·2	40	8								
Dimocarpus longan	20	0·2	26	8	13	0·1	17	5	20	0·2	67	9
Memecylon sp.	20	0·2	20	8								
Palaquium ellipticum					63	1·2	3696	64	100	2·0	511	67
Cullenia exarillata					25	0·5	1882	30	30	0·3	52	12
Drypetes elata					38	0·4	689	20	30	0·4	779	38
Nothapodytes foetida					38	0·7	127	18				
Agrostistachys meeboldii					38	0·5	137	16				
Litsea sp.					38	0·5	88	15	30	0·3	68	13
Garcinia morella					25	0·4	72	11	10	0·1	10	4
Macaranga peltata					25	0·3	23	9				
Xanthophyllum flavescens					13	0·3	32	6				
Myristica dactyloides					13	0·1	97	5	30	0·3	49	12
Unidentified sp. F					13	0·1	88	5				
					13	0·1	75	5	60	0·4	124	15

Species												
[illegible]												
Amoora sp.					13	0·1	21	5	40	0·7	123	27
Boehmeria malabarica					13	0·1	11	4				
Laportea crenulata					13	0·1	11	4				
Knema attenuata									20	0·2	80	10
Canarium strictum									10	0·1	20	4
Glochidion sp.									10	0·1	10	4
Miliusa sp.									10	0·1	10	4
SAPLINGS												
Dimocarpus longan	80	1·4	32	100					10	0·1	5	7
Litsea sp.	60	1·0	19	70	25	0·3	8	15	10	0·1	4	7
Olea dioica	20	0·6	31	53								
Clerodendrum viscosum	20	0·2	10	23								
Eugenia sp.	20	0·2	8	21	50	1·4	36	55	10	0·1	3	6
Unidentified sp. E	20	0·2	4	17								
Unidentified sp. F	20	0·2	3	16								
Myristica dactyloides					38	0·5	22	29	40	0·4	19	29
Xanthophyllum flavescens					38	0·4	13	23				
Palaquium ellipticum					38	0·4	12	22	50	0·7	39	48
Cullenia exarillata					25	0·4	12	19	50	0·6	21	37
Macaranga peltata					13	0·3	17	16				
Boehmeria malabarica					25	0·3	10	15				
Laportea crenulata					25	0·3	7	14				
Litsea coriacea					13	0·3	12	14				
Euonymus angulatus					13	0·2	8	11				
Artocarpus heterophyllus					13	0·1	9	10				
Nothapodytes foetida					13	0·1	9	10				
Syzygium laetum					13	0·1	9	10				
Callicarpa tomentosa					13	0·1	7	9				
Unidentified sp. A					13	0·1	7	9	10	0·2	5	9
Amoora sp.					13	0·1	4	9	60	1·1	50	65
Glochidion sp.					13	0·1	2	6	20	0·2	8	14
Cinnamomum macrocarpum					13	0·1	1	6	20	0·2	7	13
Mesua nagasarium									30	0·3	11	20
Miliusa sp.									10	0·1	7	8
Holigarna nigra									10	0·1	4	7
Elaeocarpus tuberculatus									10	0·1	3	6
Garcinia morella									10	0·1	3	6
Knema attenuata									10	0·1	3	6
Scolopia crenata									10	0·1	3	6
Alseodaphne sp.									10	0·1	1	5

Total tree density and total basal cover were lower as compared to the mesic upland forest.

The mesic upland forest was dominated by *P. ellipticum*, *Cullenia exarillata* and *Ficus* sp. (Table 2). However, only 16% trees belonged to *P. ellipticum* which had an IVI of 64. The total tree basal cover (103 m^2/ha) is considerably greater than the values reported (36·0–73·6 m^2/ha) for tropical rain forests from certain other regions (Dawkins 1958, 1959; Burgess 1961; Kartawinata *et al.* 1981).

The less mesic upland forest dominated by *P. ellipticum*, *Drypetes elata* and *Alseodaphne* sp. (Table 2) had the least total tree basal cover among the three sites. The total tree density in this forest was higher compared to the riparian forest but lower compared to the mesic upland forest.

These findings suggest that the tree layer in the riparian forest is not so well developed as in the upland forests. Among the two upland forests the tree layer is less extensive in the less mesic forest. It is not clear whether the less mesic condition is a result of heavier biotic disturbance or of lower rainfall, hence it cannot be stated whether or not the lower tree basal cover on this site has resulted from greater biotic stress or from water stress.

The analytic data for trees in different girth classes (Table 3) indicate that each of the eight different girth classes normally had different dominants. For example, in the mesic upland forest the dominant species was *Agrostistachys meeboldii* in 31·5–65·5 cm girth class, *Eugenia* sp. in 66–100 cm girth class, an unidentified sp. in 135–169 cm girth class, *D. elata* in 169·5–203·5 cm girth class, *C. exarillata* in 204–238 and in 238·5–272·5 cm girth classes, and *P. ellipticum* in ≥273 cm girth class (Table 3).

In general, the IVI of the dominant species in a girth class increased from lower to higher girth classes. This in part was related to the fact that in lower girth classes there was a greater number of species. As a corollary the vegetation in lower girth classes was more diverse.

Saplings

Table 2 indicates that species which were predominant in the tree layer did not dominate the sapling layer. Richards (1952) points out that in several rain-forests, the dominant species vary from one girth class to another, to the extent that in some sites the most dominant species of top canopy may have few individuals in lower girth classes. Earlier, these facts had led Aubréville (1938) to state that the combination of dominant species at a given place and time is succeeded, not by the same combination, but by a different one.

In riparian forest the dominant member of the tree layer (*E. tuberculatus*) was absent from the sapling layer and the other co-dominants were much less represented (Table 2). The total density of this layer, too, was less (3·8 saplings/100 m^2) in this forest than in upland forests.

In mesic upland forest, the dominants in the sapling layer were *Eugenia* sp., *Myristica dactyloides*, *Xanthophyllum flavescens* and *P. ellipticum* (Table 2). The maximum IVI for an individual species was less than that in the tree layer. There were a total of 5·6 saplings/100 m^2, of which 1·4 belonged to *Eugenia* sp. and 0·5 to *M. dactyloides*.

In less mesic upland forest, except for *P. ellipticum* none of the dominants of the tree layer were also dominant in the sapling layer (Table 2). *Amoora* sp. was the most common. *C. exarillata*, which was the co-dominant species in the tree layer of the mesic upland forest but not in this forest, was among the dominant species of the sapling layer. The total density of 4·7 saplings/100 m² lies between that of mesic upland and the riparian forests.

Seedlings

In the riparian forest *Dimocarpus longan* had the maximum number of seedlings (Table 4). The total seedling density was lower (16·8/100 m²) compared to the mesic upland forest (38·5/100 m²). In the latter forest, *P. ellipticum*, the dominant species of the tree layer, had the maximum seedling density; this was followed by *D. longan* which was hardly represented in higher girth classes (Table 4).

In less mesic upland forest, *Knema attenuata* which dominated neither the tree layer nor the sapling layer had maximum seedling density closely followed by *Eugenia* sp. which too was less prominent in higher girth classes (Table 4). The total seedling density of 29·8/100 m² lies between the mesic upland and the riparian forests.

Shrubs and herbs

The total density of shrubs declined in less mesic forest. It was 159 per 100 m² in riparian, 63 per 100 m² in mesic upland and 5 per 100 m² in less mesic upland forest (Table 4). The dominant shrub was *Ochlandra scriptoria* in riparian, *Strobilanthes* sp. in mesic and *Psychotria thwaitesii* in less mesic upland forest.

During the ten years following the clearance of original vegetation along the roads, a 3–4 m tall shrubby vegetation (treelets), largely dominated by *Clerodendrum* sp. (30·4 plants/100 m²) and *Macaranga peltata* (8·8 plants/100 m²), has emerged. *Macaranga* has been called a genus of 'biological nomads' by van Steenis (1958) and 'pioneer par excellence' by Whitmore (1975). The individuals of *M. peltata*, were, however in the denser regions. The shrub layer not rising above 3 m was dominated by *Leea* sp. and *Solanum torvum*. The dominant species of the herb layer of this secondary vegetation were either absent or present only in negligible numbers in the dense forests. Some of the coarse grasses, such as *Saccharum spontaneum* and *Imperata cylindrica* which dominate the grassland, were present in sizeable proportions.

The herb layer was poor under all the forests. *Pouzolzia* sp. in mesic upland as well as in less mesic upland forests and *Schumannianthus virgatus* in the riparian forest were the most frequent herbs (Table 5).

The grassland examined in the Veliaparathod area was covered with coarse tussock species. *Saccharum spontaneum*, *Imperata cylindrica* and *Themeda triandra* were dominant. *Cymbopogon* sp. and *Curcuma* sp. were also present. Scattered trees of *Emblica officinalis* were evident. Associated with these were isolated trees of *Wendlandia notoniana* and the seedlings of *Dalbergia* sp.

Woody climbers

Woody climbers occurred on 25 tree species. They were most frequent on *Eugenia* sp. (on 91% of the individuals), frequent on *Litsea coriacea* (57%), less frequent (30–40%) on *C. exarillata*, *Amoora* sp., *Nothapodytes foetida* and *Litsea* sp. and were only occasionally

TABLE 3. Analytic characters and IVI of tree components of different gbh classes in riparian forest and, mesic and less mesic upland forests

Species	Riparian forest				Mesic upland forest				Less mesic upland forest			
	Frequency (%)	Density (plants/ 100 m^2)	Total basal cover (cm^2/ 100 m^2)	IVI	Frequency (%)	Density (plants/ 100 m^2)	Total basal cover (cm^2/ 100 m^2)	IVI	Frequency (%)	Density (plants/ 100 m^2)	Total basal cover (cm^2/ 100 m^2)	IVI
31·5 to 65·5 cm gbh												
Clerodendrum viscosum	20	0·4	100	45								
Unidentified sp. B	20	0·2	61	29								
Holigarna nigra	20	0·2	57	28								
Calophyllum elatum	20	0·2	57	28								
Unidentified sp. D	20	0·2	57	28								
Litsea wightii	20	0·2	62	27								
Toona ciliata	20	0·2	40	25								
Helicia sp.	20	0·2	40	25								
Dimocarpus longan	20	0·2	26	22	13	0·1	17	9	10	0·1	24	9
Eugenia sp.	20	0·2	20	21	25	0·6	73	33				
Memecylon sp.	20	0·2	20	21								
Agrostistachya meeboldii					38	0·5	137	44				
Nothepodytes foetida					38	0·5	69	34	10	0·1	10	7
Palaquium ellipticum					25	0·5	65	29	90	1·4	236	98
Garcinia morella					25	0·4	71	27				
Litsea sp.					25	0·4	34	22	20	0·2	29	16
Macaranga peltata					25	0·3	23	15				
Xanthophyllum flavescens					13	0·3	32	15				
Unidentified sp. C					13	0·1	42	13				
Drypetes elata					13	0·1	28	11	10	0·1	30	10
Amoora sp.					13	0·1	20	10	40	0·5	570	34
Unidentified sp. A					13	0·1	18	10				
Boehmeria malabarica					13	0·1	11	9				
Leportea crenulata					13	0·1	11	9				
Litsea coriacea									30	0·3	86	30
Cullenia exarillata					13	0·2	14	9	30	0·3	52	25
Alseodaphne sp.									20	0·3	60	23
Myristica dactyloides									20	0·3	44	18
Canarium strictum									10	0·1	20	8
Knema attenuata									10	0·1	20	8
Miliusa sp.									10	0·1	10	7
Glochidion sp.									10	0·1	10	7
66 to 100 cm gbh												
Poeciloneuron indicum	40	0·6	348	70								

Species												
[illegible]	20	0·4	287	47								
Alseodaphne sp.	20	0·2	129	27					30	0·4	223	60
Unidentified sp. A	20	0·2	115	26								
Gordonia obtusa	20	0·2	102	25								
Clerodendrum viscosum	20	0·2	78	24								
Litsea wightii	20	0·2	74	24								
Palaquium ellipticum					25	0·3	116	44	40	0·6	317	85
Myristica dactyloides					13	0·1	94	32				
Unidentified sp. F					13	0·1	84	31				
Litsea sp.					13	0·1	75	30	10	0·1	45	15
Nothapodytes foetida					13	0·2	72	30				
Litsea coriacea					13	0·1	72	30	10	0·1	39	15
Unidentified sp. D					13	0·1	64	29	10	0·1	51	16
Unidentified sp. E					13	0·1	61	24				
Amoora sp.									20	0·2	78	30
Knema attenuata									10	0·1	67	18
Holigarna nigra									10	0·1	51	16
Unidentified sp. C									10	0·1	45	15
Dimocarpus longan									10	0·1	45	15
Unidentified sp. B									10	0·1	41	15
100·5 to 134·5 cm gbh												
Elaeocarpus tuberculatus	20	0·2	269	80								
Ficus sp.	20	0·2	229	76								
Unidentified sp. C	20	0·2	193	72								
Unidentified sp. D	20	0·2	193	72								
Alseodaphne sp.									10	0·2	249	300
135 to 169 cm gbh												
Cinnamomum macrocarpum	20	0·2	312	300								
Unidentified sp. B					13	0·1	224	300				
Holigarna nigra									10	0·1	156	300
169·5 to 203·5 cm gbh												
Drypetes elata					25	0·3	796	300	20	0·2	516	201
Calophyllum sp.									10	0·1	258	99
204 to 238 cm gbh												
Olea dioica	20	0·2	770	300								
Cullenia exarillata					13	0·1	447	300				
Drypetes elata									10	0·1	334	300
238·5 to 272·5 cm gbh												
Elaeocarpus tuberculatus	20	0·2	1076	300								
Cullenia exarillata					13	0·1	573	300				
≥273 cm gbh												
Palaquium ellipticum					25	0·4	7558	176				
Ficus sp.					13	0·1	2486	67				
Cullenia exarillata					13	0·1	1436	57				

TABLE 4. Tree seedlings, shrubs and climbers in Riparian forest and mesic and less mesic upland forests

Species	Riparian forest		Mesic upland forest		Less mesic upland forest	
	Frequency (%)	Density (plants/100 m^2)	Frequency (%)	Density (plants/100 m^2)	Frequency (%)	Density (plants/100 m^2)
SEEDLINGS						
Dimocarpus longan	40	4·8	63	4·5		
Eugenia sp.	40	3·2	13	2·0	60	4·4
Antidesma sp.	20	2·4				
Boehmeria malabarica	20	1·6	13	0·5		
Poeciloneuron indicum	20	1·6				
Nothophagus sp.	20	1·8				
Cinnamomum macrocarpum	20	0·8	13	1·5		
Elaeocarpus tuberculatus	20	0·8				
Syzygium caryophyllatum	20	0·8				
Palaquium ellipticum			38	10·0	30	2·4
Persea macrantha			13	3·0		
Myristica dactyloides			50	3·0	20	1·2
Mesua nagasarium			25	3·0	60	3·7
Agrostistachys meeboldii			25	2·0	20	2·4
Syzygium laetum			13	2·0		
Canarium strictum			13	2·0		
Cullenia exarillata			25	1·0	10	0·8
Alseodaphne sp.			13	1·0	20	1·6
Laportea crenulata			13	1·0		
Xanthophyllum flavescens			13	0·5		
Garcinia morella			13	0·5	20	1·6
Memecylon sp.			13	0·5		
Glochidion sp.			13	0·5	20	1·6
Amoora sp.			13	0·5	30	2·0
Knema attenuata					80	5·2
Litsea coriacea					10	1·2
Drypetes elata					10	0·5
Litsea sp.					10	0·4
Holigarna nigra					10	0·4
Chrozophora sp.					10	0·4

SHRUBS						
Ochlandra scriptoria	40	108·0				
Psychotria thwaitesii	80	40·0	38	4·0	50	3·4
Strobilanthes sp.	60	11·2	50	30·5		
Antistrophe serratifolia			50	15·5		
Leea indica			25	3·5		
Ipomaea silicosa			25	3·5	20	1·6
Lasianthus jackianus			38	1·5		
Microtropis latifolia			25	1·5		
Unidentified sp. A			13	1·0		
CLIMBERS						
Piper sp.	60	4·0	63	13·5	40	3·6
Smilax prolifera	40	2·4	13	2·0	10	0·8
Gnetum sp.	40	1·6				
Sarcostemma intermedium	40	1·6				
Randia speciosa	20	1·6			10	0·4
Caryatia sp.	20	0·8				
Jasminium sp.	20	0·8			10	0·4
Stephania sp.	20	0·8				
Mezoneuron sp.	20	0·8				
Calamus rotang			25	5·0	30	1·2
Erythropalum populifolium			38	3·0	40	3·2
Paramignya armata			38	3·0		
Cissus sp.			25	2·5		
Ancistrocladus heyneanus			25	1·5		
Pothos scandens			25	1·5	10	0·4
Thunbergia sp.			13	0·5	20	0·8
Ventilago sp.			13	0·5	30	2·4
Trichosanthes sp.			13	0·5		
Derris sp.					40	2·0
Cyclea peltata					10	0·4

TABLE 5. Percentage frequency of herbs in the riparian forest and mesic and less mesic upland forests

Species	Riparian forest	Mesic upland forest	Less mesic upland forest
Pouzolzia sp.		87·5	70·0
Amorphophalus sp.		25·0	
Sarcandra grandifolia		25·0	30·0
Ophiuros sp.		25·0	
Panicum sp.		12·5	
Pellionia sp.		12·5	
Amomum cannaecarpum	40·0	12·5	
Pandanus sp.	60·0		20·0
Chloranthus sp.	40·0		
Croton sp.			70·0
Eginolfia sp.			60·0
Elatostemma sp.			10·0
Schumannianthus virgatus	80·0		

present on *P. ellipticum* (13·5%). Among the shrubs, climbers occurred most frequently on *M. peltata* (on 75% of the individuals).

The number of species was similar (9–11) across sites. However, their total density was much higher in the mesic upland forest than the less mesic upland or riparian forests (Table 4). *Piper* sp. was most prevalent in mesic upland (13·5/100 m^2) and riparian forest (4·0/100 m^2) as well as in less mesic upland forest (3·6/100 m^2).

Profiles

Figures 1 to 3 illustrate the profile structures of the three forests. Though there was frequent overlapping, a total of six tree strata in the mesic upland forest, five in the less mesic upland forest and four in the riparian forest were frequently recognizable. Two additional strata, one of the shrubs or treelets and the other of herbs were also present. The grassland consisted mainly of grasses less than 1·5 m tall and few scattered trees of about 4 m height.

The average tree heights in the riparian forest were 34·9, 21·9, 13·8, 7·5 and 2·3 m, respectively for A4, A3, A2, A1 and B strata. The height of each stratum in this forest was lower compared to mesic upland forest even with the same species. However, girth attained by a species was more or less similar in both the forests, indicating that the trees are less slender compared to those of the mesic upland forest. In contrast, canopy depth was relatively greater in these forests than in the upland forests. The A4 stratum was sparse with a broken canopy. This stratum had one tree each of *Olea dioica* and *E. tuberculatus* within an area of 400 m^2. The A3 stratum had a denser canopy and was dominated by *Eugenia* sp. Other species such as *C. exarillata*, *Amoora* sp., *Alseodaphne* sp., *Gordonia obtusa* etc., were also present in this stratum. The A2 and A1 strata had more or less continuous canopies. *D. longan* was the most common species in these strata. The B stratum, dominated by *O. scriptoria*, was well defined with plants being very dense at places. The crowns in the different strata tended to be deep rather than wide.

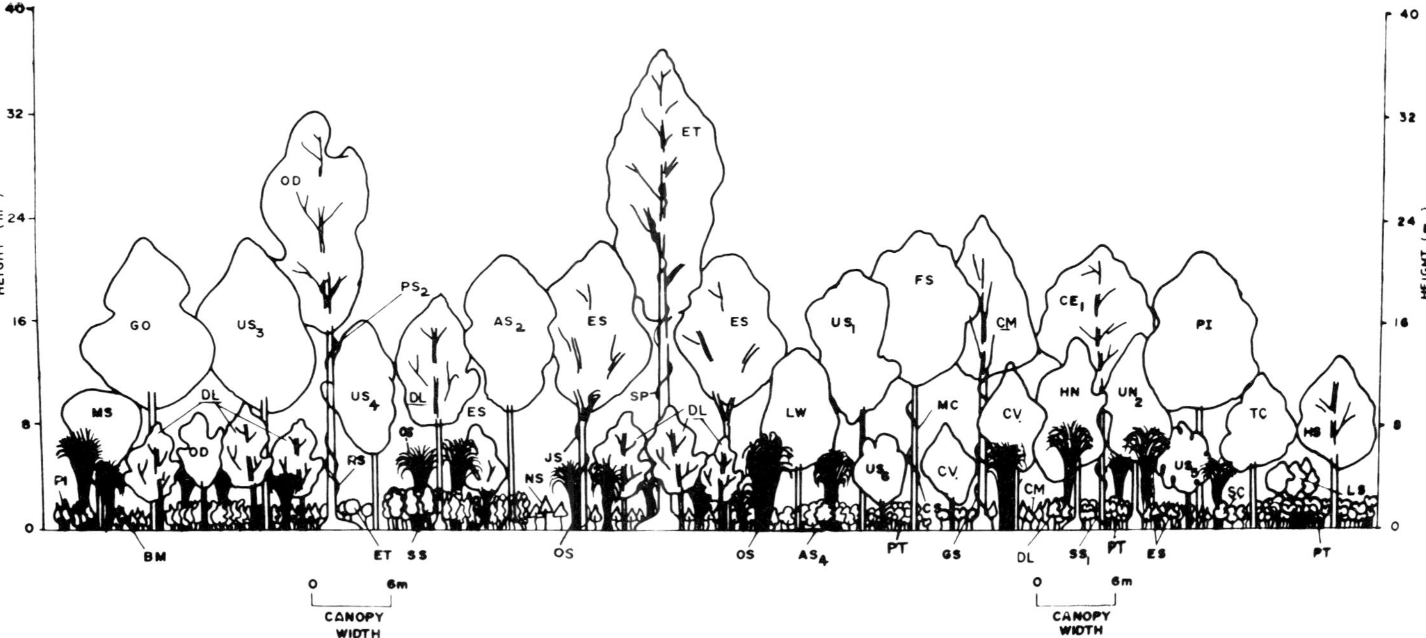

Fig. 1. Profile diagram for riparian forest representing 400 m² area.

AS₂ = *Alseodaphne* sp., AS₄ = *Antidesma* sp., BM = *Boehmeria malabarica*, CE₁ = *Calophyllum elatum*, CM = *Cinnamomum macrocarpum*, CV = *Clerodendrum viscosum*, DL = *Dimocarpus longan*, ET = *Elaeocarpus tuberculatus*, ES = *Eugenia* sp., FS = *Ficus* sp., GS = *Glochidion* sp., GO = *Gordonia obtusa*, HN = *Holigarna nigra*, HS = *Helicia* sp., JS = *Jasminum* sp., LS = *Litsea* sp., LW = *Litsea wightii*, MC = *Mezoneuron* sp., MS = *Memecylon* sp., NS = *Nothophagus* sp., OD = *Olea dioica*, OS = *Ochlandra scriptoria*, PS₂ = *Piper* sp., PI = *Poeciloneuron indicum*, PT = *Psychotria thwaitesii*, RS = *Randia speciosa*, SC = *Syzygium caryophyllatum*, SS = *Strobilanthes* sp., SS₁ = *Stephania* sp., SP = *Smilax prolifera*, TC = *Toona ciliata*, US₁ = Unidentified sp. A, UN₂ = Unidentified sp. B, US₃ = Unidentified sp. C, US₄ = Unidentified sp. D, US₅ = Unidentified sp. E, US₆ = Unidentified sp. F.

In the mesic upland forest, the canopies of the upper three strata (A6, A5, A4) were discontinuous, with sparse trees. The top layer consisted of isolated trees which emerged above others, imparting an undulating shape to the physiognomy of the forest. The canopy of the fourth stratum (A3) was comparatively continuous and the trees were dense. In general, the canopy of the fifth (A2) stratum was irregular and discontinuous. However, in places where second and third strata canopies were relatively more broken, the canopy of the fifth layer was better developed and it overlapped with the canopy of the fourth layer, forming a dense continuous canopy. The sixth stratum (A1), consisting mainly of young individuals of species which form the taller strata, was well developed. The shrub and treelet stratum (B) was also well defined. The trunk height/diameter ratio was very high giving a slender appearance to trees. The average heights were 54·6, 43·6, 36·0, 23·3, 15·0, 8·2 and 3·8 m in A6–A1 strata. The height of the uppermost layer compares well with some luxurient lowland evergreen forests of Malaya (Whitmore 1975), *P. ellipticum* and *C. exarillata* were the only occupants of this stratum. *Ficus* sp. (a 'strangler') together with *P. ellipticum* represented the A5 stratum. In the A4 stratum *D. elata* was dominant, while in the A3, A2 and A1 strata *Eugenia* sp. was dominant. The shrub layer was dominated by *Strobilanthes* sp. *Pouzolzia* sp. formed the poorly developed, almost non-existent herb layer.

The uppermost stratum (A5) of the less mesic upland forest had only two trees of *D. elata* per 400 m² area with an average height of 42·0 m. The next two strata, A4 and A3 with average heights of 29·3 and 21·5 m, respectively, were also little developed with a discontinuous canopy. A4 stratum was dominated by *Alseodaphne* sp. *P. ellipticum* dominated both the A3 and A2 strata (average height = 15·7 m). The latter layer had an almost continuous canopy. The canopy of the lowest stratum (A1) was fairly dense, with an average height of 7·6 m. The seedlings of *K. attenuata* (tree species) and *P. thwaitesii* (shrub) were dominant in the B stratum which indicated an average height of 2·2 m.

Buttresses, a characteristic feature of rain-forest were exhibited by almost all emergent and some understorey species. For example, 57% trees of the larger girth class were buttressed in *C. exarillata* and *D. elata*, about 41% in *P. ellipticum*, 75% in *Holigarna nigra*, 85% in *Alseodaphne* sp., and 14% in *M. peltata*.

In conclusion, the forests are highly stratified with the emergent trees imparting a 'bumpy look when viewed from the air' (Odum 1971). The canopy is aerodynamically rough, perhaps stimulating energy exchange between the stand and the atmosphere and generating high productivity (Brünig *et al.* 1978). The trees are typically slender often exhibiting 'flying buttresses' at the base and the vegetation is rich in epiphytes and stranglers. These characteristics unequivocally associate the forests with tropical rain forest (Odum 1971; Whitmore 1975; Ewusie 1980). The profile structure reflects the impoverishment of the less mesic upland forest and the contrasting nature of the riparian forest. Along the mesic-xeric gradient, both the height of tallest plants and degree of stratification were maximum in middle part.

Leaf and bark characteristics

The lack of massive amounts of new leaves in Spring, so characteristic of temperate deciduous forests, bears testimony to the tropical nature of these forests. Leaves were

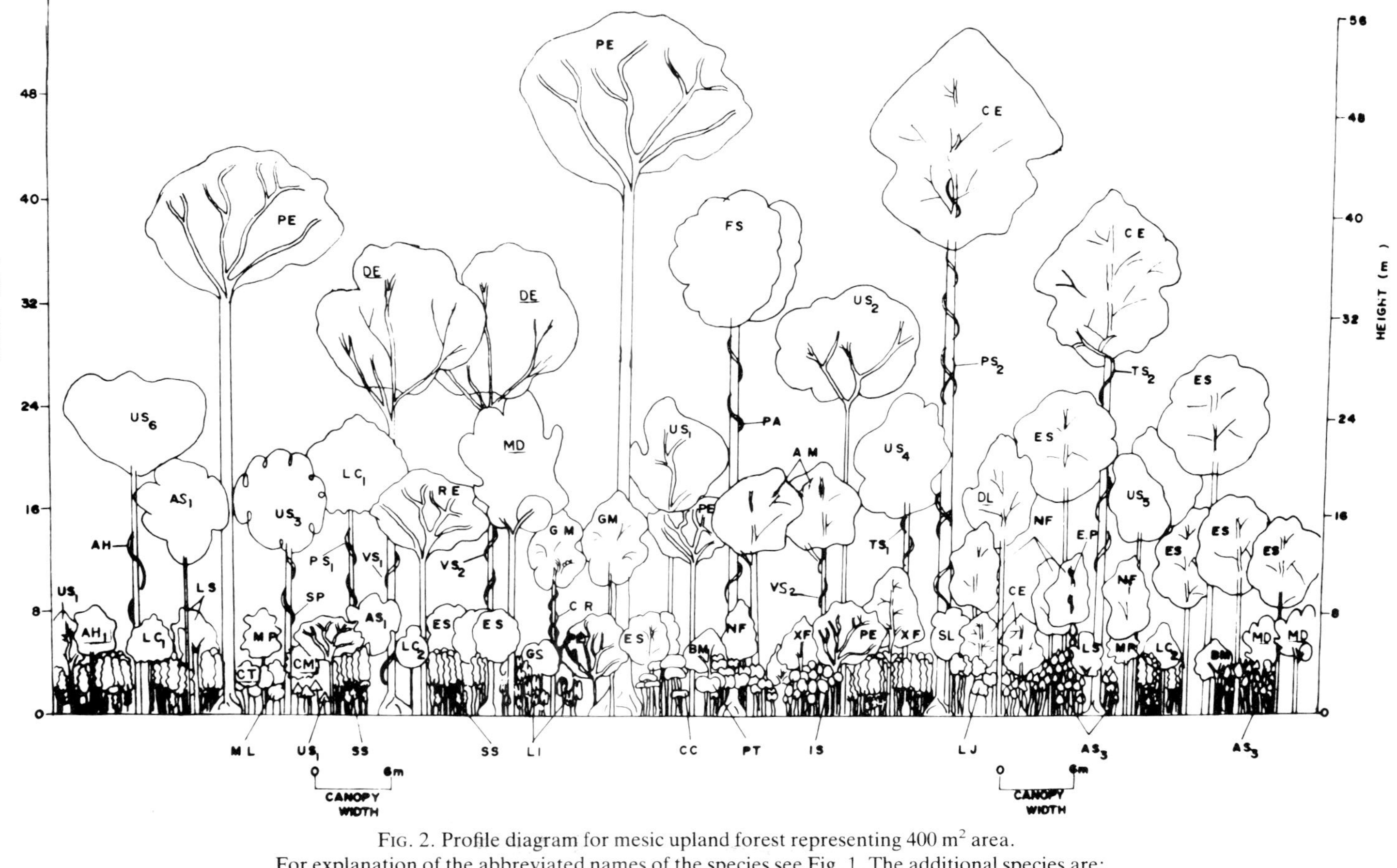

Fig. 2. Profile diagram for mesic upland forest representing 400 m^2 area.

For explanation of the abbreviated names of the species see Fig. 1. The additional species are:
AM = *Agrostistachys meeboldii*, AS$_1$ = *Amoora* sp., AS$_3$ = *Antistrophe serratifolia*, AH = *Ancistrocladus heyneanus*, AH$_1$ = *Artocarpus heterophyllus*, CE = *Cullenia exarillata*, CT = *Callicarpa tomentosa*, CR = *Calamus rotang*, CC = *Chasalia curviflora*, DE = *Drypetes elata*, EP = *Erythropalum populifolium*, GM = *Garcinia morella*, IS = *Ipomoea silicosa*, LC$_1$ = *Litsea coriacea*, LC$_2$ = *Laportea crenulata*, LI = *Leea indica*, LJ = *Lasianthus jackianus*, MD = *Myristica dactyloides*, MP = *Macaranga peltata*, ML = *Microtropis latifolia*, NF = *Nothapodytes foetida*, PE = *Palaquium ellipticum*, PS$_1$ = *Pothos scandens*, PA = *Paranignya armata*, SL = *Syzygium laetum*, TS$_1$ = *Thunbergia* sp., TS$_2$ = *Trichosanthes* sp., US$_2$ = Unidentified sp. B, VS$_1$ = *Ventilago* sp., VS$_2$ = *Cissus* sp., XF = *Xanthophyllum flavescens*.

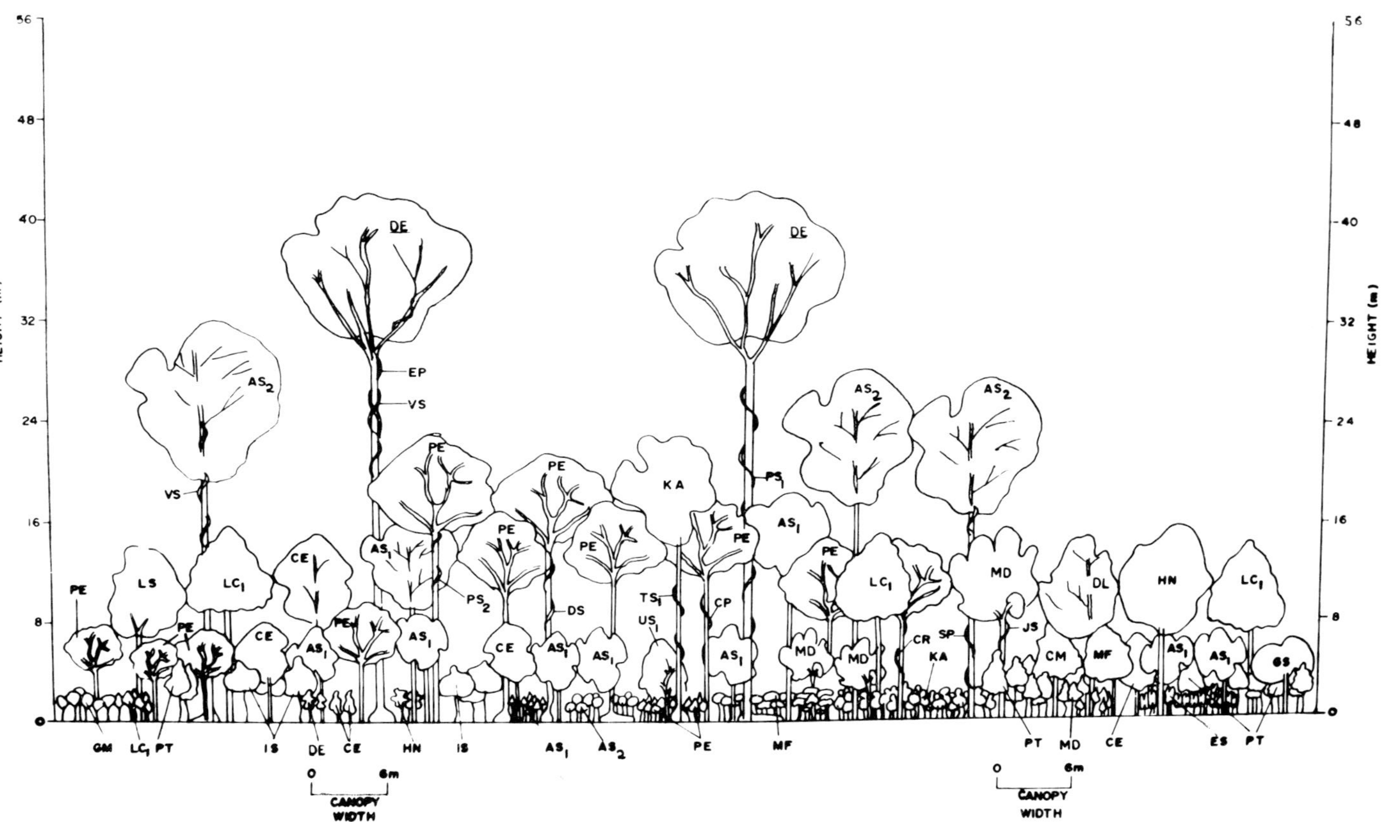

FIG. 3. Profile diagram for Less mesic upland forest representing 400 m² area:
For explanation of the abbreviated names of the species see Figs 1 and 2. The additional species are:
CP = *Cyclea peltata*, DS = *Derris* sp., KA = *Knema attenuata*, MF = *Mesua ferrea* (= *M. nagasarium*).

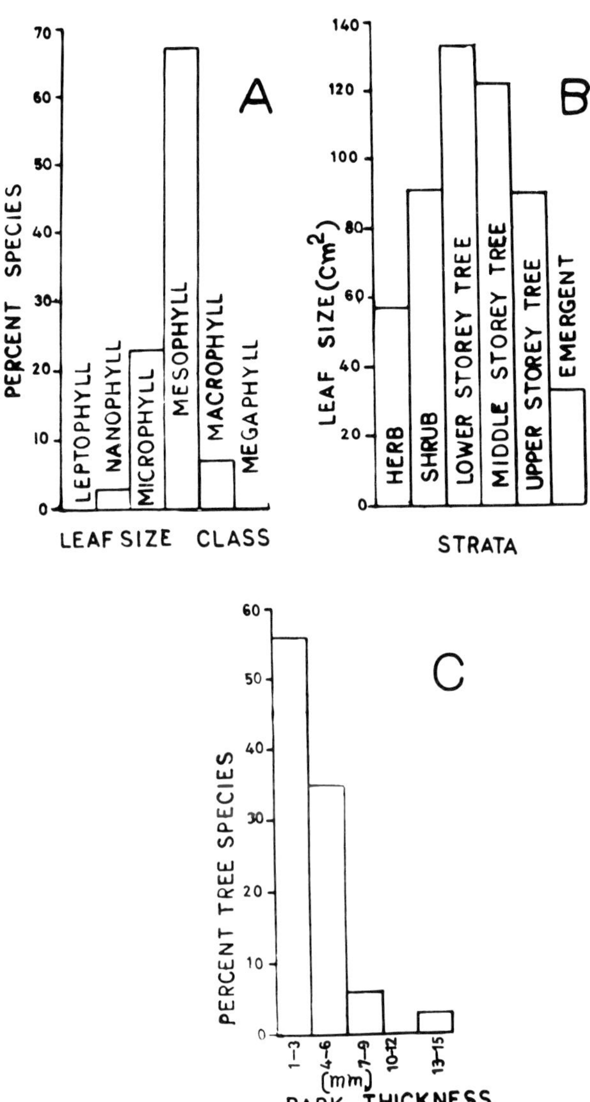

FIG. 4. (a) Leaf size spectrum for Silent Valley upland forests.   (b) Leaf size variation in different strata in Silent Valley upland forests.   (c) Bark spectrum for Silent Valley upland forests.

evergreen, laurel-like and with drip tips. Margins were mainly entire. Upper canopy leaves were thick, lower canopy leaves were thinner. Richards (1952) and Ewusie (1980) include these features among the characteristics of trees of tropical rain-forest.

An analysis of the leaf size using Raunkiaer's (1934) classification, showed a pattern (Fig. 4a) which approached that reported for other rain-forests (Richards 1952; Whitmore 1975). An overwhelmingly large percentage of the species bore mesophyll leaves; a much smaller percentage had microphyll and macrophyll leaves. The percentage of species with nanophyll leaves was negligible, and species with the lepto and megaphyll size — classes were lacking.

The leaf size increased from emergent to lower stratum trees (Fig. 4b). This fact has seldom been commented upon, but can be readily demonstrated in any rain forest community (Richards 1952). In the given site, the average leaf size was 32.7 cm^2 for emergent trees, 89.8 cm^2 for canopy trees, 121.7 cm^2 for middle storey trees, and 132.7 cm^2 for lower-storey trees. The leaf size was smaller in shrubs and herbs.

Trees of the Silent Valley forest were conspicuous by having exceptionally thin bark, about 56% of species having a bark thickness between 1–3 mm (Fig. 4c). If thin barks are an indication of year round favourable growth conditions, Silent Valley provides most favourable growth conditions for trees.

Population structure

Population structures of certain tree species are illustrated in Fig. 5. The population structure displayed by different species can be arbitrarily categorized as follows: (i) Expanding population structure, i.e., with a greater proportion of individuals in seedling and sapling stages compared to larger girth classes. Certain species, e.g. *Eugenia* sp. in riparian forest and *P. ellipticum* in mesic and less mesic upland forests exhibited expanding populations, though the pinched middle indicated that disturbance in

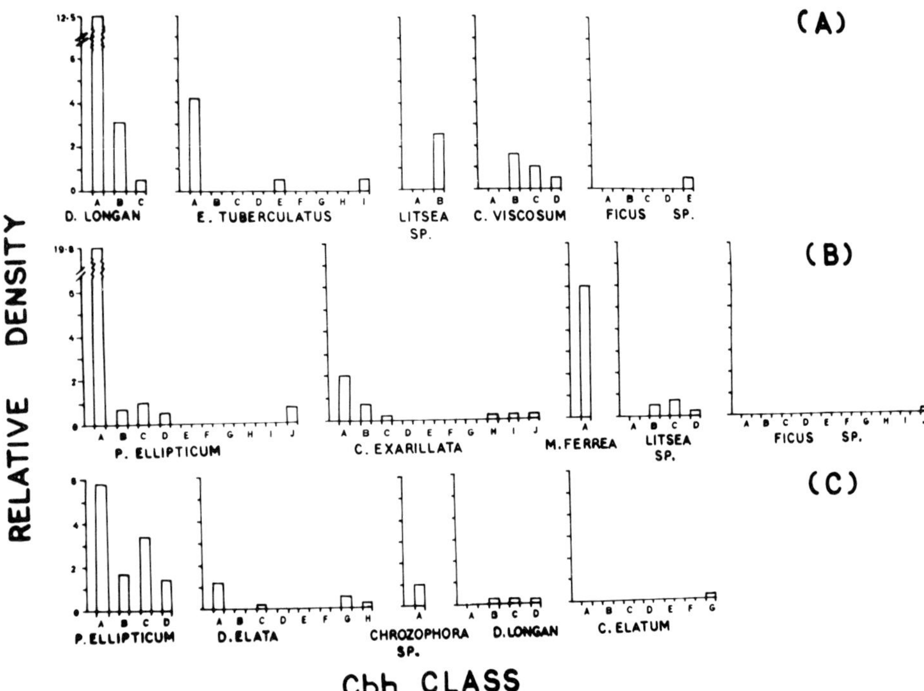

Fig. 5. Population structures of certain species. (a) riparian forest, (b) mesic upland forest and (c) less mesic upland forest. Cbh (circumference at breast height) = gbh.

regeneration had occurred at some time in the past. (ii) Declining population structure, i.e., with most of the individuals in intermediate girth classes and fewer both towards higher and lower girth classes, e.g., *Clerodendrum viscosum* in riparian, *Litsea* sp. in mesic upland and *D. longan* in less mesic upland forests. (iii) Youthful population, i.e., individuals largely confined to seedling and/or sapling size classes (e.g. *Mesua nagasarium* in upland forests, and *Litsea* sp. in riparian forest). (iv) Interrupted population structure — i.e., absence of individuals in one or other of the middle girth classes (e.g. *E. tuberculatus* in riparian, *C. exarillata* in mesic upland and *D. elata* in less mesic upland forest). Interruption may suggest gap-phase type reproduction or may indicate disturbance with a resultant reduction in survival during a given time interval. This type of reproduction may also reflect different microclimatic conditions on the forest floor which results from the change in site conditions, such as overstorey density. (v) Population structure of *Ficus* sp. and *M. peltata* in mesic upland forest and of *Calophyllum elatum* in less mesic upland forest representing a pattern which is characterized by one or two girth classes (with a very few individuals). The species following this pattern may be 'accidental' species.

A total of 31% species in riparian, 20% in mesic upland, and 11% species in less mesic upland forest had interrupted regeneration (Table 6). This gap-phase regeneration illustrates the fact that in rain-forest the combination of dominants varies in time and space (i.e., a mosaic pattern or a cyclical change in regeneration). The number of species with expanding population was maximum in less mesic upland forest (33%) followed by mesic upland (14%) and riparian forests (6%). Present results and those from Barro Calorado Island, Panama (Knight 1975), and Ivory Coast (computed on the basis of Aubréville 1938) tend to suggest that the percentage of species with expanding population structure is low in species-rich forests, even if they are virgin and mature. It appears that instability in population structure in the majority of species leads to rapid changes in species composition with time over a local spatial scale, often noticed in species-rich forests.

The data on population structure indicate an absence of regeneration of some species, including dominants. This situation in limited areas of mature tropical forests is well documented by Aubréville (1938), Richards (1952), Schulz (1960), and Baur (1964). Aubréville's mosaic theory of tropical forest regeneration was enunciated to explain the absence of their own juveniles beneath large tree spp. in virgin forest. The climax tropical forests of West Africa are spatially dynamic and it is difficult to predict the dominant species of a particular climax community (Aubréville 1938). It appears that in Silent Valley production of seedlings by the dominants requires the creation of small gaps by tree-fall, and their growth depends on the subsequent course of gap succession, i.e. light conditions being suitable for their growth. Consequently seedlings of a dominant species may be found growing at places where its old-growth trees are not evident, seedlings of other dominant species being found growing in the vicinity of old-growth trees of the former species. For instance, on the sample plot in the mesic upland forest *D. longan* had abundance of seedlings, whereas it was hardly represented in the tree layer. Similarly on less mesic upland forest site, *K. attenuata* which dominated neither tree nor the sapling layer, had maximum seedlings and on the riparian forest site, the most dominant member of tree layer was absent from the sapling layer. The shape of population structure is a function also of number of individuals sampled. Figure 6 represents population structures of two important species of mesic upland forest in Silent Valley, one for a small area (eight 10 × 10 m quadrats) and another for a larger area (entire mesic upland forest). The population structure of both the species indicates instability on a small area basis, but stability on a large area basis. Thus, the selection of the appropriate size of sampling area is important.

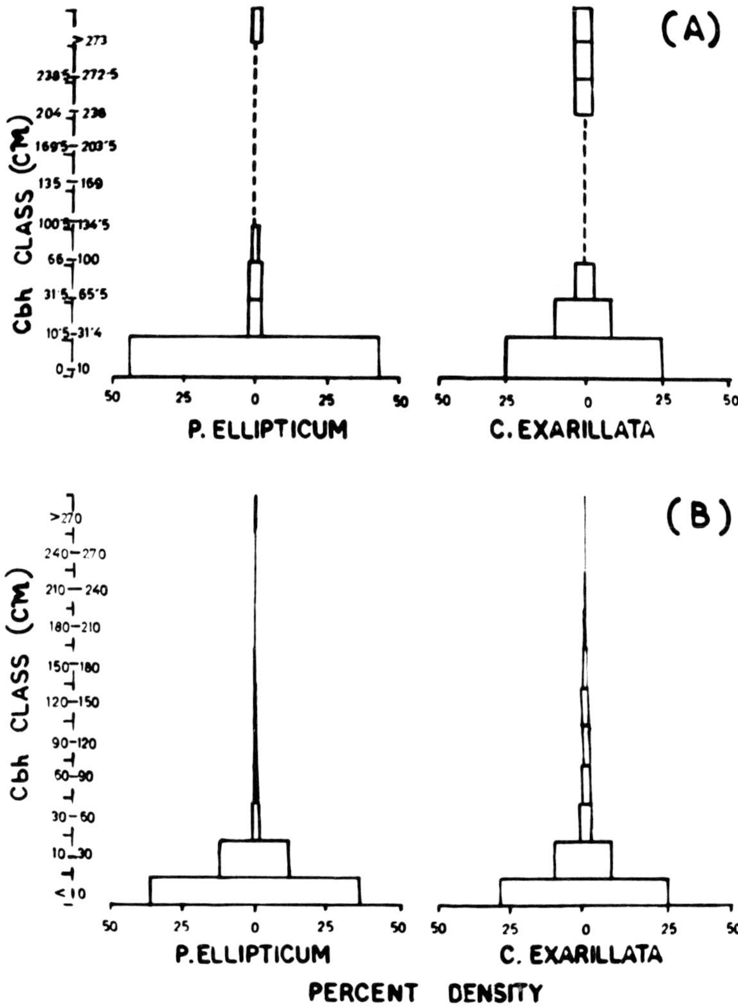

FIG. 6. Population structures of two dominants, *Palaquium ellipticum* and *Cullenia exarillata*, in mesic upland forest as represented by percentage of individuals in different gbh classes. (a) based on small area sampled in present study, (b) based on entire area of mesic upland forest (by combining the data of Chandrashekharan 1973 for individuals larger than 30 cm gbh and our data for individuals in 10–30 cm gbh range and <10 cm gbh).

Plant diversity

The plant diversity in the present forest has been examined in the context of species area curves, Shannon–Wiener function, spatial diversity and resource partitioning.

TABLE 6. Percentage of species with different population structure in the different forest types

Forest	Expanding	Declining	Youthful	Interrupted	Accidental
Riparian forest	5·7	5·7	14·3	31·4	42·9
Mesic upland forest	14·3	5·7	17·1	20·0	42·9
Less mesic upland forest	33·3	3·7	14·8	11·1	37·0

Species area curve

Species area curves are based on 8 contiguous, 10 × 10 m quadrats in the mesic upland forest, and 10 contiguous quadrats of the same size in the riparian and less mesic upland forests. All vascular plants within these quadrats, with the exception of ferns and epiphytic lower plants, were recorded. The curves (Fig. 7) for all vascular plants increased nearly exponentially in all forests. Due to the limitation of time, data could not be collected from a larger area, but as the trend of the curves indicates, species number would continue to increase with increasing area. Species area curves for a variety of tropical forests show that the number of species increases to the largest plot studied (Ross 1954; Farnworth & Golley 1974). For the species area curve for trees only, the rate of increase in number of species is somewhat lower.

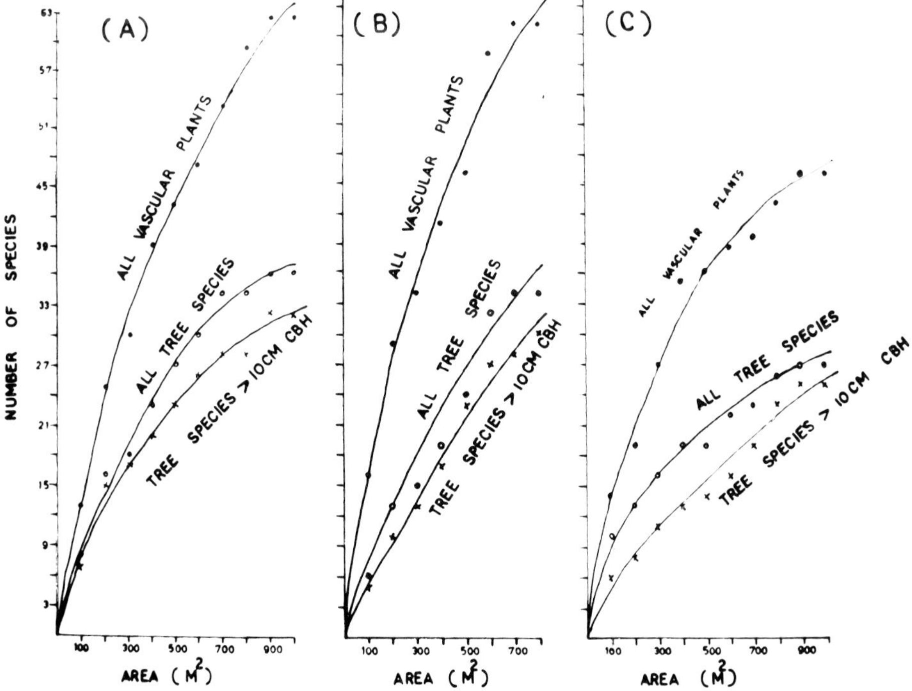

FIG. 7. Species area curves for (a) riparian forest, (b) mesic and (c) less mesic upland forests.

Spatial diversity

Rain-forests are often characterized by substrate patchiness, which is responsible for the well-known 'patchiness' effect in biological populations (MacArthur 1972; Pielou 1975).

Table 9 names the two dominant species (in terms of density) in 25 enumeration locations within the Silent Valley. *M. nagasarium, C. exarillata, P. ellipticum, Poeciloneuron indicum, Persea macrantha* and *C. elatum* dominated respectively, 6, 3, 9, 3, 2 and 2 locations out of a total of 25 locations. Considering a dominant and codominant, a total of 17 communities would seem to occur in the area; of these, 8 communities were represented at two locations each, while the rest were each confined to single locations. This reflects a high level of habitat—community heterogeneity within Silent Valley forest.

Beta-diversity, i.e. the rate of change of species composition (Whittaker 1972), was calculated for total tree species and for all ligneous species separately, following Whittaker (1975), by taking five contiguous quadrats, each 10 × 10 m, beginning with the stream bank and moving perpendicularly away within the riparian forest (Fig. 8). The computed value of beta-diversity was 2·9 for tree species and 3·1 for all ligneous plants. There was a continuous decline in Shannon–Wiener function and a concomitant increase in the density of *O. scriptoria* as one approached the stream. Thus vegetation longitudinally along the stream is simpler, because of the domination of a single species and there is a rapid change as one moves away from the stream.

Resource partitioning

Dominance-diversity curves for all forests are plotted in Fig. 9 on the basis of relative tree basal cover, in order to interpret the community organization in terms of resource share

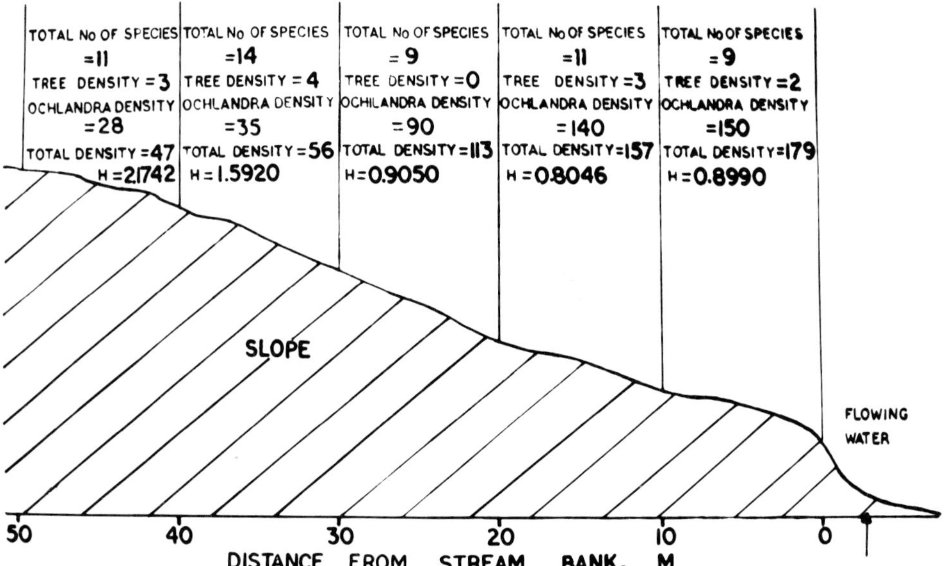

FIG. 8. Changes in community characteristics of the forest located along a transect running perpendicular to a stream. The number of species and density values are per 100 m². H = diversity index.

TABLE 9. Dominant species and tree density in Silent Valley (Based on Mohammad 1967)

Enumeration compartment	Dominant species	Trees (No./ha) 10–94 cm gbh	>94 cm gbh	Total (No./ha)
1	*Cullenia exarillata* *Persea macrantha*	476·6	61·5	538·1
2	*Palaquium ellipticum* *Mesua ferrea*	1577·1	203·5	1780·6
3	*Palaquium ellipticum* *Mesua ferrea*	992·0	128·0	1120·0
4	*Palaquium ellipticum* *Calophyllum elatum*	1294·2	167·0	1461·2
4a	*Palaquium ellipticum* *Bischofia javanica*	31·0	4·0	35·0
5	*Palaquium ellipticum* *Persea macrantha*	887·3	114·5	1001·8
6	*Palaquium ellipticum* *Persea macrantha*	1030·7	133·0	1163·7
7	*Persea macrantha* *Palaquium ellipticum*	333·2	43·0	376·2
8	*Poeciloneuron indicum* *Palaquium ellipticum*	1170·2	151·0	1321·2
8a	*Palaquium ellipticum* *Poeciloneuron indicum*	453·3	58·5	511·8
9	*Poeciloneuron indicum* *Palaquium ellipticum*	1267·1	163·5	1430·6
9a	*Palaquium ellipticum* *Poeciloneuron indicum*	1065·6	137·5	1203·1
10	*Poeciloneuron indicum* *Mesua ferrea*	484·3	62·5	546·8
10a	*Mesua ferrea* *Calophyllum elatum*	160·8	20·7	181·5
10b	*Mesua ferrea* *Persea macrantha*	48·4	6·2	54·6
11	*Mesua ferrea* *Palaquium ellipticum*	699·4	90·2	789·6
11a	*Mesua ferrea* *Calophyllum elatum*	395·2	51·0	446·2
11b	*Persea macrantha* *Hopea parviflora*	120·1	15·5	135·6
12	*Palaquium ellipticum* *Cullenia exarillata*	711·0	91·7	802·8
12a	*Mesua ferrea* *Persea macrantha*	790·5	102·0	892·5
12b	*Calophyllum elatum* *Persea macrantha*	151·1	19·5	170·6
13	*Cullenia exarillata* *Palaquium ellipticum*	1081·1	139·5	1220·6
14	*Cullenia exarillata* *Palaquium ellipticum*	4121·0	531·7	4652·8
14a	*Mesua ferrea* *Palaquium ellipticum*	1114·0	143·7	1257·8
14b	*Calophyllum elatum* *Dysoxylum purpureum*	21·3	2·7	24·0

Mesua ferrea = *M. nagasarium*

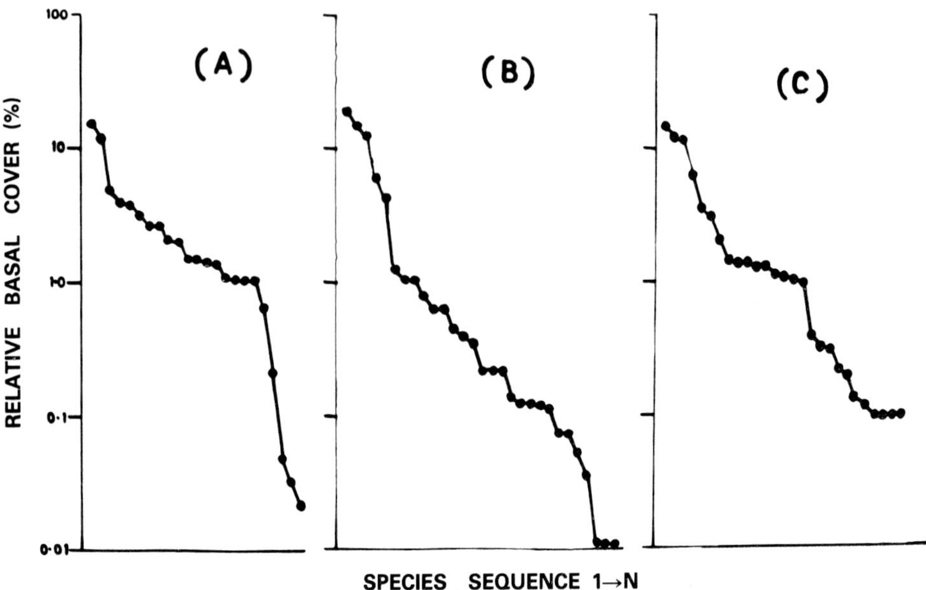

FIG. 9. Dominance-diversity curves for (a) riparian forest, (b) mesic and (c) less mesic upland forests.

and niche space. These curves approach Preston's (1948) lognormal distribution type. Whittaker (1975) opined that this type of distribution is representative of species-rich tropical rain-forest. There is limited dominance in resource partitioning by two or three species, followed by relatively equitable segments of the resource being shared by groups of species. These curves again indicate a high level of diversity in these forest ecosystems.

CONCLUSIONS

Several features often attributed to a typical tropical rain-forest, viz., preponderance of woody vegetation and species with leaves in the mesophyll size class, tall slender trees with flying buttress and thin bark, multilayering of vegetation with abundance of epiphytes and stranglers, evergreenness, a strong tendency for change in species composition in time and space and high alpha and beta diversities were displayed by the forests of Silent Valley. A relatively high species richness indicates that this valley possesses virgin forest and conditions for growth which are very favourable. Because of the terrain, heterogeneity in habitat is well marked.

ACKNOWLEDGMENTS

We thank Professor P. S. Ramakrishnan and Drs O. P. Toky and Jasbir Singh for participating in the field work. Dr R. R. Rao and Mr P. Bhargavan helped with the identification of plants. Dr N. C. Nair of the Botanical Survey of India, Coimbatore, and the officers of the Kerala State Electricity Board provided the logistic support. Discussions with Professors Madhav Gadgil and V. M. Meher-Homji were helpful. We thank the Department of Environment, India for funding support, and to Dr Ted St John for reading through the manuscript. Thanks are also due to Professor A. K. Sharma for his keen interest in this study.

REFERENCES

Aubréville, A. (1938). La foret coloniale: les forets de l'Afrique occidentale francaise. *Annals Academie des Sciences Colonies, Paris*, **9**, 1–245.

Baur, G.N. (1964). *The ecological basis of Rain forest management.* Forest Commission of New South Wales, Sydney, Australia.

Brünig, E.F., Heuveldop, J., Smith, J. & Alder, D. (1978). Structure and functions of a rainforest. The International Amazon ecosystem project: Floristic stratification and variation of some features of stand structure and precipitation. In Singh and Gopal (eds) Glimpses of ecology. Professor R. Misra commemoration volume. *International Scientific Publications*, Jaipur, pp. 125–144.

Burgess, P.F. (1961). The structure and composition of lowland tropical rain forest in North Borneo. *Malaysian Forester*, **24**, 66–80.

Campbell, R.C. (1974). *Statistics for biologists.* Cambridge University Press, U.K.

Champion, H.G. & Seth, S.K. (1968). *A revised survey of the forest types of India.* Government of India Publications, New Delhi, India.

Chandrashekharan, C. (1973). *Forest resources of Kerala; a quantitative assessment.* Kerala Forest Department, Trivandrum.

Curtis, J.T. & McIntosh, R.P. (1950). The interrelations of certain analytic and synthetic phytosociological characters. *Ecology*, **31**, 434–455.

Curtis, J.T. (1959). *The vegetation of Wisconsin.* University of Wisconsin Press, Madison, U.S.A.

Dawkins, H.C. (1958). The management of natural tropical high forest with special reference to Uganda. *Commonwealth Forestry Institute*, paper 34.

Dawkins, H.C. (1959). The volume increment of natural tropical high forest and limitations on its improvement. *Empire Forest Review*, **38**, 178–180.

Ewusie, J.Y. (1980). *Elements of tropical ecology.* Heinemann, London, U.K.

Farnworth, E.G. & Golley, F.B, eds (1974). *Fragile Ecosystems.* Springer, New York, U.S.A.

Janzen, D.H. (1970). Herbivores and the number of tree species in tropical forests. *American Naturalist*, **104**, 501–528.

Kartawinata, K., Adisoemarto, S., Riswan, S. & Vayda, A.P. (1981). The impact of man on a Tropical forest in Indonesia. *Ambio*, **10** (2–3), 115–119.

Knight, D.H. (1963). A distance method for constructing forest profile diagrams and obtaining structural data. *Tropical Ecology*, **4**, 89–94.

Knight, D.H. (1975). A phytosociological analysis of species-rich tropical forest on Barro Colorado Island, Panama. *Ecological Monographs*, **45**, 259–284.

MacArthur, R.H. (1972). *Geographical ecology. Pattern in the distribution of species.* Harper and Row, New York, U.S.A.

Mohammad, E. (1967). *Revised working plan for Palghat Forest Division, 1959–1960 to 1973–1974.* Kerala State Forest Department, Trivandrum, India.

Odum, E.P. (1971). *Fundamentals of Ecology.* Saunders Co., Philadelphia, U.S.A.

Phillips, E.A. (1959). *Methods of vegetation study.* Holt, Rinehart & Winston, Inc., New York, U.S.A.

Pielou, E.C. (1975). *Ecological diversity.* Wiley, New York, U.S.A.

Preston, F.W. (1948). The commonness, and rarity, of species. *Ecology*, **29**, 254–283.

Raunkiaer, C. (1934). *The life-forms of plants and statistical plant geography.* Oxford University Press, U.K.

Richards, P.W. (1952). *The tropical rain forest.* Cambridge University Press, London, U.K.

Risser, P.G. & Rice, E.L. (1971). Diversity in tree species in Oklahoma upland forests. *Ecology*, **52**, 876–880.

Ross, R. (1954). Ecological studies on the rain forest of southern Nigeria. III. Secondary succession in the Shasha forest reserve. *Journal of Ecology*, **42**, 259–282.

Schulz, J.P. (1960). Ecological studies on forests in northern Surinam. *Verhandlungen der K. nederldsche akademie van wetenschappen A natuukunde*, **53**, 1–267.

Shannon, C.E. & Wiener, W. (1963). *The mathematical theory of communication.* University of Illinois Press, Urbana, U.S.A.

Simpson, E.H. (1949). Measurement of diversity. *Nature*, **163**, 688.

Singh, J.S., Singh, S.P., Saxena, A.K., & Rawat, Y.S. (1984). India's Silent Valley and its threatened rain-forest ecosystems. *Environmental Conservation* (in press).

van Steenis, C.G.G.J. (1958). Rejuvenation as a factor for judging the status of vegetation types: The biological nomad theory. In *Proceedings of the Kandy symposium on study of tropical vegetation.* UNESCO, Paris, France, pp. 159–163.

von Lengerke, H.J. (1977). The Nilgiris. Weather and climate of a mountain area in south India, *Beitrage zur Sudasienforschung*, **32**, Wiesbaden, Steiner.

von Lengerke, H.J. (1980). Heavy rainfall areas in Peninsular India. Arch. Met. Geoph. Biokl., Series B, **28**, 115–122.

Whitford, P.B. (1949). Distribution of woodland plants in relation to succession and clonal growth *Ecology*, **30**, 199–200.

Whitmore, T.C. (1975). *Tropical rain forests of the far east.* Clarendon Press. Oxford, U.K.

Whittaker, R.H. (1965). Dominance and diversity in land plant communities. *Science*, **147**, 250–260.

Whittaker, R.H. (1972). Evolution and measurement of species diversity. *Taxon*, **21**, 213–251.

Whittaker, R.H. (1975). *Communities and ecosystems.* Macmillan, New York, U.S.A.

Whittaker, R.H. (1977). Evolution of species diversity in land communities. *Evolutionary biology*, **10**: 1–67.

The present status of the Mangrove Forest Ecosystem of Segara Anakan, Cilacap, Java

SUKRISTIJONO SUKARDJO

Herbarium Bogoriense, LBN-LIPI Bogor, Indonesia

SUMMARY

1 The structural and floristic characteristics of the largest mangrove forest area in Java and Bali are described in summary form and related to the topography, soils and tidal flow of the region.

2 The threats to the mangrove environment from pollution and illicit exploitation are outlined.

3 The way in which mangrove forest management and development has proceeded in recent years is summarized and the prospects for conservation are investigated.

4 A series of recommendations are presented which will allow for optimum long term development and preservation whilst encouraging further research and understanding of the complexity of the factors influencing the future of the mangroves.

INTRODUCTION

The mangrove forest ecosystem of Segara Anakan is the largest area of mangrove in Java and Bali, covering an area of approximately 21 090 ha. Forty-four per cent constitutes production forest managed by the Perum Perhutani (The State Forestry Corporation), providing an important source of forest products (firewood, poles, tannin). The ecosystem also provides many tangible and intangible benefits to the local population.

The forest has a well-developed flora and fauna. During the last decade the mangrove of Segara Anakan has been damaged by oil pollution (Hardjosuwarno *et al.* 1975, 1980; Surjowinoto *et al.* 1977), mining activities (ECI 1974), village development and agricultural land expansion, indiscriminate conversion into tambak (fish ponds), and dumping of sediments (Soerianagara 1968). Degraded ecological conditions may lead to poor natural regeneration of the more useful species, such as *Rhizophora* and *Bruguiera*. Because of the important long-term benefits of the mangroves of Segara Anakan for the region, it is desirable to assess their present status in order to devise an integrated management and development policy that will ensure that the balance of nature is maintained.

The purpose of this paper is to give an overview of the status of mangroves in Segara Anakan, and to outline a plan for acquiring and using the information needed for the management of mangrove resources for sustained yield and maximization of value.

ENVIRONMENT OF SEGARA ANAKAN

The region includes all-year wet and mid-year dry climates (Kartawinata 1979). The annual rainfall varies from 2553 to 4711 mm (Berlage 1949), while the ratio between dry

CONCLUSIONS AND RECOMMENDATIONS

In recent years the mangrove ecosystem of Segara Anakan has been adversely affected by factors such as poorly executed logging operations, pollution, Pertamina activities, alluvial and sedimental deposits, drainage canals, and indiscriminate building of tambak, tambak tumpang sari and sawah. It is clear that the biological and nature conservation values of the ecosystem are being lost because of indiscriminate exploitation. Nevertheless, the rapid growth of human population in the Cilacap region, particularly in coastal villages, makes it necessary that such developments must be allowed to proceed in selected areas; sufficient knowledge already exist, however, to implement immediately conservation measures which ensure that the developments proceed in a proper manner. The initial conservation efforts must be directed to the creation of forest reserves in the region. This could facilitate the integrated use of the forest for both fishery forestry and scientific purposes (cf. Haan 1953). The reserves could be of two categories:

(1)   Reserves for the preservation of the flora and fauna of the forest

(2)   Reserves for forest development, research and exploitation purposes. In addition, a research programme should be constituted to cover all aspects of mangrove forest area ecology.

The aims of the research programme would be to provide the knowledge on which to base the management of the mangrove areas of Segara Anakan, so that all-round productivity may be optimized for man and so that the optimum economic value be obtained on a long-term basis, without destroying the ecosystem. The initiation and successful conduct of a research programme on the mangrove ecosystem of Segara Anakan must aim to be based on a quantitative knowledge of the abundance and distribution of the major components of the ecosystem and the inventory may take the form of a series of maps which provide the following general categories of information:

(1)   The distribution of all mangrove species (flora and fauna) including estimates of their respective densities in the mangrove ecosystem of Segara Anakan.

(2)   The spatial distribution of the types of mangrove ecosystem giving details of water courses, mudflats, backwater areas, and saltflats.

(3)   The description of the distribution and occurrence of specific characteristics or features of the mangrove ecosystem of Segara Anakan and associated marine areas.

(4)   The distribution of soil sediment types with corresponding information on their physical and chemical characteristics and suitability as habitats for the living components of the ecosystem.

Referring to short and long-term pressures (human activities, pollution, sediment, mining activities) on the mangrove ecosystem of Segara Anakan, it is desirable to study without delay:

(1)   The change with time in the structure and composition of the mangrove ecosystem, supplemented by the use of remote sensing, aerial photography and conventional survey methods.

(2)   The nature and magnitude of the stresses such as reduction of fresh water flow, or input of toxic chemicals, which are responsible for the changes observed above.

(3)   The effects of these stresses on the composition of the fauna and flora, the

organization of the dynamics and the productivity of the mangrove ecosystem of Segara Anakan.

It is desirable also to quantify losses, subsidies and gains of natural resources of the Cilacap region, if a thorough understanding is to be gained of the factors regulating the mangrove system and the long-term needs of the surrounding communities (cf. Bird & Soegiarto 1980; Sukardjo 1980a). In order to get a clear picture of this, the following areas of research are indicated:

(1)   Determination of the ecology of the principal components of the biota characterizing the region, particularly those biota of commercial value

(2)   Determination of the present and potential labour skills of the community as they relate to the mangrove ecosystem of Segara Anakan.

Finally, dealing with the potential for fishery products in the mangrove ecosystem, Polunin and Sukardjo (1980) stated that studies of the fate of detrital organic matter in mangrove forests such as that of Segara Anakan are badly needed, so that the contributions of the mangrove forest and its environment to the fisheries sector of Indonesia can be evaluated clearly and understood properly.

ACKNOWLEDGMENTS

I thank Mr Paul Lunberg of the East West Center, Hawaii U.S.A., for his valuable suggestion during the preparation of the manuscript, and Professor E. C. F. Bird and Dr M. Barson of the Department of Geography, University of Melbourne, Australia for their critical reading of the manuscript.

REFERENCES

Adiwirjono, I. S. (1981). The floristic study on mangrove forest in Segara Anakan Cilacap, South coast of Central Java. Paper presented at the Seminar on Coastal Resources of Segara Anakan, Central Java, 18 August 1981.

Berlage, H.P. (1949). Rainfall in Indonesia. Verhandelingen no. 37.

Bird, E.C.F. & Soegiarto, A. (1980). The Proceedings of the Jakarta Workshop on Coastal Resources Management. UN-University, Tokyo. 106 pp.

Boswezen. (1930). Bedrijfsplan van de definitief Ingerichte vloed bosschen van de afdeling Tjilatjap bosdistrict Banyumas voor de period January 1930 t/m 31 December 1939.

Burbridge, P.R. & Koesoebiono. (1980). Management of mangrove exploitation in Indonesia. Paper presented at the Symposium on mangrove environment: research and management. University of Malaya, Kuala Lumpur, Malaysia, 25–29 August 1980.

Dinas Hidro-Oseanologi, A.L. (1981). Daftar arus pasang surut. Jawatan Hidro-Oseanologi ALRI, Jakarta. 130 pp.

Djawatan Kehutanan (1952). Rencana sambungan dari afdeling hutan Banyumas Barat untuk jangka waktu 1 Januari 1942 s/d 31 Desember 1955.

ECI (1974). Feasibility report for reclaimation of the Segara Anakan and its environs. The Citanduy river basin development project. Denver, Colorado, USA-Banjar, Indonesia. 89 pp.

Endert, F.H. (1930). Tourneeverslag van 25 July 1930 naar de vloedbosschen van Angke. Document Herbarium Bogoriense, Bogor.

Fernandes, D.A. (1934). Over mangrove culture, Naschrift. *Tectona*, **26**, 300–303.

Haan, J.H. de (1931). Het een en andercover de Tjilatjapsche vloedboschen. *Tectona*, **24**, 39–76.

Haan, J.H. de (1953). Reisrapport no. 17 Naar het panglonggebried. In: Djoebar, Rimba Indonesia, **2**(8–9), 365–369.

Hardjosuwarno, S., Tanjung, S.D., Pujoarinto, A. & Purwoto (1975). Study mengenai ekosistem dari mangrove community Cilacap. Fakulti Biologi, Universiti Gadjan Mada. 42 pp.

Hardjosuwarno, S., Hadisumarmo, S. & Martopo, S. (1980). Excursion guide to Segara Anakan mangrove. Paper presented at the Workshop on coastal resources management, Yogjakarta, 20 August–10 September, 1980.

Hesse, P.R. (1961a). Some differences between the soils of *Rhizophora* and *Avicennia* mangrove swamp in Sierra Leone. *Plant and Soil*, **14**(4), 335–346.

Hesse, P.R. (1961b). The decomposition of organic matter in a mangrove swamp soil. *Plant and Soil*, **14**(3), 249–263.

Jennings, J.H. & Bird, E.C.F. (1967). Regional geomorphological characteristics of some Australian estuaries (G. H. Lauff, Ed.). pp. 121–128. American Association for the Advancement of Science Publ. No. 83. Washington, D.C. xv + 575 pp. Illustrated.

Jong, B. de. (1934). Over mangrove culturen. *Tectona*, **27**, 238–298.

Kartawinata, K. (1979). The ecological zones of Indonesia. Paper presented at the 13th Pacific Sci. Cong. Vancouver, 18–20 August 1979.

LPTP (1966). Peta tanah tinjau Jawa-Madura. LPTP, Bogor.

Mantra, I.M. (1980). Population and its problem in fishery community at Segara Anakan region. A case study of Ujung Gagak village. Paper presented at the Workshop and Training on Coastal Resources Management, Yogjakarta, 20 August–10 September 1980.

Napitupulu, N., Kikkeri, L.V. & Ramu, P.E. (1980). Development of Segara Anakan area in Central Java. Paper presented at the Workshop and Training on coastal resources management, Yogjakarta, 20 August–10 September, 1980.

Perum Perhutani (1976). Pokok-pokok pemikiran penyelesaian masalah patimuan dan rehabilitasi hutan payau KPH Banyumas Barat. Mimeorg.

Polunin, N.V.C. & Sukardjo, S. (1980). Proposal for the study of the fate of detrital organic matter in Indonesian mangrove forest. Paper presented at the International Wetlands Conference, New Dehli, India, 10–17 September 1980.

Pool, D.J., Snedaker, S.C. & Lugo, A.R. (1977). Structure of mangrove forests in Florida, Puerto Rico, Mexico and Coasta Rica. Biotropica 9: 195–212.

Rielle, H.J.TE. (1937). Verlag van de bodemkundige kaartering van de vlakten van Krawang. Document LPTP No. 21/29-13-6(1937), LPTP Bogor.

Soegiarto, A. (1973). Impact of human activities upon coastal environment in Indonesia. In: B. Marton (Ed.) Pacific Science Association Special Symposium in Marine Science, Hong Kong, 8–14 December 1973. Symposium paper, 111–113.

Soegiarto, A. (1979). The state of pollution in the water environment of Indonesia. Paper presented at the 13th Pacific Science Congress Vancouver, 18–28 August 1979.

Soerianagara, I. (1968). Penyebab kematian pohon-pohon tancang (*Bruguiera* spp.) di hutan payau daerah Cilacap, Jawa Tengah. *Rimba Indonesia*, **12**(1, 2, 3, 4), 1–11.

Soerianagara, I. (1971). Characteristics and classification of mangrove soils of Java. *Rimba Indonesia*, **16**(3, 4), 141–150.

Sukardjo, S. (1980a). The mangrove in the new Cimanuk delta. In: Proceedings on Cimanuk delta, W. Java (Rosengren and Ongkosongo, Eds.).

Sukardjo, S. (1980b). The mangrove ecosystem of the northern coast of West Java. In: Bird and Soegiarto (Eds.). Proceedings of the Jakarta Workshop on Coastal Resource Management, pp. 54–64.

Sukardjo, S. (1980c). Mangroves of Jakarta Bay need conservation. Paper presented at the 'Diskusi Kelestarian Teluk Jakarta', Jakarta 3 Juni 1980.

Sukardjo, S. (1982). Soils in the mangrove forest of Cimanuk delta. Paper presented at the Symposium on the Mangrove Forest Ecosystem Productivity, Bogor, 19–22 April 1982.

Sukardjo, S. & Akhmad, S. (1982). The mangrove forest of Java and Bali. Paper presented at the Symposium on the Mangrove Forest Ecosystem Productivity, Bogor 19–20 April 1982.

Sukartiko, B. (1980). Itensifikasi tumpang sari tambak di hutan payau Cilacap. Paper presented at the Workshop on 'Pengalaman dengan Agroforestry di Jawa, Indonesia', Yogjakarta 9 October 1980.

Sulthoni, A., Hardjosuwarno, S., Martopo, S. & Sarido, A.S.A. (1980). Penilaian lingkungan wilayah

Cilacap. Paper presented at the Workshop & Training on Coastal Resources Management. Yogjakarta 25 August–10 September 1980.

Sumarna, K. 1974. Tabel volume bakau-bakau (*Rhizophora* spp.) di daerah Bengkalis, Riau. Pengumuman No. 101, Lembaga Penelitian Hutan Bogor.

Sumatra, I.M. 1980. Insecticide residue monitoring in sediments, water, fishes and mangroves at the Cimanuk delta. Paper presented at the Seminar on coastal resources of Cimanuk delta, West Java. Jakarta, 18 August 1980.

Surjowinoto, M., Hardjosuwarno, S., Sukahar, A. Tanjung, S.B., Pujoarinto, A. & Purwoto (1977). Base line study data lingkungan hidup di daerah.

Versteegh, F. (1952). Problems of silviculture and management of mangrove forests in Indonesia. Paper presented at the Asia Pacific Forestry Commission Conference, Singapore, December, 1952.

Watson, J.C. (1928). Mangrove forest of the Malay Peninsula. *Malay Forestry Record*, **6**, 1–275.

Wirjodarmodjo, H., Suroso Sa. & Sukartiko, B. (1979). Pengelolaan hutan payau Cilacap. Proseeding Seminar Ekologi Hutan Mangrove. pp. 72–80. LHL 26.

Wirjodihardjo, M.W. (1953). Ilmu Tubuh Tanah, III. Noordhoff Kolif. Jakarta.

Wisaksono, W. (1974). Beberapa aspek pencemaran minyak di perairan Indonesia. Paper presented in the Environmental Week, Jakarta 21–26 January, 1974, 25 pp. + 4 maps.

SECTION II
NUTRIENT CYCLING

personal communications from the authors) which are not referenced. A dash (—) means information not available.

(b)   Unless mentioned in the notes below the tables, the litterfall was collected in traps; the size limits of the woody litterfall fraction are not defined; there are no details of a trash fraction; there are no details of flower or fruit fall; the litterfall was oven dried but the temperature is not known.

(c)   Where possible an indication of the reliability of the mean values is given by $\pm$ (standard deviation) or $\pm$ S.E. (standard error) or $\pm$ C.L. (95% confidence limits). For studies which have extended for two or more years the range of yearly values is given in parentheses below the means.

(d)   In the great majority of cases where seasonal variation of litterfall has been recorded the greater part falls during a relatively dry time of the year. Known exceptions to this pattern are noted.

Notes on Tables 7–8

Table 7 summarizes chemical analyses for total small litterfall. Where leaf analyses for the same studies have been reported these are in Table 8 (along with those from papers which have given data only for leaves). The separation of these data into two tables is justified because the components of total small litterfall vary greatly and the leaf fraction is often better defined (Proctor 1983).

ACKNOWLEDGMENTS

I am indebted to the following for help: K. Balasubramanyan, H. Brasell, J. R. Bray, N. M. Collins, H. C. Dawkins, P. J. Edwards, H. W. Fassbender, I. F. Fergus, H. Fölster, J. I. Furtado, F. B. Golley, W. K. Gong, A. Hladik, B. Hopkins, C. F. Jordan, G. Josens, M. Kellman, H. Klinge, H. Laudelout. E. G. Leigh, M. T. Lim, N. Manokaran, I. Markova, E. Medina, B. A. Mitchell, D. M. Newbery, P. Newbould, J. I. Pitman, R. Pitman, D. Ryelandt, S. N. Rai, K. P. Singh, S. C. Snedaker, A. V. Spain, N. M. Stark, T. D. Steinke, M. D. Swaine, M. J. Swift, E. V. J. Tanner, P. M. Vitousek and T. C. Whitmore.

Miss M. Keilt and Mrs E. M. Walker are thanked for typing the manuscript.

TABLE 1. Litterfall measurements in African tropical forests

Country and locality	Forest type	Latitude	Annual Rainfall (mm)	Mean annual temp. (°C)	Altitude (m)	Total small litterfall ($t\,ha^{-1}yr^{-1}$)	Leaf litterfall ($t\,ha^{-1}yr^{-1}$)	Litterfall sample area (m^2)	Number of litterfall samples	Collection intervals of litterfall samples (weeks)	Total sampling period (months)	Area of sample site (ha)	Authors	Study No.
IVORY COAST:	Evergreen													
Banco (plateau)		5°N	2100	26	100	11·9 (11·3–13·4)	8·2 (7·2–9·2)	1 for leaves, 4 for other litter	10 (of each size)	1	24 (36 for leaves at Banco)	0·25	Bernhard (1970)	1
Banco (valley)					50	9·3 (9·0–9·6)	7·4 (7·2–7·9)							2
Yapo (plateau)		6°N	1800		70	9·6 (9·2–10·1)	7·1 (6·6–7·6)							3
Yapo (valley)					70	9·0 (8·3–9·8)	6·3 (5·7–6·8)							4
SENEGAL: Sahel	*Acacia senegal* savanna	14°N	300	–	–	–	0·4 (0·4–0·4)	–	–	–	24	–	Bernhard-Reversat & Poupon (1980)	5
ZAÏRE: Ituri	Mixed	2°N	–	–	1650	–	8·5	–	–	–	–	0·003	J. Brynaert (unpublished)	6
NIGERIA: Mokwa	Southern Guinea savanna	9°N	1200	27	180	3·1	2·4±0·62 C.L.	0·25 for leaves, 10 for wood	16 (of each size)	1–2	12	6	Collins (1977)	7
GHANA: Tafo	Old secondary semi-deciduous	6°N	1600	25	250	8·7	–	–	–	–	12	–	Cunningham (1963)	8
IVORY COAST: Lamto	P1, old secondary;	6°N	1300	27	–	5·6±0·6	5·0±0·4	1	10	1	12	0·01	Devineau (1976)	9
	P2, old secondary;					7·4±3·5	5·2±0·3	1	10		12			10
	VG, waterlogged;					8·1±0·8	6·5±0·5	0·64	16		12			11
	TR6, riverine;					6·9±1·3 (6·6–7·1)	5·4±0·6 (5·2–5·6)	1	10		24			12
	MS, gallery, riverine;					8·5±1·0	7·6±0·6	0·64	16		12			13
	TR4, gallery, riverine;					6·2±1·5 (5·6–6·8)	4·4±0·5 (4·2–4·7)	1	10		24			14

Table 1 continued

Country and locality	Forest type	Latitude	Annual Rainfall (mm)	Mean annual temp. (°C)	Altitude (m)	Total small litterfall ($t\,ha^{-1}yr^{-1}$)	Leaf litterfall ($t\,ha^{-1}yr^{-1}$)	Litterfall sample area (m^2)	Number of litterfall samples	Collection intervals of litterfall samples (weeks)	Total sampling period (months)	Area of sample site (ha)	Authors	Study No.
	TR2, gallery riverine;					5·3±0·8 (5·2–5·3)	4·3±0·3 (4·2–4·3)	1	10		24			15
	BD, gallery riverine					7·7±0·8	6·7±0·5	0·64	16		12			16
GABON: Ipassa	Evergreen	1°N	1700	26	500	13·3	6·5	0·8	120	2–3	12	–	Hladik (1978)	17
NIGERIA: Olokomeji	Derived savanna;	7°N	1200	22	100	–	0·88 (0·87–0·88)	0·25	10	4	25	–	Hopkins (1966)	18
	Semi-deciduous;				140		4·6 (4·5–4·7)							19
Omo	Evergreen	6°N	2100	26	60		7·2				12			20
GHANA: Kade	Old secondary, evergreen/ semi-deciduous	6°N	1700	28	150	9·7±0·46 C.L.	7·4 (7·3–7·5)	1	20	4	26	2	John (1973)	21
SENEGAL: Bambey	*Acacia albida*	15°N	500	–	20	2·7	0·58	2	10	4–7	12	–	Jung (1969)	22
ZAÏRE: Yanganbi	Mixed; *Brachystegia*; *Macrolobium*; *Musanga cecropioides* (>15 yr old)	1°N	1700	25	300	12·4 12·3 15·3 14·9	–	2	10	–	12	–	Laudelout & Meyer (1954)	23 24 25 26
TANZANIA: Mazumbai	Mixed	5°S	1200	–	1400	8·8 (8·5–9·1)	5·5 (5·5–5·5)	0·16	20	1	24	0·037	Lundgren (1978)	27
NIGERIA: Ibadan	Secondary (>15 yr old)	7°N	1200	27	250	5·6	3·7	1	6	2	13·5	0·023	Madge (1965)	28
ZAÏRE: Lubumbashi	Miombo (woodland)	11°S	1300	20	1210	4·3 (3·9–5·5)	2·9 (2·5–3·4)	1	10	4	72	–	Malaisse (1978)	29
ZAÏRE: Lubumbashi	Evergreen; Riparian	11°S 12°S	1300	20	1210 1190	9·1 5·9	4·7 4·5	–	–	–	–	–	Malaisse *et al.* (1975)	30 31

IVORY COAST:	Open savanna,	6°N	1500				0·9 (0·8–1·0)	12·0	1	1	18	0·125	Menaut (1974)	32
Lamto	Closed savanna						1·8 (1·5–2·1)	625				0·0625		33
GHANA: Kade	Old secondary, evergreen/ semi-deciduous	6°N	1700	28	150	10·5	7·0	1·7	6	2	12	–	Nye (1961)	34
SOUTH AFRICA: Mgeni Estuary	Mangrove: *Avicennia*;	30°S	1000	21	0	–	7·2 (4·8–9·5)	0·25	15	2	24	1·25	Steinke & Charles (1983)	35
	Bruguiera						8·6 (7·8–9·5)		10			0·67		36
GHANA: Shai Hills	South-east Outlier;	6°N	760	–	170	5·6 (4·7–6·4)	3·8 (3·0–4·6)	1	5	4	36	–	M.D. Swaine, J.B. Hall &	37
Ankasa	Wet Evergreen	5°N	2000		60	9·0 (8·9–9·8)	6·3 (5·8–6·8)			4·5	24		D. Lieberman (unpublished)	38

NOTES

Study No.	
1–4	Wood, flower and fruit litterfall collected from ground. Flower and fruit fall ($t\,ha^{-1}yr^{-1}$) (means with ranges for two years' collections in parenthesis): Banco (plateau), 1·1 (0·98–1·2); Banco (valley), 0·67 (0·39–0·94); Yapo (plateau), 1·1 (0·78–1·3); Yapo (valley), 0·54 (0·41–0·66). Confidence limits (95%) of litterfall were (as a percentage of yearly estimates, presumably) Banco, *c.* 35% (wood, flowers and fruits), 8–12% (leaves); Yapo, *c.* 50% (wood, flowers and fruits), 16% (leaves). Dried at 70°C.
5	Litterfall collected under scattered trees over several ha.
6	Litterfall drying method not known.
7	Wood fall collected from ground. Total includes a wood fall of 0·70 $t\,ha^{-1}yr^{-1}$ (with woody fruits) $\leqslant 2$ cm diameter. An additional larger wood fall (>2 cm diameter) of 0·68 $t\,ha^{-1}yr^{-1}$ was recorded. Dried at 100°C.
9–16	Fruit fall $t\,ha^{-1}yr^{-1}$ (means with ranges for two years' collections in parenthesis): P1, 0; P2, 0·2; VG, 0·9; TR6, 0·3 (0·2–0·4); MS, 0·4; TR4, 0·65 (0·1–1·2); TR2, 0 (0–0); and BD, 0·1. P1, P2, VG, TR6 and MS showed a marked dry-season peak of leaf fall; TR4, TR2 and BD (riverine forests) showed less seasonality in leaf litterfall and although they had a peak in the dry season there was another during the wet season. Dried at 80°C.
17	Total litterfall included a 'dust' fraction. A value of 13·9 $t\,ha^{-1}$ total litterfall was recorded in the same paper from a sub-sample of forty of the 120 traps. Litter traps were placed 10 m apart in a line along two 600 m transects. Leaf and wood fall were highest in the rainy seasons, least during the major dry season. Litterfall dried in open dryer and retained 5% of its weight as moisture.
18–20	Dried at 105°C.
21	Total litterfall included a 'trash' fraction and wood $<2·5$ cm diameter. Fruit, seed and flower fall was 0·39 $t\,ha^{-1}yr^{-1}$. The litter traps were in eight 0·25 ha areas with contrasting drainage. Dried at 98°C.
22	Litter traps placed in pairs under five trees. Flower and fruit fall was 1·7 $t\,ha^{-1}yr^{-1}$ (62% of the total). Jung expressed his results for a tree density of 43 ha^{-1}. I have changed this to apply for 10 trees ha^{-1} (the mean density for the area). Leaf fall was maximum in the rainy season, that of flowers and fruits maximum in the dry season. Dried at 105°C.
23–26	Litterfall dried at about 100°C. *Brachystegia* forest is called 'Forest' by Bartholomew, Laudelout & Meyer (1953) who gave the same litterfall value for this site.
27	Flower and fruit fall was 0·61 $t\,ha^{-1}yr^{-1}$ (0·52–0·70).
28	Litterfall air-dried.
29	Litterfall collected from the ground; wood fall $<2·0$ cm diameter. Flower and fruit fall has a mean (over six years) of 0·51 $t\,ha^{-1}yr^{-1}$ with a wide range of 0·099–2·01 $t\,ha^{-1}yr^{-1}$.
32, 33	Leaf litterfall collected from ground over all sampling area. Litterfall so seasonal that two seasons of fall covered in 18 months sampling. G. Josens (pers. comm.) has given further values for total small litterfall of trees of: open savanna, 1·7 $t\,ha^{-1}yr^{-1}$; closed savanna, 6·4 $t\,ha^{-1}yr^{-1}$. These values supersede that given for 'derived savanna' at this site by Collins (1977).
34	Litter traps moved after each collection.
35, 36	Litterfall dried at 70°C.
37 & 38	Wood fall $<5·0$ cm diameter. Litterfall weights expressed on a dry weight (*c.* 100°C) basis.

TABLE 2. Litterfall measurements in South American and Hawaiian tropical forests

Country and locality	Forest type	Latitude	Annual Rainfall (mm)	Mean annual temp. (°C)	Altitude (m)	Total small litterfall ($t\,ha^{-1}yr^{-1}$)	Leaf litterfall ($t\,ha^{-1}yr^{-1}$)	Litterfall sample area (m^2)	Number of litterfall samples	Collection intervals of litterfall samples (weeks)	Total sampling period (months)	Area of sample site (ha)	Authors	Study No.
BRAZIL: Manaus	Igapo	3°S	1800	27	c. 50	6·8±0·91 S.E.	5·3±0·66 S.E.	0·25 & 1	5–12	4–8	10	1	Adis, Furch & Irmler (1979)	39
VENEZUELA: Merida	Montane	9°N	1500	13	2300	7·0±1·6 S.E.	3·4±0·47 S.E.	1	36	2	12	0·75	Fassbender & Grimm (1981)	40
COLOMBIA: Magdalena Valley	On terrace;	7°N	3200	28	120	12·0	6·5±1·2 S.E.	0·75	6	3	12–15	–	Fölster & de las Salas (1976)	41
	On slope;					8·7	6·6±1·1 S.E.							42
	Secondary (16 yr old)					9·5	7·4±0·74 S.E.							43
VENEZUELA: Caparo	Mixture of evergreen and deciduous stands	7°N	1800	25	100	8·6±2·3 S.E.	6·1±1·4 S.E.	1	100	2	15	2·5	Franco (1979)	44
BRAZIL: Manaus	Riverine;	3°S	1800	27	c. 50	6·4	4·3±1·5 S.E.	1	10	1	12	0·5	Franken, Irmler & Klinge (1979)	45
	Terra firme					7·9 (7·8–8·0)	6·4±2·0 S.E. (6·1–6·8)				24			46
BRAZIL: Espirito Santo	Lower montane	20°S	1600	17	850	–	4·5	1·44	26	4	11·5	–	Jackson (1978)	47
COLOMBIA: Calima	Lowland;	4°N	9100	27	30	8·5	–	1	1	–	12	–	Jenny, Gessel & Bingham (1949)	48
Chinchima	Upland	5°N	2800	21	1630	11·1	–	1	2		19	–		49
VENEZUELA: San Carlos	Mixed;	2°N	3500	26	120	5·8 (5·2–6·3)	–	0·12	42	4	60	–	Jordan & Murphy (1982)	50
	Caatinga					4·8 (3·8–6·2)					48			51
BRAZIL: Belém	Terra firme;	1°S	2300	25	<100	9·9	8·0	0·25	16	2	22	3·7	Klinge (1977)	52
	Varzea;			26		9·0	7·5					2·0		53
	Igapo			26		7·8	6·7					–		54

BRAZIL: Manaus	Terra firme	3°S	1800	27	90	7·3±1·9 S.E. (6·7–7·9)	5·6±1·5 S.E. (4·8–6·4)	0·25	10	1	24	0·5	Klinge & Rodrigues (1968a)	55
VENEZUELA: Calabozo Rancho	Deciduous;	9°N	1300	27	100	8·2	–	1	6	2	11	–	Medina & Zelwer (1972)	56
Grande	Montane		1800	19	1000	7·8					12			57
HAWAII:	Montane	20°N	4400	–	1420	5·2	–	0·5	15	–	12	–	D. Mueller-Dombois,	58
		20°N	4400		1220	5·2							Gerrish & P.M.	59
		19°N	2200		1200	6·3							Vitousek (unpublished)	60
FRENCH GUIANA: Sinnamary	Rain forest	5°N	3400	–	50	8·7	5·8	1	60	2	12	1·0	Puig (1980)	61
BRAZIL: Reserva Ducke & Rio Negro-Branco	Terra firme	3°S	1800	27	50	21·9	–	1	44	<1	6	–	Stark (1971)	62

NOTES

Study No.	
39	Flower and fruit fall, 0·46±0·47 S.E. t ha^{-1}yr^{-1}. Litterfall least during the rainy season but twice as high during the inundation phase as it is during the emersion phase. Dried at 60°C.
40	Flower and fruit fall, 1·1±0·28 t ha^{-1}yr^{-1}. Dried at 105°C.
41–43	Flower and fruit fall (t ha^{-1}yr^{-1}): terrace forest, 0·36; slope forest, 0·12; secondary forest (16 yr old), 0·21. Terrace forest total litterfall includes a contribution of 2·1 t ha^{-1}yr^{-1} from large palm leaves which fell very irregularly. Terrace and secondary forests had their maximum litterfall at the end of the dry season; the slope forest early in the wet season. Wood < 3·5 cm diameter.
44	Flower and fruit fall, 1·2±0·81 S.E. t ha^{-1}yr^{-1}.
45 & 46	Flower and fruit fall (t ha^{-1}yr^{-1}): riverine forest, 0·96; *terra firme* forest, 0·47. Leaf fall standard error calculated as mean standard error for wet and dry seasons.
47	Leaf litterfall calculated from author's figure. Highest leaf litterfall in wet season.
48 & 49	Trap placed '6 feet from a tree trunk'. Dried at 105°C.
50 & 51	The values in this table supersede those of Herrera (1979) for the caatinga and of Murphy (in Jordan & Escalante 1980) for the mixed forest. Total litterfall was leaf litterfall and twigs <1 cm diameter.
52–54	In the igapo forest traps were placed along a 960 m transect. Flower and fruit fall (t ha^{-1}yr^{-1}): *terra firme*, 0·6; varzea, 0·7; igapo, 0·4. Highest leaf fall in wet season.
55	The fruit fraction of litterfall included 'non-recognizable' plant parts. Flower and fruit fall (t ha^{-1}yr^{-1}), 0·4±0·4 S.E. (year 1, 0·2±0·3; year 2, 0·5±0·4). Dried at 105°C.
56 & 57	Values in paper expressed in g m^{-2}d^{-1} for litterfall at Rancho Grande should all be increased by 0·45 g m^{-2}d^{-1} (E. Medina pers. comm.). The litterfall of 7·8 tha^{-1}yr^{-1} given above is the corrected value. Authors mention litterfall for the next year at Calabozo as 6·5 t ha^{-1}. Dried at 100°C.
61	Fifteen traps each in four 0·25 ha areas of forest on different soils. Litterfall peak not obviously related to rainfall pattern. Flower and fruit fall was 0·95 t ha^{-1}yr. Dried at 100°C.
62	Litterfall collected from the ground; the litterfall value combines collections from two sites at Reserva Ducke and Rio Negro-Branco. Dried at 65°C.

Table 3 continued

Country and locality	Forest type	Latitude	Annual Rainfall (mm)	Mean annual temp. (°C)	Altitude (m)	Total small litterfall ($t\,ha^{-1}\,yr^{-1}$)	Leaf litterfall ($t\,ha^{-1}\,yr^{-1}$)	Litterfall sample area (m²)	Number of litterfall samples	Collection intervals of litterfall samples (weeks)	Total sampling period (months)	Area of sample site (ha)	Authors	Study No.
U.S.A.: Florida: Naples	Mangrove: Riverine;	26°N	–	–	0	11·8	–	–	–	–	12	–	Sell (1977)	95
Everglades	Riverine					11·8								96
U.S.A.: Florida: Rookery Bay Ten Thousand	Mangrove: Basin;	26°N	–	–	0	7·4	–	0·25	20	2–3	54	–	Snedaker & Brown (1981)	97
Islands	Fringe;					9·8			20		37			98
	Riverine;					10·7			10		37			99
	Riverine;					11·7			10		37			100
	Overwash					10·2			10		37			101
Turkey Point	Fringe;					10·8			20		28			102
	Hammock;					7·5			20		28			102
	Dwarf;					1·7			8		27			104
	Dwarf					2·7			8		27			105
JAMAICA: Blue Mountains	Upper montane: Mor Ridge;	18°N	2200	16	1550	6·6	4·9	1	10	2	12	0·02	Tanner (1980)	106
	Mull Ridge;					5·5	5·3							107
	Wet Slope;					5·6	4·4							108
	Gap					6·5	5·5							109
U.S.A.: Florida: Biscayne Bay	Mangrove: Fringe;	26°N	–	–	0	8·8	–	–	–	–	12	–	Teas (1974)	110
	Dwarf					4·5								111
PUERTO RICO: El Verde	Lower montane: Radiation Center;	18°N	3800	22	420	–	5·0	0·5	30	4–8	12	2	Wiegert (1970)	112
South Control Center							4·7		25	4–13				113

Study No.	
63	Dried at 60°C.
64 & 65	Traps were placed equidistant between large *Mora* trees. Two leaf fall peaks, one in the dry and the other in the wet season.
67	Authors' results for fertilized areas are not included here. Leaf litterfall and reproductive part ($0.049\ t\ ha^{-1}yr^{-1}$) data for second year of study only. Dried at 65°C. Original trap size 2–3 m^2 changed after 6 months to small traps which were regularly positioned. Authors give results (not reviewed here in detail) for annual litterfall in several cypress forests in the U.S.A. The litterfall (for undisturbed sites with latitude lower than 30°N) ranged from 3.4–$6.2\ t\ ha^{-1}yr^{-1}$.
68 & 69	Litterfall mass calculated from calorific values in Dugger's paper using the conversion factor: 4.49 kilocalories $\equiv 1$ g organic matter.
71	Dried at 70°C. Flower and fruit fall $0.97\ t\ ha^{-1}yr^{-1}$. Traps placed at base of, and 1 m away from, trees. Litterfall seems extraordinarily high.
75–77	Wood fall >2 cm diameter collected from the ground. For the 'tropical moist forest' a value of $9.8\ t\ ha^{-1}yr^{-1}$ was reported for total (called 'leaf' by the authors) small litterfall excluding branches >2 cm diameter and collected from the 1 m^2 traps only.
78	Samples collected over 1–2 week periods in January 1958, May 1959 and May 1960.
79	'The twig and bark fraction was made up of material greater than 4 mm but less than 25 mm in diameter; it included numerous rachises of compound leaves'. Litterfall was dried over light bulbs for a week. Results include a trash fraction <4 mm diameter. Fruit fall was $1.2\ t\ ha^{-1}yr^{-1}$.
81	Small woodfall <2 cm diameter. Fruit fall $3.3\ t\ ha^{-1}yr^{-1}$. Dried at 80°C.
82	Traps were located under varying densities of the canopy so that they would yield a representation of the total accumulation.
84 & 85	Litterfall values corrected for weight loss during stay in traps ($t\ ha^{-1}yr^{-1}$): Plot I, 10.6 (total) and 8.1 (leaves); Plot II, 11.5 (total) and 8.7 (leaves). Flower and fruit fall (means with ranges for two years) ($t\ ha^{-1}yr^{-1}$): Plot I, 1.1 (0.73–1.4); Plot II, 0.43 (0.38–0.48). Peak leaf fall at end of dry season continuing into first rains. Wood fall peak well into rainy season. Dried at 85°C.
86	Dried at 60°C.
87	Total litterfall calculated from values for the study from 1971–1974 in Leigh (1975) and leaf litterfall for 1971–1975 in Leigh & Smythe (1978). Fruit fall (1971–1974): $1.2\ t\ ha^{-1}yr^{-1}$ (ranging from 0.8–$1.9\ t\ ha^{-1}yr^{-1}$). Standard error for leaf fall is about 10% of the mean. Dried at 60°C.
89	Dried at 70°C. Litterfall includes a miscellaneous fraction. Flower and fruit fall (mean and range for 2 yrs): 0.20 ± 0.02 S.E. (0.18–0.22) $t\ ha^{-1}yr^{-1}$. Traps regularly placed.
90 & 91	Leaf litterfall included a 'miscellaneous fraction'. Dried at 70°C.
97–105	Litterfall includes a miscellaneous fraction. Dried at 70°C. In dwarf mangroves litterfall collected by enclosures around individual plants. Traps and enclosures arranged at regular intervals along transects.
106–109	Leaf fraction includes 'other material'. For Mull Ridge forest a second study (2 years after the first) was made with thirty-eight $0.29\ m^2$ traps emptied at 4-week intervals over a year. Results were very similar ($t\ ha^{-1}yr^{-1}$): 5.8 (total litterfall); 5.6 (leaf litterfall). Dried at 100°C.
112 & 113	Authors 'leaf litterfall' seems to include other fractions of litter except fruit fall which was $0.51\ t\ ha^{-1}yr^{-1}$ in the Radiation Center and $0.22\ t\ ha^{-1}yr^{-1}$ in the South Control Center (Odum 1970).

TABLE 4. Litterfall measurements in tropical forests from India and Sri Lanka

Country and locality	Forest type	Latitude	Annual Rainfall (mm)	Mean annual temp. (°C)	Altitude (m)	Total small litterfall ($t\,ha^{-1}yr^{-1}$)	Leaf litterfall ($t\,ha^{-1}yr^{-1}$)	Litterfall sample area (m^2)	Number of litterfall samples	Collection intervals of litterfall samples (weeks)	Total sampling period (months)	Area of sample site (ha)	Authors	Study No.
INDIA: Pondicherry	Dry formation	12°N	1500	30	–	3·8 (3·4–4·1)	2·9 (2·6–3·1)	0·55	20	4	36	26	K. Balasubramanyan (unpublished)	114
INDIA: Varanasi	Dry deciduous	25°N	840	–	350	7·7	6·2	–	–	–	–	–	Bandhu (1973)	115
INDIA: Gundar	Montane	10°N	1200	14	2100	5·6 (3·9–7·3)	3·9 (2·0–5·0)	0·44–0·78	39	4	36	1	Blasco & Tassy (1975)	116
INDIA: Udaipur	Dry deciduous	25°N	660	–	590	4·0	–	–	20	2	6	–	Garg & Vyas (1975)	117
INDIA: Varanasi	Dry deciduous	25°N	1100	26	350	1·5 1·8	1·3 1·7	1	20	4	24	1	Gaur & Pandey (1978)	118 119
SRI LANKA: Wilpattu	Semi-arid semi deciduous;	8°N	1000	27	0	3·9	–	1	100	3–4	11	–	Hladik (1978)	120
Polonn-aruwa	Dry semi-deciduous;	8°N	1700	26	60	4·6	2·4		72	3–4	7			121
Horton Plains	Montane evergreen	7°N	2000	15	2100	5·9	3·5		70	4	12			122
SRI LANKA: Sinharadja	Lowland evergreen	6°N	3800	28	700	6·4	–	1	70	4	6	–	Hladik & Hladik (1972)	123
INDIA: Varanasi	Dry deciduous	25°N	1100	26	350	1·7	–	0·5–1	5–20	4	–	–	Pandey, Gaur & Singh (1980)	124
INDIA: Karnataka: Agumbe	Evergreen	14°N	7700	22	575	4·2 (3·9–4·5)	3·6 (3·3–3·9)	0·5	50	4	24	0·5	Rai (1981)	125
Bannadpare;		12°N	5300	27	200	4·1 (4·0–4·1)	3·2 (3·2–3·3)		100			1		126
Kagneri		13°N	6100	29	300	4·0 (3·5–4·5)	3·4 (3·0–3·9)		100			1		127
South Bhadra		13°N	6500	22	800	3·4 (3·2–3·7)	2·9 (2·6–3·2)		50			0·5		128
INDIA: Udaipur	Dry deciduous	25°N	660	–	590	–	4·8	0·25	20	–	6	–	Ranawat & Vyas (1975)	129
INDIA: Rajustan	Dry savanna	–	–	–	–	3·2	2·9	–	–	–	–	–	Rodin, Prakash & Bazilevich (in Rodin & Brazilevich 1967)	130
INDIA: Varanasi	Dry deciduous	25°N	–	–	300	2·1	1·5	–	–	–	–	–	Sharma (1981)	131
INDIA: Varanasi	Dry deciduous	25°N	1100	26	90–370	–	–	1	10	–	24	–	Singh (1968)	

	Tectona;					(0·1–0·4) 5·0±0·12 S.E. (5·0–5·1)								133
	Diospyros- *Anogeissus*;					4·2±0·26 S.E. (4·2–4·3)								134
	Shorea- *Buchaniana*;					3·2±0·16 S.E. (2·8–3·6)								135
	Butea (open and dry degraded)					1·0±0·20 S.E. (0·91–1·1)								136
INDIA: Varanasi	Dry deciduous (40 yr old secondary)	25°N	1100	26	–	7·8	–	–	–	–	–	–	Singh (1975)	137
INDIA: Varanasi	Dry deciduous 'Natural';	25°N	1300	26	140–300	5·7±0·23 S.E. 5·1	4·2±0·19 S.E. 3·9	1	18	4	12	1·5	Singh & Misra (1978)	138
	'Degraded'													139
INDIA: Meghalaya	Humid, sub-tropical (50 yr old secondary) Undisturbed zone Disturbed zone	26°N	2200	18	–	6·5 4·5	4·7 3·8	1	20	4	12	–	Singh & Ramakrishnan (1982)	140 141
INDIA: Nilgiri Hills	Shola forest (wet montane)	11°N	–	–	–	2·1	–	1·5	5	4	12	–	Venkataraman & Chinnamani (1978)	142
INDIA: Sagar	Dry deciduous: Open *Butea* forest; *Butea-* *Diospyros*; *Tectona-* *Terminalia*; *Anona-* *Madhuca*	24°N	1100	28	–	–	1·6 2·3 8·2 9·4	0·84	5	1	1	–	Upadhyaya (1955)	143 144 145 146

Study No. NOTES

114	Flower and fruit fall (mean with range over three years) (t ha^{-1}yr^{-1}): 0·35 (0·21–0·45). Dried at 85°C.
115	This assumed to be the same forest as that discussed by Misra (1972). Values for litterfall of 6·8 t ha^{-1}yr^{-1} and for leaf litterfall of 5·7 t ha^{-1}yr^{-1} were given for a forest of similar description by Bandhu (1981).
116	Woodfall < 2 cm diameter. Mean litterfall values have an 'erreur à craindre ± 10 à 15%'. Fruit fall (with range over three years) (t ha^{-1}yr^{-1}): 0·32 (0·24–0·41). Litterfall maximum in wet period. Dried at 70°C.
117	Dried at 85°C.
118&119	Dried at 80°C.
120–123	Litter traps placed at 10 m intervals along transects.
124	Litterfall results are the means for two forests. Dried at 80°C.
125–128	Dried at 85°C. Litter traps placed at 10 m intervals along transects.
132–136	Litterfall collected from the ground.
138&139	Total litterfall includes twigs < 1 cm diameter. Litterfall collected from the ground. Dried at 80°C.
140&141	Authors report a litterfall of 9·7 t ha^{-1}yr^{-1} in a 20 yr old forest dominated by bamboo in the Meghalaya area. Dried at 80°C.
143–146	Litterfall (probably leaf) sampled from ground in April after leaf-fall period in February–April.

TABLE 5. Litterfall measurements in tropical forests in south-east Asia

Country and locality	Forest type	Latitude	Annual Rainfall (mm)	Mean annual temp. (°C)	Altitude (m)	Total small litterfall ($t\,ha^{-1}yr^{-1}$)	Leaf litterfall ($t\,ha^{-1}yr^{-1}$)	Litterfall sample area (m^2)	Number of litterfall samples	Collection intervals of litterfall samples (weeks)	Total sampling period (months)	Area of sample site (ha)	Authors	Study No.
THAILAND: Chanwat Chantaburi	Mangrove	13°N	–	27	0	9·3	–	1	32	4	12	–	Aksornkoae & Khemnark (1980)	147
JAVA: Pringombo	Lower montane forest	7°S	4600	22	650	6·8	5·4±0·59 S.E.	1	5	2–4	8	0·5	Bruijnzeel (1982)	148
MALAYA: Tasek Bera	Freshwater swamp	3°N	2000	30	30	9·2 (6·2–10·9)	7·2 (5·2–8·7)	1	8	1	31	–	Furtado *et al.* (1980)	149
MALAYA: Pasoh	Lowland dipterocarp	3°N	2100	23	100	9·2	6·8	1	6	–	5	–	Gong (1972)	150
MALAYA: Penang	Lowland dipterocarp	5°N	3400	27	70–300	7·5 (7·0–7·9)	5·4 (5·3–5·4)	1	10–80	4	24	–	Gong & Ong (1983)	151
MALAYA: Matang, Perak	*Rhizophora* mangroves: Secondary (15 yr old);	5°N	–	–	0	10·0	8·0	1	15	4	12	–	Gong *et al.* (1980)	152
	Secondary (20 yr old);					10·3	8·1							153
	Secondary (25 yr old)					11·4	8·4							154
	Primary					7·6	5·8							155
PHILLIPINES: South-east Mindanao	Secondary (19 yr old)	7°N	4200	23	965	9·4	–	0·0625	12	3–6	1·5–3	–	Kellman (1970)	156
	Secondary (21 yr old)				1085	12·5								157
	Secondary (19 yr old)				980	7·6								158
	Secondary (19 yr old);				1030	11·1								159
	Secondary (19 yr old);				950	12·2								160
	Secondary				925	10·0								161

	(27 yr old); Secondary					1235	7·0								162
	(27 yr old); Lowland dipterocarp					1185	5·3								163
THAILAND: Khao Chong	Rain forest	8°N	2700	27	–	23·3	11·9	10·8	1	<1–2	1·5	–	Kira *et al.* (1964)	164
MALAYA: Pasoh	Lowland dipterocarp	3°N	2100	23	100	8·9 (7·5–10·2)	6·4 (5·4–7·4)	1	50	1	36	–	Lim (1978)	165
MALAYA: Bikam, South Perak	Dipterocarp	4°N	3300	26	200	7·2 (6·9–7·5)	–	0·63	2	2	36	–	Mitchell (1960)	166
Lumut, South Perak			1900	27	60	5·5 (3·9–7·4)		0·63	2		36			167
Ulu Gombak			1800	24	500–600	6·3		0·84	15 or 20		24			168
Bukit Lagong	Secondary	3°N	2700	26	230	8·2 (7·1–9·3)		0·31	3		24			169
					300	10·5 (10·2–10·7)			2		24			170
					450	14·3 (13·3–15·2)			3		24			171
JAPAN: Okinawa	Mangroves: *Bruguiera gymnorrhiza;*	26°N	–	–	0	5·9	–	–	–	–	12	–	Nishira (1983)	172
	B. gymnorrhiza;					4·5								173
	Kandelia candel;					2·8								174
	Bruguiera-Kandelia					3·0								175
MALAYA: Pasoh	Lowland dipterocarp	3°N	2100	23	100	10·6	6·3	1	30	1	21	–	Ogawa (1978)	176
MALAYA: Sungai Mabok	*Rhizophora* with *Bruguiera;*	6°N	–	–	–	10·6	7·3	1	10	–	2	–	Ong, Gong & Wong (1980)	177
	Rhizophora;					14·9	10·4							178

TABLE 8. Concentrations (as % oven-dry weight) of nitrogen, phosphorus, potassium, sodium, calcium and magnesium in leaf litterfall from tropical forests

Country	Study No.	Litterfall $t\,ha^{-1}yr^{-1}$	N	P	K	Na	Ca	Mg	Authors
Brazil	39	5·3	1·5	0·024	0·29	0·007	0·53	0·13	Adis, Furch & Irmler (1979)
	46	6·4	1·5	0·026	0·21	0·05	0·48	0·18	
India	115	6·2	1·8	0·14	–	–	1·6	–	Bandhu (1973)
Ivory Coast	1	8·7	1·5	0·069	0·22	–	0·56	0·46	Bernhard (1970)
	2	7·9	1·8	0·16	0·91	–	0·95	0·41	
	3	6·4	1·4	0·050	0·28	–	1·32	0·29	
	4	5·9	1·4	0·053	0·49	–	1·36	0·32	
Senegal	5	0·4	2·0	–	–	–	–	–	Bernhard-Reversat & Poupon (1980)
Java	148	5·4	1·1	0·055	0·48	0·046	2·2	0·39	Bruijnzeel (1982)
Trinidad	64	6·8	0·90	0·050	0·17	–	1·00	0·22	Cornforth (1970)
	65	7·0	0·80	0·030	0·15	–	0·82	0·21	
U.S.A.	67	4·1	–	0·030	–	–	–	–	Deghi, Ewel & Mitsch (1980)
New Guinea	202	6·1	1·3	0·074	0·40	–	1·3	0·27	Edwards (1982)
Venezuela	40	3·4	1·2	0·062	0·57	0·0041	0·73	0·26	Fassbender & Grimm (1981)
Colombia	41	6·5	1·3	0·035	0·13	–	0·80	0·19	Fölster & de las Salas (1976)
	42	6·6	1·2	0·041	0·33	–	1·4	0·13	
	43	7·4	1·3	0·025	0·20	–	0·58	0·19	
Venezuela	44	6·1	1·6	0·15	0·74	–	2·1	0·40	Franco (1979)
Brazil	45	4·3	1·3	0·028	0·26	0·066	0·35	0·017	Franken (1979)
Malaya	149	7·2	0·91	0·019	0·30	0·13	1·4	0·34	Furtado *et al.* (1980)
Brazil	52	8·0	1·7	0·041	0·17	0·074	0·31	0·28	Klinge (1977)
	53	7·5	1·2	0·036	0·26	0·069	0·87	0·30	
	54	6·7	1·2	0·036	0·32	0·072	0·80	0·38	
Brazil	55	5·6	1·5	0·030	0·18	0·067	0·22	0·18	Klinge & Rodrigues (1968a, b)
Malaya	165	6·4	1·2	0·030	0·38	–	0·70	0·22	Lim (1978)

TANZANIA	27	5·5	1·8	0·10	0·43	–	1·3	0·30	Lundgren (1978)
MALAYA	178	10·4	0·49	0·06	0·71	1·2	1·0	0·30	Ong, Gong & Wong (1980)
GHANA	34	7·0	2·1	0·087	1·0	–	2·0	0·54	Nye (1961)
HONG KONG	182	4·3	0·80	0·17	0·86	0·16	1·1	0·22	R. Pitman & J.I. Pitman (unpublished)
SARAWAK	183	6·6	0·90	0·027	0·26	0·006	2·4	0·20	Proctor et al. (1983)
	184	5·4	0·95	0·011	0·45	0·009	0·15	0·11	
	185	5·6	0·57	0·014	0·23	0·005	0·89	0·16	
	186	7·3	1·2	0·038	0·16	0·013	3·1	0·33	
SARAWAK	187	6·7	1·0	0·017	0·43	0·0079	0·51	0·12	Proctor, Anderson & Vallack (1983)
	188	5·7	0·81	0·021	0·37	0·0051	0·19	0·18	
	189	2·3	0·74	0·026	0·18	0·010	0·19	0·20	
INDIA	132	6·2	0·87	0·44	0·41	–	3·0	0·48	Singh (1968)
	133	5·0	0·72	0·16	0·40	–	2·4	0·22	
	134	4·2	0·60	0·071	0·74	–	2·0	0·40	
	135	3·2	0·66	0·41	0·25	–	1·0	0·34	
	136	1·0	1·8	0·030	0·59	–	1·5	0·40	
INDIA	138	4·2	1·2	0·088	0·37	–	–	–	Singh & Misra (1978)
	139	3·9	1·2	0·084	0·42	–	–	–	
INDIA	140	4·7	0·80	0·50	0·43	–	2·2	0·59	Singh & Ramakrishnan (1982)
	141	3·8	0·79	0·46	0·39	–	2·2	0·57	
JAMAICA	106	4·9	0·60	0·018	0·23	0·13	0·58	0·33	Tanner (1977)
	107	5·3	0·84	0·025	0·59	0·087	0·91	0·32	
	108	4·4	0·66	0·039	0·41	0·099	1·01	0·42	
	109	5·5	0·93	0·038	0·59	0·11	0·95	0·28	
AUSTRALIA	215	7·4	1·8	0·14	0·56	–	1·8	–	Webb et al. (1969)
	216	4·5	0·98	0·046	0·21	–	0·95	–	
	217	6·5	0·63	0·021	0·13	–	0·38	–	

NOTES

Study
No.

67 Leaf litterfall for second year of study.
202 Values calculated for the whole of the non-woody material fraction of which 96% is from leaves.

REFERENCES

Adis, J., Furch, K. & Irmler, U. (1979). Litter production of Central-Amazonian blackwater inundation forest. *Tropical Ecology*, **20**, 236–245.

Aksornkoae, S. & Khemnark, C. (1980). Nutrient cycling in mangrove forest of Thailand. *Asian Symposium on Mangrove Environment and Management*, pp. 1–14. University of Malaya, Kuala Lumpur, Malaysia.

Arnason, J.T. & Lambert, J.D.H. (1982). Nitrogen cycling in the seasonally dry forest zone of Belize, Central America. *Plant and Soil*, **67**, 333–342.

Bandhu, D. (1973). Chakia project. Tropical deciduous forest ecosystem. *Modelling forest ecosystems* (Ed. by L. Kern), pp. 39–61. Oak Ridge National Laboratory, Tennessee, U.S.A.

Bandhu, D. (1981). Chakia, India. *Dynamic Properties of Forest Ecosystems. International Biological Program*, 23 (Ed. by D. E. Reichle), p. 588. Cambridge University Press, U.K.

Bartholomew, W.V., Meyer, J. & Laudelout, H. (1953). Mineral nutrient immobilization under forest and grass fallow in the Yangambi (Belgian Congo) region. *Publications de l'Institut National pour l'Étude Agronomique du Congo Belge. Série Scientifique*, **57**, 1–27.

Bevege, I.D. (1978). *Biomass and nutrient distribution in indigenous forest ecosystems.* Technical Paper No. 6, Department of Forestry, Queensland, Australia.

Bernhard, F. (1970). Étude de la litière et de sa contribution au cycle des éléments minéraux en forêt ombrophile de Côte-d'Ivoire. *Oecologia Plantarum*, **5**, 247–266.

Bernhard-Reversat, F. & Poupon, H. (1980). Nitrogen cycling in a soil-tree system in a Sahelian Savanna. Example of *Acacia senegal. Nitrogen cycling in West African Ecosystems* (Ed. by T. Rosswall), pp. 363–369. Scope-Unep, Royal Swedish Academy of Sciences, Stockholm, Sweden.

Birk, E. (1979). Overstory and understory litterfall in a eucalyptus forest: spatial and temporal variability. *Australian Journal of Botany*, **27**, 145–156.

Blasco, F. & Tassy, B. (1975). Étude d'un écosystème forestier montagnard du Sud de l'Inde. *Bulletin d'Ecologie*, **6**, 525–539.

Brasell, H.M., Unwin, G.L. & Stocker, G.C. (1980). The quantity, temporal distribution and mineral-element content of litterfall in two forest types at two sites in tropical Australia. *Journal of Ecology*, **68**, 123–139.

Bruijnzeel, L.A. (1982). *Hydrological and Biogeochemical Aspects of Man-Made Forests in South-Central Java, Indonesia.* Vrije Universiteit te Amsterdam, Holland.

Christensen, B. (1978). Biomass and primary production of *Rhizophora apiculata* Bl. in a mangrove in southern Thailand. *Aquatic Botany*, **4**, 43–52.

Collins, N.M. (1977). Vegetation and litter production in Southern Guinea Savanna, Nigeria. *Oecologia*, **28**, 163–175.

Cornforth, I.S. (1970). Leaf fall in a tropical rain forest. *Journal of Applied Ecology*, **7**, 603–608.

Cruz, de la, Acosta A. (1964). A preliminary study of organic detritus in a tropical forest ecosystem. *Revista de Biologica Tropicale*, **12**, 175–185.

Cunningham, R.K. (1963). The effect of clearing a tropical forest soil. *Journal of Soil Science*, **14**, 334–345.

Deghi, G.S., Ewel, K.C. & Mitsch, W.J. (1980). Effects of sewage effluent application on litterfall and litter decomposition in cypress swamps. *Journal of Applied Ecology*, **17**, 397–408.

Devineau, J.-L. (1976). Données preliminaires sur la litière et la chute feuilles dans quelques forestières semi-décidues de moyenne Côte d'Ivore. *Oecologie Plantarum*, **11**, 375–395.

Dugger, K.R. (1978). Observaciones en tres bosques de climas distintas en Puerto Rico. *Quinto Simposio de los Recursas Naturales*, pp. 27–41. Departmento de Recursos Naturales, San Juan, Puerto Rico.

Edmisten, J. (1970). Preliminary studies of the nitrogen budget of a tropical forest. *A Tropical Rain Forest.* (Ed. by H. T. Odum and R. F. Pigeon), pp. H-211–H-214. United States Atomic Energy Commission, Oak Ridge, Tennessee, U.S.A.

Edwards, P.J. (1977). Studies of mineral cycling in a montane rain forest in New Guinea II. The production and disappearance of litter. *Journal of Ecology*, **65**, 971–992.

Edwards, P.J. (1982). Studies of mineral cycling in a montane rain forest in New Guinea V. Rates of cycling in throughfall and litterfall. *Journal of Ecology*, **70**, 807–827.

Enright, N.J. (1979). Litter production and nutrient partitioning in rain forest near Bulolo, Papua New Guinea. *Malaysian Forester*, **42**, 202–207.

Ewel, J.J. (1976). Litterfall and leaf decomposition in a tropical forest succession in eastern Guatemala. *Journal of Ecology*, **64**, 293–308.

Fassbender, H.W. & Grimm, U. (1981). Ciclos bioquímicos en un ecosistema forestal de los Andes Occidentales de Venezuela II. Producción y descomposición de los residuos vegetales. *Turrialba*, **31**, 39–48.

Fölster, H. & de las Salas, G. (1976). Litter fall and mineralizaton in three tropical evergreen forest stands, Colombia. *Acta Cientifica Venezolana*, **27**, 196–202.

Fournier, L.A. & Comacho de Castro, L. (1973). Producción y descomposición del mantillo en un bosque secundario húmedo de premontano. *Revista de Biologia Tropical*, **21**, 59–67.

Franco, W. (1979). *Die Wasserdynamik einiger Waldstandorte der West-Llanos Venezuelas und Ihre Beziehung zur Saisonalität des Laubfalls. Dissertation.* Universität Göttingen, West Germany.

Franken, M. (1979). Major nutrient and energy contents of the litterfall of a riverine forest of Central Amazonia. *Tropical Ecology*, **20**, 211–224.

Franken, M., Irmler, U. & Klinge, H. (1979). Litterfall in inundation, riverine and *terra firme* forests of Central Amazonia. *Tropical Ecology*, **20**, 225–235.

Furtado, J.I., Verghese, S., Liew, K.S & Lee, T.H. (1980). Litter production in a freshwater swamp forest, Tasek Bera, Malaysia. *Tropical Ecology and Development. Proceedings of the Vth International Symposium of Tropical Ecology* (Ed. by J. I. Furtado), pp. 815–822. International Society of Tropical Ecology, Kuala Lumpur, Malaysia.

Garg, R.K. & Vyas, L.N. (1975). Litter production in deciduous forest near Udaipur (South Rajasthan) India. *Tropical Ecological Systems: Trends in Terrestrial and Aquatic Research* (Ed. by F. B. Golley & E. Medina), pp. 131–135. Springer, New York, U.S.A.

Gaur, J.P. & Pandey, H.N. (1978). Litter production in two tropical deciduous forest communities at Varanasi, India. *Oikos*, **30**, 570–575.

Gessel, S.P., Cole, D.W., Johnson, D. & Turner, J. (1980). The nutrient cycles of two Costa Rican forests. *Progress in Ecology*, pp. 23–44. Today & Tomorrow's Printers & Publishers, New Delhi, India.

Gist, C.S. (1973). *Some Tropical Modelling Efforts.* Ecology Center, Utah State University, Logan, Utah, U.S.A.

Golley, F.B., McGinnis, J.T., Clements, R.G., Child, G.I., Duever, M.J. (1975). *Mineral Cycling in a Tropical Moist Forest Ecosystem.* University of Georgia Press, Athens, Georgia, U.S.A.

Golley, F.B., Odum, H.T. & Wilson, R.F. (1962). The structure and metabolism of a Puerto Rican red mangrove forest in May. *Ecology*, **43**, 9–19.

Gong, W.K. (1972). *Studies on the Rates of Fall, Decomposition and Nutrient Element Release of Leaf Litter of Representative Species in a Lowland Dipterocarp Forest.* B.Sc. (hons.) thesis, University of Malaya.

Gong, W.K. & Ong, J.E. (1983). Litter production and decomposition in a coastal hill dipterocarp forest. *British Ecological Society Rain Forest Symposium* (Ed. by S. Sutton, A. Chadwick & T. C. Whitmore), pp. 275–285. Blackwell Scientific Publications, Oxford, U.K.

Gong, W.K., Ong, J.E., Wong, C.H. & Dhanarajan, G. (1983). Productivity of mangrove trees and its significance in a managed mangrove ecosystem in Malaysia. *Mangrove Environment: Research and Management* (Ed. by E. Soepadmo). University of Malaya (in press).

Haines, B. & Foster, R.B. (1977). Energy flow through litter in a Panamanian forest. *Journal of Ecology*, **65**, 147–155.

Hawkins, P.J. (1966). Seed production and litterfall studies of *Callitris columellaris*. *Australian Forest Research*, **2**, 3–16.

Heald, E.J. (1969). *The Production of Organic Detritus in a South Florida Estuary.* Ph.D. dissertation, University of Miami.

Herrera, R. (1979). *Nutrient Distribution and Cycling in an Amazonian Caatinga Forest on Spodosols in Southern Venezuela.* Ph.D. thesis, University of Reading.

Hladik, A. (1978). Phenology of leaf production in rain forest of Gabon: distribution and composition of food for folivores. *The Ecology of Arboreal Folivores* (Ed. by G. G. Montgomery), pp. 51–71. Smithsonian Institute Press, Washington D.C., U.S.A.

Hladik, C.M. & Hladik, A. (1972). Disponsibilities alimentaires et domaines vitaux des primates à Ceylan. *La Terre et la Vie*, **26**, 149–215.

Hopkins, B. (1966). Vegetation of the Olokemeji forest reserve, Nigeria. IV. The litter and soil with special references to their seasonal changes. *Journal of Ecology*, **54**, 687–703.

Hutton, R. & Tyson, E. (1966). Forest litter. Environment data base for regional studies in the humid tropics. Semi-annual report 1 and 2. *USATECOM project 9-4-0013-01*, pp. 71–76.

Jackson, J.F. (1978). Seasonality of flowering and leaf fall in a Brazilian subtropical lower montane forest. *Biotropica*, **10**, 38–43.

Jenny, H., Gessel, S.P. & Bingham, F.T. (1949). Comparative study of decomposition rates of organic matter in temperate and tropical regions. *Soil Science*, **68**, 419–432.

John, D.M. (1973). Accumulation and decay of litter and net production of forest in tropical West Africa. *Oikos*, **24**, 430–435.

Jordan, C.F. (1971). Productivity of a tropical forest and its relation to a world pattern of energy storage. *Journal of Ecology*, **59**, 127–142.

Jordan, C.F. & Escalante, G. (1980). Root productivity in an Amazonian rain forest. *Ecology*, **61**, 14–18.

Jordan, C.F. & Murphy, P.G. (1982). Productivity and mortality of two forest types in the Amazon territory of Venezuela. *Nutrient Dynamics of a Tropical Rain Forest Ecosystem and Changes in the Nutrient Cycle due to Cutting and Burning*, pp. 122–166. Annual Report to U.S. National Science Foundation, Institute of Ecology, University of Georgia, U.S.A.

Jordan, C.F., Kline, J.R. & Sasscer, D.S. (1972). Relative stability of mineral cycles in forest ecosystems. *American Naturalist*, **106**, 237–253.

Jung, G. (1969). Cycles biogéochimiques dans un écosystème de région tropicale sèche *Acacia albida* (Del.) sol ferrugineux tropical peu lessivé (Dior). (Note préliminaire). *Oecologia Plantarum*, **4**, 195–210.

Kawanabe, S. (1977). A subtropical broad-leaved forest at Yona, Okinawa. *Primary Productivity of Japanese Forests*. (Ed. by T. Shidei & T. Kira), pp. 268–279. University of Tokyo Press, Japan.

Kellman, M.C. (1970). *Secondary Plant Succession in Tropical Montane Mindanao*. Publication BG/2, Research School of Pacific Studies. Australian National University, Canberra.

Kira, T. (1978). Community architecture and organic matter dynamics in tropical lowland rain forests of Southeast Asia with special reference to Pasoh forest, West Malaysia. *Tropical Trees as Living Systems* (Ed. by P. B. Tomlinson and M. H. Zimmerman), pp. 561–590. Cambridge University Press, London, U.K.

Kira, T., Ogawa, H., Yoda, K. & Ogino, K. (1964). Primary production by a tropical rainforest of southern Thailand. *Botanical Magazine Tokyo*, **77**, 428–429.

Klinge, H. (1977). Fine litter production and nutrient return to the soil in three natural forest stands of Eastern Amazonia. *Geo-Eco-Trop*, **1**, 159–167.

Klinge, H. & Rodrigues, W.A. (1968a). Litter production in an area of Amazonian *terra firme* forest. Part I. Litter-fall, organic carbon and total nitrogen contents of litter. *Amazoniana*, **1**, 287–302.

Klinge, H. & Rodrigues, W.A. (1968b). Litter production in an area of Amazonian *terra firme* forest. Part II. Mineral nutrient content of the litter. *Amazoniana*, **1**, 303–310.

Kunkel-Westphal, I. & Kunkel, P. (1979). Litter fall in a Guatemalan primary forest, with details of leaf shedding by some common tree species. *Journal of Ecology*, **67**, 665–686.

Lambert, J.D.H., Arnason, J.T. & Gale, J.L. (1980). Leaf-litter and changing nutrient levels in a seasonally dry tropical hardwood forest, Belize, C.A. *Plant and Soil*, **55**, 429–443.

Laudelout, H. & Meyer, J. (1954). Les cycles d'éléments mineraux et de matière organique en forêt équatoriale congalaise. *Transactions of the 5th International Congress of Soil Science*, **2**, 267–272.

Leigh, E.G. (1975). Structure and climate in tropical rain forest. *Annual Review of Ecology and Systematics*, **6**, 67–86.

Leigh, E.G. & Smythe, N. (1978). Leaf production, leaf consumption and the regulation of folivory on Barro Colorado Island. *The Ecology of Arboreal Folivores* (Ed. by G. G. Montgomery), pp. 33–50. Smithsonian Institute Press, Washington D.C., U.S.A.

Lim, M.T. (1978). Litterfall and mineral nutrient content of litter in Pasoh Forest Reserve. *Malayan Nature Journal*, **30**, 375–380.

Lugo, A.E., Cintron, G. & Goenaga, C. (1983). Mangrove ecosystems under stress. *Stress Effects on Natural Ecosystems* (Ed. by G. Barrett & R. Rosenberg). John Wiley, New York, U.S.A.

Lugo, A.E., Gamble, J.F. & Ewel, K.C. (1978). Organic matter budget in a mixed hardwood forest in North-Central Florida. *Environmental Chemistry and Cycling Processes.* (Ed. by D. C. Adriano & I. L. Brisbin, Jr). pp. 790–800. DOE Symposium Series 45 (CONF — 760429).

Lugo, A.E., Gonzalez-Liboy, J.A., Cintron, B. & Dugger, K. (1978). Structure, productivity and transpiration of a subtropical dry forest in Puerto Rico. *Biotropica,* **10,** 278–291.

Lundgren, B. (1978). Soil conditions and nutrient cycling under natural and plantation forests in Tanzanian Highlands. *Reports in Forest Ecology and Forest Soils,* **31,** Swedish University of Agricultural Sciences.

Madge, D.S. (1965). Leaf fall and litter disappearance in a tropical forest. *Pedobiologia,* **5,** 273–288.

Malaisse, F. (1978). The miombo ecosystem. *Tropical Forest Ecosystems,* pp. 589–606. Natural Resources Research 14, UNESCO.

Malaisse, F., Freson, R., Goffinet, G. & Malaisse-Mousset, M. (1975). Litter fall and litter breakdown in Miombo. *Tropical Ecological Systems. Trends in Terrestrial and Aquatic Research* (Ed. by F. B. Golley & E. Medina), pp. 137–152. Springer, New York, U.S.A.

Medina, E. & Zelwer, M. (1972). Soil respiration in tropical plant communities. *Tropical Ecology with an Emphasis on Organic Production* (Ed. by P. M. Golley & F. B. Golley) pp. 245–269. University of Georgia, Athens, U.S.A.

Menaut, J.C. (1974). Chute des feuilles et apport au sol de litière par les ligneux dans une savane preforestière de Côte d'Ivoire. *Bulletin d'Ecologie,* **5,** 27–39.

Misra, R. (1972). A comparative study of net primary productivity of dry deciduous forest and grassland of Varanasi, India. *Tropical Ecology with an Emphasis on Organic Production* (Ed. by P. M. Golley & F. B. Golley), pp. 279–293. University of Georgia, Athens, U.S.A.

Mitchell, B.A. (1960). Comparison and assessment of site fertility under various crops and after various uses. Sub-project No. 1, deposition of organic matter. *Research Pamphlet,* **26A,** pp. 9–11. Forest Research Institute, Malaya.

Müller, D. & Nielsen, J. (1965). Production brute pertes par respiration et production nette dans la forêt ombrophile tropicale. *Det Forstlige Forsøgsvaesen I Danmark,* **29,** 73–160.

Nishira, M. (1983). Aspects of Japanese mangroves. *Proceedings of the UNESCO Regional Seminar on Human Uses of Mangrove Environment and its Management Implications.* BANSDOC, Dacca, Bangladesh (in press).

Nye, P.H. (1961). Organic matter and nutrient cycles under moist tropical forest. *Plant and Soil,* **13,** 333–346.

Odum, H.T. (1970). Summary: an emerging view of the ecological system at El Verde. *A Tropical Rain Forest* (Ed. by H. T. Odum & R. F. Pigeon), pp. I-191 to I-289. Division of Technical Information. U.S. Atomic Energy Commission, Oak Ridge, Tennessee, U.S.A.

Ogawa, H. (1978). Litterfall and mineral nutrient content of litter in Pasoh Forest. *Malayan Nature Journal,* **30,** 375–380.

Ogawa, H., Yoda, K. & Kira, T.A. (1961). A preliminary survey of the vegetation of Thailand. *Nature and Life in South East Asia,* **1,** 21–157.

Ong, J.E., Gong, W.K. & Wong, C.H. (1980). *Ecological Survey of the Sungei Merbok Estuarine Mangrove System.* School of Biological Sciences, Universiti Sains Malaysia, Penang, Malaysia.

Ong, J.E., Gong, W.K., Wong, C.H. & Dhanarajan, G. (1981). Productivity of a managed mangrove forest in West Malaysia. *Proceedings of the International Conference on Trends in Applied Biology in South East Asia,* pp. 274–284. Universiti Sains Malaysia, Penang, Malaysia.

Pandey, H.N., Gaur, J.P. & Singh, R.N. (1980). Litter input and decomposition in tropical dry deciduous forest, grassland and abandoned crop field communities at Varanasi, India. *Acta Oecologica/ Oecologia Plantarum,* **1,** 317–323.

Pool, D.J., Lugo, A.E. & Snedaker, S.C. (1975). Litter production in mangrove forests of Southern Florida and Puerto Rico. *Proceedings of the International Symposium on the Biology and Management of Mangroves,* Volume I (Ed. by G. E. Walsh, S. C. Snedaker & H. J. Teas), p. 213. University of Florida, Gainesville, U.S.A.

Proctor, J. (1983). Tropical forest litterfall I. Problems of data comparison. *Tropical Rain Forest: Ecology and Management* (Ed. by S. L. Sutton, T. C. Whitmore & A. C. Chadwick), pp. 267–273. Blackwell Scientific Publications, Oxford.

Proctor, J., Anderson, J.M., Fogden, S.C.L. & Vallack, H.W. (1983). Ecological studies in four contrasting lowland rain forests in Gunung Mulu National Park, Sarawak II. Litterfall, litter standing crop and preliminary observation on herbivory. *Journal of Ecology*, **71**, 261–283.

Proctor, J., Anderson, J.M. & Vallack, H.W. (1983). Comparative studies on soils and litterfall in forests at a range of altitudes on Gunung Mulu, Sarawak. *Malaysian Forester*, 46, 60–76.

Puig, H. (1980). Production de litière en forêt guyanaise: résultats preliminairies. *Bulletin Societe Histoire Naturelle Toulouse*, **115**, 338–346.

Rai, S.N. (1981). *Productivity of Tropical Rain Forests of Karnataka*. Ph.D. thesis, University of Bombay.

Ranawat, M.P.S. & Vyas, L.N. (1975). Litter production in deciduous forests of Koriyat, Udaipur (South Rajasthan), India. *Biologia (Bratislava)*, **30**, 41–47.

Rodin, L.E. & Bazilevich, N.I. (1967). *Production and Mineral Cycling in Terrestrial Vegetation*. Oliver & Boyd, London.

Rogers, R.W., Westman, W.E. (1977). Seasonal nutrient dynamics of litter in a subtropical Eucalypt forest, North Stradboke Island. *Australian Journal of Botany*, **25**, 47–58.

Rozanov, B.G. & Rozanova, I.M. (1964). The biological cycle of nutrient elements of bamboo in the tropical forests of Burma. *Botanicheskii Zhurnal*, **49**, 348–357.

Sell, M.G., Jr (1977). *Modelling the Response of Mangrove Ecosystems to Herbicide Spraying, Hurricanes, Nutrient Enrichment and Economic Development*. Ph.D. thesis, University of Florida, Gainesville.

Sharma, V.K. (1981). Chakia forest, Varanasi, India. *Dynamic properties of forest ecosystems. International Biological Program 23* (Ed. by D. E. Reichle), pp. 5 and 7. Cambridge University Press, London, U.K.

Singh, J. & Ramakrishnan, P.S. (1982). Structure and function of a sub-tropical humid forest of Meghalaya II. Litter dynamics and nutrient cycling. *Proceedings of the Indian Academy of Science (Plant Science)*, **91**, 255–268.

Singh, K.P. (1968). Litter production and nutrient turnover in deciduous forests of Varanasi. *Proceedings of The Symposium on Recent Advances in Tropical Ecology*. (Ed. by R. Misra & B. Gopal), pp. 655–665. International Society for Tropical Ecology, Varanasi, India.

Singh, K.P. & Misra, R. (1978). *Structure and functioning of natural, modified and silvicultural ecosystems of Eastern Uttar Pradesh*. Technical Report. UNESCO programme on man and the biosphere. Banaras Hindu University, Varanasi, India.

Singh, R.P. (1975). Biomass, nutrient and productivity structure of a stand of dry deciduous forest of Varanasi. *Tropical Ecology*, **16**, 104–109.

Snedaker, S.C. & Brown, M.S. (1981). *Water Quality and Mangrove Ecosystem Dynamics*. United States Environmental Protection Agency. Office of Pesticides and Toxic Substances. Gulf Breeze, Florida, U.S.A.

Specht, R.L. & Brouwer (1975). Seasonal shoot growth in *Eucalyptus*. *Australian Journal of Botany*, **23**, 459–474.

Stark, N. (1971). Nutrient cycling II: nutrient distribution in Amazonian vegetation. *Tropical Ecology*, **12**, 177–201.

Steinke, T.D. & Charles, L.M. (1983). Productivity and phenology of *Avicennia marina* (Forsk.) Vierh, and *Bruguiera gymnorrhiza* (L.) Lam. in Mgeni Estuary, South Africa. *Proceedings of the Second International Symposium in Mangrove Biology and Management*, Port Moresby. W. Junk, The Hague.

Tanner, E.V.J. (1977). *Mineral Cycling in Montane Rain Forests in Jamaica*. Ph.D. dissertation, University of Cambridge.

Tanner, E.V.J. (1980). Litterfall in montane rain forests of Jamaica and its relation to climate. *Journal of Ecology*, **68**, 833–848.

Teas, H.J. (1974). *Mangroves of Biscayne Bay*. Report to Metropolitan Dade County Commission, Miami, Florida, U.S.A.

Thaiutsa, B., Suwannapinunt, W., & Kaitpraneet, W. (1978). *Preliminary Study of Production and Chemical Composition of Forest Litter in Thailand*. Forest Research Bulletin 52, Faculty of Forestry, Kasetsart University, Bangkok, Thailand.

Upadhyaya, S.C. (1955). *Soil Formation in Relation to Plant Cover*. Ph.D. thesis, University of Sagar, India.

Venkataramanan, C. & Chinnamani, S. (1978). A preliminary note on the return of nutrient by the leaf-litter of wet (montane) evergreen Shola forests of Nilgiris. *Indian Forester*, **104**, 450–456.

Webb, L.J., Tracey, J.G., Williams, W.T. & Lance, G.N. (1969). The pattern of mineral return in leaf litter of three subtropical Australian forests. *Australian Forestry*, **33**, 99–110.

Wiegert, G.R. (1970). Effects of ionising radiation on leaf fall, decomposition and litter microarthropods of a montane rain forest. *A Tropical Rain Forest* (Ed. by H. T. Odum and R. F. Pigeon), pp. H-89–H-100. United States Atomic Energy Commission, Oak Ridge, Tennessee, U.S.A.

Wilcox, D.G. (1960). Studies in the Mulga pastoral zone 2. Some aspects of the value of the Mulga scrub. *Journal of Agriculture, Western Australia*, **1** (4th Series), 581–586.

Yamada, I. (1976). Forest ecological studies of the montane forest of Mt. Pangrango, West Java III. Litter fall of the tropical forest near Cibodas. *South East Asian Studies*, **14**, 194–229.

Zonn, S.V. & Li, C.K. (1962). Dynamics of the breakdown of litter and humus. *Soobshcheniya Laboratorii lesovedeniya*, **6**, 144–152.

SECTION IIIA
MAINTENANCE OF DIVERSITY
ECOPHYSIOLOGY

Ecophysiology and habitat preference of Trinidadian epiphytic bromeliads

H. GRIFFITHS,[1,*] J. A. C. SMITH,[2] M. E. BASSETT[1] AND N. M. GRIFFITHS[1]

[1]*Department of Biological Sciences, University of Dundee, DD1 4HN, Tayside, U.K.*
[2]*Institut für Botanik, Technische Hochschule Darmstadt, D-6100, Darmstadt, F.R.G.*

SUMMARY

1 The well documented ecology of rain-forest types and of the Bromeliaceae in Trinidad provided the background to our investigation of Crassulacean acid metabolism (CAM) in epiphytic bromeliads.

2 Field measurements of xylem-sap tension and leaf diffusion resistance were related to sap osmotic pressure, titratable acidity and plant carbon isotope composition.

3 CAM and non-CAM members of the Bromeliaceae were compared with regard to biochemical and physiological adaptions of the photosynthetic mechanism, water relations and habitat preference.

INTRODUCTION

The Bromeliaceae are adapted to a wide range of neotropical habitats, and although there is contention over the direction of evolution of both the epiphytic habit and possession of crassulacean acid metabolism (CAM) (Medina 1974 cf. Benzing & Renfrow 1971, Benzing 1980), the family provides an outstanding opportunity to study the response of CAM to environmental variables. As a site for investigating bromeliad physiology, Trinidad has a number of advantages. It is a mountainous island and the wide range of vegetational types, found within such a relatively small area, have been extensively investigated and classified by Beard (1946). Furthermore, the unparalleled monograph of Pittendrigh (1948) has detailed the ecology of the bromeliad flora, and the staff and plant collection of the National Herbarium, St Augustine, provided further invaluable aids to research.

CAM is a photosynthetic adaptation to arid environments: CAM plants open stomata at night to take up CO_2, thus conserving water. The CO_2 is fixed as C_4 acids and is then regenerated during the day, when stomata are closed, and re-assimilated via the C_3 pathway. CAM may be monitored by studying diurnal changes in stomatal aperture, plant-water status and cell-solute concentration and titratable acidity. If water and light are plentiful, the acids formed at night may be decarboxylated rapidly, stomata may then open during the day and the plant perform conventional 'C_3' type photosynthesis (Osmond 1978). The proportion of each photosynthetic pathway is reflected in plant carbon isotope content ($\delta^{13}C$), which can be determined mass spectrometrically from dried plant material (O'Leary 1981).

*Present address: Department of Plant Biology, University of Newcastle upon Tyne, NE1 7RU, U.K.

Termitarium cohabitation in Amazônia

ALAN E. MILL
Department of Biology, University of Southampton, U.K.

SUMMARY

1   A quantitative investigation was made of the inhabitants of all arboreal and epigeal termitaria in two 1 ha study areas in evergreen rain-forest within the Amazon basin. A total of 292 termite nests were examined, 54% of which contained animals cohabiting with the host colony.

2   6·5% of the nests contained termitophiles, 4·4% contained vertebrate inquilines and 49·6% contained invertebrate inquilines. One nest of *Syntermes solidus* held 34 colonies of inquilinous ants and termites, in addition to other inquilines.

INTRODUCTION

Nest-sharing, inquilinism, termitophily and other associations with termites in the neotropics have often been studied. A large body of general descriptive reports and isolated observations have built up, from Berg's (1900) 'Termitariophilie', to the present. Wheeler (1936) studied ant–termite relationships, Seevers (1957) and Kistner (1969, 1982) described termitophilous staphylinids and Mathews (1977) reported on termite inter-relationships. Among the vertebrates using termite nests, studies have been made on reptiles (Hermann 1920), amphibians (Araujo 1970), small mammals and birds (Goodland 1965). Although there is a wide selection of literature describing different associations, there are no quantitative studies on termitarium cohabitation in the neotropics. This paper presents the results of the first such study.

In describing the different associations, the terms termitophile and inquiline will be used. A termitophile is an animal which has become an obligate member of a termite community while an inquiline has little or no association with the host termite colony.

LOCALITY AND METHODS

During the period June 1980 to July 1981, the termite faunas at several sites in the Amazonian rain-forest in Brazil were studied. The data relating to termitarium-sharing, termitophily and the use of termitaria by other animals are reported here. These data were collected at two ecological reserves, Maracá and Iquê-Juruena, within Brazilian Amazônia. Maracá (3° 27′ N, 61° 21′ W) lies in the territory of Roraima and Iquê-Juruena (12° 00′ S, 59° 30′ W) in the State of Mato Grosso. Both reserves are located in regions of dense evergreen tropical rain-forest. They were established in the late 1970s and are maintained by the Special Environmental Agency (S.E.M.A.) of the Brazilian Interior Ministry.

At each locality a 1 ha plot, 100 m by 100 m, was marked out with tape and all epigeal and arboreal termitaria within the plots were broken open. Samples of the different inhabitants were collected and preserved in 75% alcohol for later identification. A record was kept of the inhabitants of each nest and notes made on the relative proportion of the nest occupied by each inhabitant, their feeding habits and the degree of aggression between the inhabitants of a nest.

RESULTS

All the nests examined were still occupied by their original builders. Table 1 lists the number of termitaria at each site, their original builder, the mean number of termite and ant colonies per nest and any other cohabitants recorded. A summary and analysis of these data are provided in Table 2.

The epigeal termitaria were free-standing structures from 10 cm to 200 cm tall, composed of soil cemented into a matrix of variable thickness and durability. The nests of *Cornitermes* spp. were the hardest, those of *Parvitermes* n.sp the softest. At Maracá, the commonest epigeal mounds were built by *Cornitermes* (15 mounds ha^{-1}). At Iquê-Juruena, *Cornitermes* was absent and there was no dominant mound builder.

The arboreal termitaria were generally spherical and were attached either to the trunk or to the branches of a variety of trees. The nests of *Microcerotermes* spp. and *Nasutitermes* spp. were formed of a brittle but hard carton made from semi-digested plant material and a cement produced by the termite workers. The nests of *Armitermes holmgreni* Snyder, *Labiotermes labralis* (Holmgren) and *Ruptitermes arboreus* (Emerson) were made from cemented soil of a hardness comparable to the harder epigeal termitaria. At both sites the commonest arboreal nest builders were *Nasutitermes*: 8 spp. and 70 nests ha^{-1} at Maracá; 7 spp. and 72 nests ha^{-1} at Iquê-Juruena.

A total of 292 termite nests was examined in the two 1 ha sites and 158 of these nests contained other animals in addition to the original termite builder. The nests inhabited by several different animals rarely differed in external appearance from those inhabited by the builder only. Nest occupied by birds and meliponine bees had obvious exits for these occupants, but the overall appearance of the termitarium was not altered.

DISCUSSION

Barely 6·5% of all nests examined contained termitophiles, while 54% contained inquilines. This low abundance of termitophiles may be due to the difficulties inherent in getting from one host nest to the next where the nests are widely separated. For example, the staphylinid *Spirachtha eurymedusa* (Schiodte) living with *Nasutitermes peruanus* (Holmgren) at Iquê-Juruena had a host density of nine nests ha^{-1}, yet it was present in only four nests. The frequency of occurrence was considerably less for the other termitophiles discovered.

Termitophiles

Seevers (1957) and Kistner (1969, 1982) deal extensively with the ecology of termitophilous Staphylinidae and nothing further will be added here. Less well-known than

TABLE 1. A record of cohabitants from the termitaria examined during this study. All psocids, staphylinids and termitaphids listed in this Table are termitophiles; other cohabitants are inquilines

Termite host	Termitarium location	Number examined	Number with cohabitants	Mean number of cohabitant colonies per nest (maximum in parentheses)		Other cohabitants
				Termite	Ant	
MARACÁ						
Microcerotermes arboreus	arboreal	10	3	–	–	beetle larvae
Neocapritermes n.sp.	epigeal	3	0	–	–	–
Orthognathotermes gibberorum	epigeal	5	2	2 (3)	–	staphylinids
Termes fatalis	epigeal	3	2	3 (4)	–	termitaphids
T. hispaniolae	epigeal	7	3	1 (2)	–	–
Termes n.sp.	epigeal	4	1	1 (1)	–	–
Armitermes holmgreni	arb/epig	6	4	3 (4)	2 (2)	staphylinids
A. neotenicus	epigeal	5	3	2 (5)	2 (3)	centipedes, woodlice
Cornitermes ovatus	epigeal	9	9	5 (8)	4 (8)	spiders, beetle larvae
C. pugnax	epigeal	6	6	4 (7)	6 (10)	centipedes, false scorpions
Nasutitermes brevioculus	arboreal	11	6	–	1 (1)	–
N. callimorphus	arboreal	12	7	1 (1)	1 (1)	–
N. crassirostris	arb/epig	10	5	–	–	parakeets
N. geigei	arboreal	8	5	–	–	beetle larvae, melip. bees
N. globiceps	arboreal	7	2	1 (1)	2 (4)	meliponine bees, beetles
N. nigriceps	arboreal	8	3	–	–	parakeets
N. surinamensis	arboreal	7	2	–	1 (1)	meliponine bees
N. tuichensis	arboreal	10	6	–	–	beetle larvae
Parvitermes n.sp.	epigeal	4	0	–	–	–
Rotunditermes bragantinus	epigeal	3	0	–	–	–
Syntermes calvus	epigeal*	5	5	15 (17)	11 (14)	spiders, beetle larvae
S. solidus	epigeal*	5	5	10 (15)	10 (19)	spiders, scorpions, beetle larvae
Rupitermes arboreus	arboreal	4	4	–	1 (1)	psocids
Totals		148	83			

Table 1 continued

Termite host	Termitarium location	Number examined	Number with cohabitants	Mean number of cohabitant colonies per nest (maximum in parentheses)		Other cohabitants
				Termite	Ant	
IQUÊ-JURUENA						
Microcerotermes strunkii	arboreal	15	4	–	1 (2)	beetle larvae
Termes fatalis	epigeal	3	1	3 (5)	–	–
Crepititermes verruculosus	epigeal	8	2	1 (1)	1 (1)	–
Armitermes holmgreni	arb/epig	6	4	3 (4)	2 (2)	staphylinids
A. neotenicus	epigeal	5	3	2 (5)	2 (3)	centipedes, scorpions
Labiotermes labralis	arboreal	10	7	1 (3)	2 (5)	beetle larvae, spiders
Nasutitermes acangussu	arboreal	12	5	–	–	parakeets
N. ephratae	arboreal	14	3	1(1)	–	meliponine bees
N. guyanae	arboreal	10	5	–	–	beetle larvae, false scorpions
N. macrocephalus	arboreal	12	7	–	1(1)	lepid. larvae, beetle larvae
N. octipilis	arboreal	10	8	–	1 (1)	centipedes, beetle larvae
N. peruanus	arboreal	9	4	1 (1)	1 (3)	staphylinids
N. surinamensis	arboreal	5	2	–	1 (1)	meliponine bees
Syntermes brevimalatus	epigeal*	4	4	8 (14)	10 (19)	spiders, false scorpions
S. lighti	epigeal*	6	6	11 (19)	9 (15)	spiders, beetles, scorpions
S. spinosus	epigeal*	6	6	5 (11)	7 (14)	centipedes, beetles
Ruptitermes arboreus	arboreal	4	4	–	1 (1)	–
Totals		144	75			

Note: * — *Syntermes* termitaria are largely subterranean but frequently have an epigeal portion 2–4 m in diameter and up to 1 m tall

the ubiquitous staphylinid beetles, a number of phorid flies, termitaphid bugs and a few psocids are also true termitophiles and several were discovered during this study. The phorids may act as cleaners in the termitarium, removing detritus etc., but no detailed studies of termitophilous phorid flies have yet been published.

Myers (1932) and Usinger (1942) provide brief accounts of the ecology of termitaphids and their relationships with termites. In the present study it was found that the termitaphids fed on the hyphae of fungi in termite foraging galleries. They were not molested by the termites and may have been protected from predators by living within the termite community.

Townsend (1912) provides the only published ecological data on termitophilous psocids. Observations from the present study suggest that, as with termitaphids, psocids in termitaria feed on micro-epiphytes within termite galleries, e.g. fungal hyphae, fungal spores and unicellular algae. They are tolerated by their host, but the full extent of the relationship is unknown.

Inquilines

The commonest inquilines discovered in the present study were other termites and ants. The data summary in Table 2 shows that 43·1% of the termite nests examined contained either ants or termites or both.

TABLE 2. A summary of the data presented in Table 1

Number of termitaria with inquilines

Location	Number of nests examined	Termites only	Ants only	Termites and ants only	Termites, ants and other arthropods	Termites and arthropods only	Ants and arthropods only	Arthropods only	Vertebrates only	Number of termitaria with termitophiles
Maracá	148	4	6	7	34	4	6	14	8	12
Iquê-Juruena	144	1	4	2	34	3	21	5	5	8
Total	292	5	10	9	68	7	27	19	13	19
as percentage of nests examined		1·7	3·4	3·1	23·3	2·4	9·2	6·5	4·4	6·5

54

Table 1 shows that a single termitarium of *Syntermes solidus* Emerson held a total of 34 colonies. 34·9% of all the nests examined contained arthropods in addition to ants or termites (Table 2). In contrast, only 4·4% of the termite nests examined contained

strategy is particularly interesting. Mortality to the young stages is high because of abortion of young seeds and pods (Hopkins & Hopkins in prep.), and the strategy is apparently very wasteful. It has been reported previously only on *Prosopis* which is the second most diverse non-cultivated legume genus in terms of its interactions with Bruchidae (Hopkins 1983). This strategy will probably only be found where bruchid diversity is high, and when interspecific competition is presumably intense.

ACKNOWLEDGMENTS

This work was supported by a Fellowship from the Royal Commission for the Exhibition of 1851. I am grateful to the directors and staff of the Instituto Nacional de Pesquisas da Amazônia, in Manaus and of the Museu Paraense 'Emílio Goeldi', in Belém for their help and cooperation, to the Força Aérea Brasileira for transport to the Serra do Cachimbo; to E. Lleras, N. Fernandes, B. Nelson, D. Charlewood and J. Revilla for help with equipment and transport and for field assistance, to an anonymous reviewer for comments on an earlier draft, and especially to H. C. Hopkins for assistance with all stages of this research.

REFERENCES

Bridwell, J.C. (1920). Notes on the Bruchidae (Coleoptera) and their parasites in the Hawaiian Islands, 3rd paper. *Proceedings of the Hawaiian Entomological Society*, **4**, 403–409.

Hopkins, H.C. (1981). *Taxonomy and reproductive biology of, and evolution in the bat-pollinated genus Parkia.* D.Phil. Thesis, Oxford University.

Hopkins, M.J.G. (1983). Unusual diversities of seed beetles (Coleoptera: Bruchidae) on *Parkia* (Leguminosae: Mimosoideae) in Brazil. *Biological Journal of the Linnean Society*, **19**, 329–338.

Janzen, D.H. (1971). The fate of *Scheelea rostrata* fruits beneath the parent tree: predispersal attack by bruchids. *Principes*, **15**, 89–101.

Janzen, D.H. (1975). Interactions of seeds and their insect predators/parasitoids in a tropical deciduous forest. *Evolutionary strategies of parasitic insects and mites* (Ed. by P. W. Price), pp. 154–186. Plenum Press, New York, U.S.A.

Janzen, D.H. (1976). Two patterns of pre-dispersal seed predation by insects on Central American deciduous forest trees. *Tropical trees: Variation, Breeding and Conservation* (Ed. by J. Burley and B. T. Styles), pp. 179–188. Academic Press, London, U.K.

Janzen, D.H. (1980). Specificity of seed attacking beetles in a Costa Rican deciduous forest. *Journal of Ecology*, **68**, 929–952.

Janzen, D.H. (1981). Patterns of herbivory in a tropical deciduous forest. *Biotropica*, **13**, 271–282.

Johnson, C.D. (1981a). Interactions between bruchid (Coleoptera) feeding guilds and behavioral patterns of pods of the Leguminosae. *Environmental Entomology*, **1**, 249–253.

Johnson, C.D. (1981b). Seed beetle host specificity and the systematics of the Leguminosae. *Advances in Legume Systematics* (Ed. by R. M. Polhill & P. H. Raven), pp. 995–1027. Royal Botanic Gardens, Kew, London, U.K.

Johnson, C.D. & Kingsolver, J.M. (1976). Systematics of *Stator* of North and Central America (Coleoptera: Bruchidae). *Technical Bulletin of the United States Department of Agriculture*, number 1537.

Johnson, C.D. & Slobodchikoff, C.N. (1979). Coevolution of *Cassia* (Leguminosae) and its seed beetle predators (Bruchidae). *Environmental Entomology*, **8**, 1059–1064.

Kingsolver, J.M., Johnson, C.D., Swier, S.R. & Teran, A. (1977). Prosopis fruits as a resource for invertebrates. *Mesquite, its biology in two desert scrub ecosystems* (Ed. B. B. Simpson), pp. 108–122, US/IBP Synthesis series 4. Dowden, Hutchinson & Ross, Stroudsburg, Pennsylvania, U.S.A.

Prevett, P.F. (1966). Observations on biology in the genus *Caryedon* Schönherr (Coleoptera: Bruchidae) in northern Nigeria, with a list of associated parasitic Hymenoptera. *Proceedings of the Royal Entomological Society, London* (A), **41**, 9–16.

Southgate, B.J. (1979). Biology of the Bruchidae. *Annual Review of Entomology*, **24**, 449–473.

Wilson, D.E. & Janzen, D.H. (1972). Predation on *Scheelea* palm seeds by bruchid beetles: seed density and distance from the parent palm. *Ecology*, **53**, 954–959.

Nest tree selectivity and density of stingless bee colonies in a Panamanian forest

LESLIE K. JOHNSON AND STEPHEN P. HUBBELL

Department of Zoology, The University of Iowa, Iowa City, Iowa 52242, U.S.A.
Smithsonian Tropical Research Institute, Apartado 2072, Balboa, Panama

SUMMARY

1   The trunks of trees $\geqslant 20$ cm dbh in a 15·6 ha plot of tropical moist forest in Panama were systematically searched for tree cavity nests of stingless bees (Apidae: Meliponinae). We found twenty-two nests of nine species: *Trigona capitata* (1), *T. testaceicornis* (1), *T. frontalis* (1), *T. dorsalis* (3), *T. pectoralis* (4), *T. fulviventris* (4), *T. jaty* (5), *Melipona fasciata* (1), and *M. marginata* (2).

2   The mean size of the searched trees was 43 cm dbh. Compared to these trees, the trees used for nest sites were disproportionately large ($\bar{x} = 95$ cm dbh). The trees being investigated for nest sites by scout bees were also significantly larger ($\bar{x} = 115$). *Trigona fulviventris* nested in significantly bigger trees than did the other bee species ($\bar{x} = 169$).

3   Empty cavities (i.e., potential nest sites) were found in 161 trunks; mean size of these trees was 62 cm dbh.

4   The densities of nests of *T. dorsalis*, *T. pectoralis*, and *T. fulviventris* were 19, 26, 26 km^{-2}, respectively, densities comparable to those found for these species in a tropical dry forest of Costa Rica. A minimum reserve size of 4–5 km^2 we estimate is needed to maintain a deme of 100 colonies of each of these *Trigona* species.

INTRODUCTION

The importance to mankind of creating reserves of tropical forest has been increasingly emphasized (Myers 1980; National Academy of Sciences 1980; Whitmore 1980; Norman 1981). The question of what size reserves are needed, however, remains unanswered (Norman 1981). One must consider not only what size plot would contain and permit the survival of a significantly large sample of local tree species, but also what size plot is needed to maintain the animals the trees depend on for pollination and seed dispersal.

Stingless bees (Apidae: Meliponinae) comprise an important class of pollinators in the tropics (Baker 1973; Bawa 1980). Stingless bees, close relatives of the honeybee, live chiefly in tree cavities in social colonies numbering up to tens of thousands of workers. Despite the abundance of these bees at flowers, and their importance as pollinators of neotropical trees and shrubs (Nogueira-Neto, Carvalho & Antunes Filho 1959; Bawa 1977; Augspurger 1980), little is known about the density of stingless bee colonies or what the bees require in a nest tree. Knowledge of the natural density of stingless bees would permit an estimate of the minimum critical size of the reserve that would maintain bee populations. Knowledge of tree species and tree size requirements would allow one to suggest which species would suffer a decline in potential nesting sites in tree plantations or in forests subject to selective logging. We undertook to provide some of this necessary

                    Exudate feeding in marmosets

TABLE 3. Exudate sources used by *Callithrix penicillata kuhlii*. * A = observations of the study group, B = observations of other groups. **The growth habit of the species, T = tree, E = emergent tree, C = creeper. The rest of the table shows the months (June to November) in which *C. penicillata* were observed feeding on the species. The plants were identified by A. M. de Carvalho of the Division of Botany, CEPLAC/CEPEC, Itabuna, Bahia. The numbers in brackets are the collector's reference of specimens at the Herbarium, CEPEC

						Month			
*	Species	Family	**	J	J	A	S	O	N
AB	*Parkia pendula*	Leguminosae, Mim.	E	×	×	×	×	×	×
AB	*Inga* sp.	Leguminosae, Mim.	T	×	×	×	×	×	×
B	Unidentified (19/80)	Annonaceae	T	×		×	×	×	×
B	Unidentified (25/80)	Cyclanthaceae	C			×			
B	*Anacardium* sp.	Anacardiaceae	T		×		×	×	×
A	Unidentified (24/80)	Sapindaceae	T			×	×	×	
A	*Cupania* sp.	Sapindaceae	T				×		
A	Unidentified (28/80)	Flacourtiaceae	T			×	×	×	
A	Unidentified (37/80)	Sapotaceae	T			×			
AB	*Sloanea* sp.	Elaeocarpaceae	T				×		

portion of the feeding records (58·8% and 24·9% respectively). Fruit feeding was correspondingly reduced, contributing only 32·0% of the plant feeding records in April and 52·9% in May. In May 20·6% of the records were for feeding on flowers.

During November and the wet season, the abundant fruit crops eaten by the *C. humeralifer* study group were those of *Cecropia sciadophylla*, *Sorocea opima* and *Pourouma acuminata* of the family Moraceae, and *Inga thibaudiana* (Leguminosae) and *Pouteria* (Sapotaceae), which accounted for between 50·4% and 66·5% of the feeding records each month (Rylands 1982). In the dry season the study group were feeding mainly on fruits of *Cecropia*, *Pourouma palmata* and *Ficus* (Moraceae). However, in April, there was an evident hiatus in the availability of these fruits. *Inga* had finished fruiting and the *Cecropia* fruits were still largely unripe. There were no other abundant or large crops of fruits within the range of the group and exudate-feeding increased dramatically both in terms of the time spent tree-gouging and exudate-feeding and the number of species they used (Fig. 2). Exudate from a *Didymopanax* (Araliaceae) tree ranked second in the diet in April, contributing 11·2% of the feeding records.

Fruit was also the main component of the plant part of the diet of the *C. penicillata* study group, comprising between 63·2% and 69·5% of the plant feeding records for each of the three months (Fig. 3). Exudate-feeding contributed between 30·5% and 34·4% of the plant feeding records each month. Flowers were eaten only in August (3·3% of the records).

The most abundant of the fruit crops eaten by the *C. penicillata* study group were from various species of the family Melastomataceae, which formed large stands in second growth forest patches. In contrast to *C. humeralifer*, the *C. penicillata* group fed extensively from holes gouged in the branches of *P. pendula* trees. Although *C. penicillata* used fewer species (Fig. 4), exudate from *P. pendula* ranked second in the diet in all three months of the study, comprising between 23·4% and 27·6% of the total plant feeding records in each month.

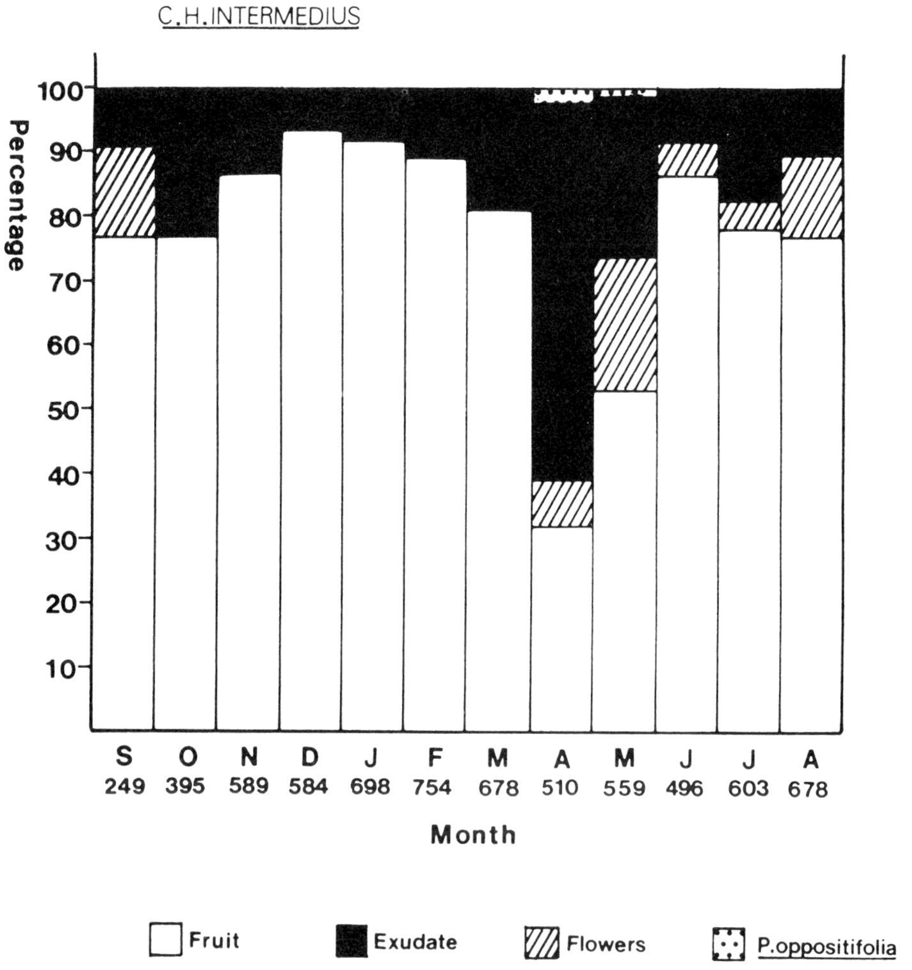

FIG. 1. Monthly changes in the plant part of the diet of *Callithrix humeralifer intermedius*. The figure shows the proportion of time recorded for feeding on each plant food type as a percentage of the total plant feeding records (shown on the abscissal scale) obtained during scan-sampling each month. The food eaten from shoot tips of *Parkia oppositifolia* (Leguminosae) was not identified.

DISCUSSION

There are a number of different types of exudate which are released by plants suffering physical damage. Sap is the circulating fluid of the plant vascular system. Resins are acidic phenols or terpene derivatives, insoluble in water, and produced by resin ducts (Harder *et al.* 1965). They are exuded in response to injury or infection and harden in the air to form a solid yellow, brown or white mass. Gums are complex polysaccharides and appear as a thick glutinous mass which is believed to serve particularly in preventing water loss.

 Exudate feeding in marmosets

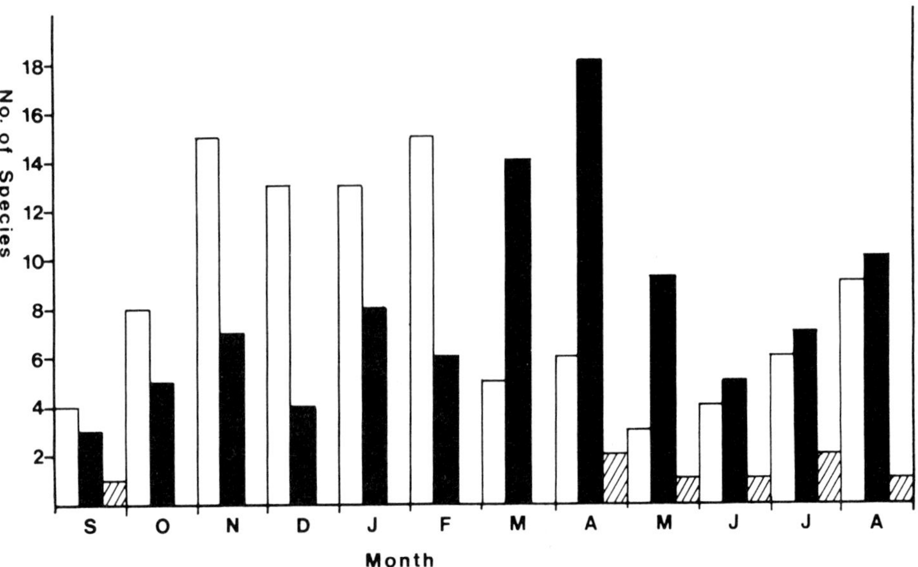

FIG. 2. The number of plant species in the diet of the *Callithrix humeralifer intermedius* study group each month according to the plant parts eaten. Open columns = fruits, black columns = exudates, striped columns = flowers.

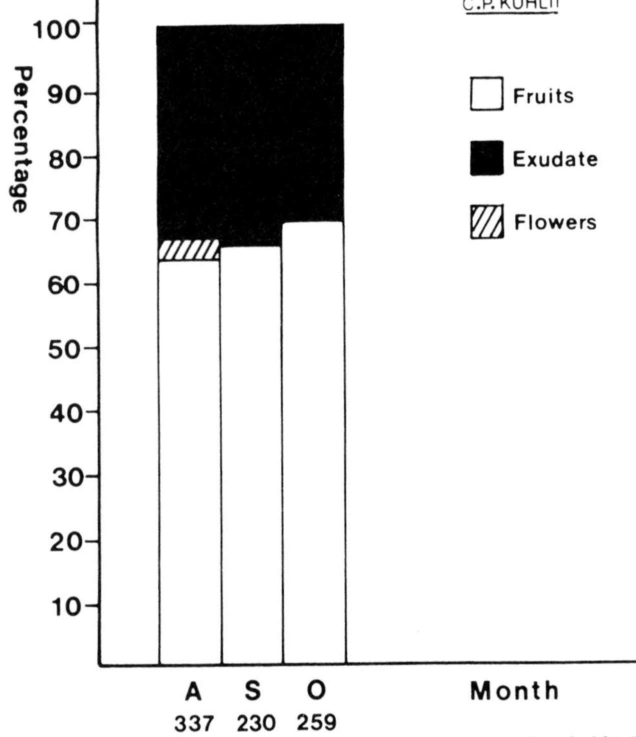

FIG. 3. Monthly changes in the plant part of the diet of *Callithrix penicillata kuhlii*. The figure shows the proportion of time recorded for feeding on each plant food type as percentages of the total plant feeding records (shown on the abscissal scale) obtained during scan-sampling each month.

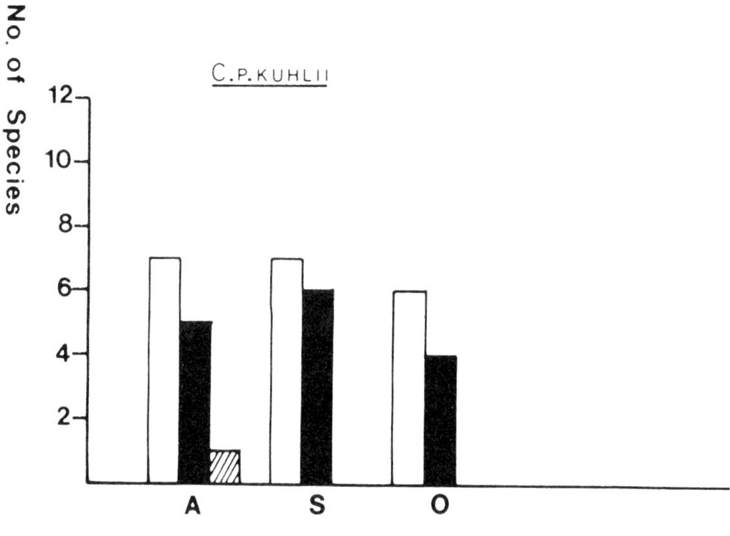

Fig. 4. The number of plant species in the diet of the *Callithrix penicillata kuhlii* study group each month according to the plant parts eaten. Open columns = fruits, black columns = exudates, striped columns = flowers.

They also contain a protein fraction and trace minerals, such as iron, aluminium, calcium, silicon, potassium, sodium and magnesium (Anderson *et al.* 1972; Bearder & Martin 1980). Latex is an equivalent of gum, but is milky coloured (red or yellow), and when exposed to air, coagulates into a solid rubbery mass. It is produced mainly by such families as Apocynaceae, Euphorbiaceae, Moraceae and Compositae. It too is believed to be important in preventing water loss and contains terpenes, tannins and resin elements, as well as small amounts of protein and non-reducing sugars (Buttery & Boatman 1976).

All species of marmosets have been observed tree-gouging and exudate-feeding (Table 4), and in most cases the substance eaten is gum. It is unlikely that marmosets eat resins because they are highly toxic, although locals in Aripuanã and Una reported that they eat the exudate of *Protium* sp. (Burseraceae) which is aromatic and resinous. Rizzini & Coimbra-Filho (1981) report that *C. p. penicillata* Thomas eats a red latex of *Hancornia speciosa* (Apocynaceae). The latex is slightly sweet, but contains only very small quantities of a non-reducing sugar, inositol. It also has a resin fraction and a small amount of protein (Guimarães & Chaves 1944, quoted by Rizzini & Coimbra-Filho 1981). Marmosets also eat the latex from the peduncles of *Artocarpus heterophyllus* (Moraceae) (Coimbra-Filho & Mittermeier 1977). In the case of gums, the polysaccharide sugars probably provide the nutritive value of the food but it is not known what is nutritive in latex or resins (Coimbra-Filho & Mittermeier 1977; Bearder & Martin 1980; Rizzini & Coimbra-Filho 1981).

The pygmy marmoset, *Cebuella*, spends up to 67% of its feeding time tree-gouging and exudate-feeding (Ramirez *et al.* 1977) and fruits comprise only a small portion of

TABLE 4. Observations of *Callithrix* species exudate-feeding and tree-gouging. The table shows the species and family of trees eaten. *Observed in captivity only. **Latex eaten from unripe fruit stems. ***Latex eaten. References are as follows: 1 — Coimbra-Filho (1972); 2 — Coimbra-Filho *et al.* (1973); 3 — Coimbra-Filho & Mittermeier (1977); 4 — Coimbra-Filho *et al.* (1981); 5 — Rizzini & Coimbra-Filho (1981); 6 — Stevenson & Rylands (in press); 7 — Torres de Assumpção (1983); 8 — Fonseca *et al.* (1980); 9 — Pers. obs. at Aripuanã (1979)

C. jacchus

Anacardium occidentale	Anacardiaceae	1, 6
Tapirira guianensis	Anacardiaceae	1, 6
Astronium fraxinifolium	Anacardiaceae	6
Spondias macrocarpa	Anacardiaceae	6
Spondias mombin	Anacardiaceae	6
Terminalia catappa	Combretaceae	1
Terminalia sp.	Combretaceae	6
Piptadenia colubrina	Leguminosae, Mim.	2
Anadenathra macrocarpa	Leguminosae, Mim.	6
Acacia sp.	Leguminosae, Mim.	6
Enterolobium sp.	Leguminosae, Mim.	6
Jatropha sp.	Euphorbiaceae	6
*Artocarpus heterophyllus***	Moraceae	3

C. p. penicillata

*Anacardium occidentale**	Anacardiaceae	1
Tapirira guianensis	Anacardiaceae	8
Piptadenia peregrina	Leguminosae, Mim.	5
Piptadenia sp.	Leguminosae, Mim.	8
Platymenia reticulata	Leguminosae, Mim.	5
Vochysia rufa	Vochysiaceae	5
Vochysia pyramidalis	Vochysiaceae	8
Vochysia tucanorum	Vochysiaceae	8
Vochysia tyrsoidea	Vochysiaceae	8
Qualea parviflora	Vochysiaceae	5, 8
Callisthene major	Vochysiaceae	5, 8
Didymopanax macrocarpum	Araliaceae	8
Simaruba versicolor	Simarubaceae	8
*Hancornia speciosa****	Apocynaceae	5

C. flaviceps

*Anacardium occidentale**	Anacardiaceae	1
Piptadenia peregrina	Leguminosae, Mim.	4

C. geoffroyi

*Anacardium occidentale**	Anacardiaceae	1

C. a. aurita

Astronium graveolens	Anacardiaceae	7

C. argentata melanura

Spondias lutea	Anacardiaceae	9
Diplotropis sp.	Leguminosae, Pap.	9
Sterculia stipulifera	Sterculiaceae	9

their diet (Soini 1982). Whereas *Cebuella* may be classified as an exudate-feeder and insectivore, the diets of the marmosets *C. penicillata* and *C. humeralifer* are principally fruits, with exudate, flowers and animal prey taking a secondary role. Seasonal changes in the diet of *C. humeralifer* indicate that exudate is eaten more extensively when fruit is scarce, suggesting that it is important particularly at times of food shortage as predicted by Coimbra-Filho & Mittermeier (1977). A similar situation has been observed for two other exudate-feeding mammals. Bearder & Martin (1980) report the findings of C. Harcourt that the bushbaby, *G. senegalensis* E.Geoffroy, eats more exudate at times when insects are scarce. The same is reported for the sugar glider, *P. breviceps*, by Smith (1982).

There also appears to be a relationship between the size of the home range and the amount of exudate in the diet of marmosets. The *C. humeralifer* group studied occupied a home range of approximately 28 ha and, except in April, they had access to abundant supplies of fruit. The *C. penicillata* group, on the other hand, had a smaller home range (approx. 10 ha) which was centred round a single *P. pendula* tree in a situation more similar to *Cebuella* which occupy very small home ranges (0·1–0·5 ha) also centred on a single, principal, exudate tree (Soini 1982). *C. penicillata* evidently depended more on exudate than *C. humeralifer*. The only other marmoset which has been studied in the wild is *C. jacchus* Linnaeus (Stevenson & Rylands, in press). Stevenson studied *C. jacchus* groups in a 500 ha patch of forest in north-east Brazil. Population densities were very high (estimated between eight and 24 individuals per ha) and the ranges of the groups were very small, approximately 0·5 ha. Stevenson believes that they were able to survive in these very high densities due to abundant supplies of gums in nearby *Anacardium occidentale* (Anacardiaceae) plantations. Both *C. jacchus* and *C. p. penicillata* range into xerophytic semi-deciduous woodland and scrub of the *cerrado* of central Brazil. Exudate-feeding is probably an important factor enabling their survival in these relatively harsh environments but whether they rely more on plant exudates than Amazonian *Callithrix* is not known.

The tamarins, *Saguinus* Hoffmannsegg, and lion tamarins, *Leontopithecus* Lesson, also eat gums (Castro & Soini 1977; Garber 1980; Rylands 1982) but they are evidently opportunists rather than specialists, only eating exudates when they are readily available. The question remains, if the marmosets eat gums when fruit is in short supply, what is the strategy of the tamarins? Janson *et al.* (1981) report that *S. fuscicollis* and *S. imperator* supplement their diet with nectar at times of fruit shortage. It is possible that they are also more insectivorous than the marmosets and that there are important differences in the animal as well as in the vegetable part of the diets of these animals.

Adaptations for tree-gouging and exudate-feeding in callitrichids

Bearder & Martin (1980) list five traits characteristic of the two most specialized exudate-feeding prosimians, *Galago elegantulus* and *Phaner furcifer*, and believe that callitrichids show parallel adaptations.

The traits are as follows:

1. Pointed, keeled nails which allow animals to cling to broad tree trunks and branches. Garber (1980) describes in detail the importance of the callitrichid claw-like nails with regard to gum feeding, particularly in *Saguinus oedipus* Linnaeus. He argues that exudate forms an important part of the diet of all callitrichids, including *Saguinus*,

and that claw-like nails are an adaptation for clinging to broad tree trunks, rather than a direct result of phyletic dwarfism (see Ford 1980). However, although exudate-feeding by *Saguinus* appears to be widespread, the evidence suggests that it is opportunistic rather than a specialization.

2. A long, narrow and conspicuously roughened tongue. This does not apply to callitrichids. Hershkovitz (1977, p. 111) concludes that there is no character or combination of characters regarding tongue morphology that separates callitrichids from cebids.

3. A relatively well-developed tooth-scraper. Rosenberger (1978) discusses dental adaptations for tree-gouging in *Callithrix* and *Cebuella*. Of particular interest is the loss of lingual enamel and hypertrophy of the buccal enamel of the lower incisor teeth, resulting in a chisel-like structure, which is ideal for gouging and scraping.

4. A large caecum and hind-gut in relation to the foregut to aid digestion of gums. Bearder & Martin (1980) believe that the digestion of the carbohydrate fraction of gums may require a symbiotic bacterial flora in an enlarged caecum. Coimbra-Filho *et al.* (1980) have shown that *C. jacchus* has a relatively large caecum, with well-developed superficial sulci and internal taenias, in comparison to those of *Saguinus midas* Linnaeus and *Leontopithecus r. rosalia* Linnaeus, which are smooth. This may be a parallel adaptation for exudate feeding. However, *S. midas* and *L. r. chrysomelas* Kuhl also eat gums (van Roosmalen, pers. comm.; Rylands 1982), if only when they are readily available, and to a much lesser extent than *Callithrix* or *Cebuella*. Coimbra-Filho *et al.* (1980) suggest that the difference in caecum structure may be related to a higher fibre content of the diet of *Callithrix*, through their tree-gouging and the ingestion of bark containing exudate droplets. The *C. humeralifer* group studied were observed stripping and chewing bark of *Inga* and *Diplotropis* (Leguminosae), but whether they ingested the bark is not known. Gums, resins and latexes contain secondary compounds such as phenols and tannins which act as digestion inhibitors of both carbohydrates and proteins (Wrangham & Waterman 1981). Intestinal flora are known to have the capacity to detoxify toxic compounds (Waterman *et al.* 1980). Considering, therefore, that *Callithrix* are specialized exudate-feeders, whereas *Saguinus* exudate-feeding is opportunistic, it is possible that the large and folded caecum of *C. jacchus* may be an adaptation to house a flora capable of detoxifying these secondary compounds. The observation that *C. humeralifer*, *C. penicillata* and the *C. jacchus* studied by Stevenson (Stevenson & Rylands, in press) eat exudate from one tree of a particular species while ignoring trees of the same species nearby, may be related to the different levels of toxic secondary compounds in the exudate of different individual trees.

5. A regular use of a succession of gum sources. This was not true for the *C. humeralifer* group studied where a large number of widely-dispersed exudate sources were used intermittently. However, for *Cebuella* a single gum source usually acts as a focus for the ranges of the groups (Soini 1982) and the *C. penicillata* group made regular visits to a single *P. pendula* tree in the centre of their range.

Garber (1980) points out that small size and an insectivorous diet are also characteristic of exudate-eating primates.

Bearder and Martin (1980) believe that the mineral content of gums may be important in supplementing the fruit and insect portion of the diet of *G. senegalensis*. The same may be true for *Callithrix*. However, the carbohydrate component is probably sufficient to explain their exploitation of this food resource. Chemical defences of the plants and the usually small quantities available, however, result in the need for specialization if exudate is to form more than a minor part of the diet. The specialized dentition and gouging behaviour of the marmosets overcome the problem of supply and, although little studied, it is possible that a specialized intestinal flora in an enlarged caecum is important for de-toxifying the exudates when a wide range of plant species are exploited.

ACKNOWLEDGMENTS

This work was carried out while I was employed by the Conselho Nacional de Desenvolvimento Científico e Tecnológico (CNPq) of Brazil at the Instituto Nacional de Pesquisas da Amazônia (INPA), Manaus. My thanks to Professor P. A. Jewell, Dr T. H. Clutton-Brock, Dr A. F. Coimbra-Filho, Dr R. A. Mittermeier and Dr M. Stevenson for many useful discussions. My thanks also to Dr Paulo de Tarso Alvim for permission to work at the Lemos Maia Experimental Station, Una and to the Centro de Pesquisas do Cacao (CEPEC) for logistic support and accommodation at Una. Financial support was provided by the World Wildlife Fund — U.S. primate programme, the Fauna and Flora Preservation Society and the Conder Conservation Trust.

REFERENCES

Anderson, D.M.W., Hendrie, A. & Munro, A.C (1972). The amino acid and amino sugar composition of some plant gums. *Phytochemistry*, **11**, 733–736.

Bearder, S.K. & Martin, R.D. (1980). Acacia gum and its use by bushbabies, *Galago senegalensis* (Primates, Lorisidae). *International Journal of Primatology*, **1**, 103–128.

Buttery, B.R. & Boatman, S.G. (1976). Water deficits and the flow of latex. *Water Deficits and Plant Growth* (Ed. by T. T. Kozlowski), Vol. IV, pp. 233–289. Academic Press, London, U.K.

Castro, R.N. & Soini, P. (1977). Field studies on *Saguinus mystax* and other callitrichids in Amazonian Peru. *The Biology and Conservation of the Callitrichidae* (Ed. by D. G. Kleiman), pp. 73–78. Smithsonian Institution Press, Washington, D.C., U.S.A.

Charles-Dominique, P. (1977). *Ecology and Behaviour of Nocturnal Primates*, Duckworth, London, U.K.

Charles-Dominique, P. & Petter, J.J. (1980). Ecology and social life of *Phaner furcifer*. *Nocturnal Malagasy Primates: Ecology, Physiology and Behaviour* (Ed. by P. Charles-Dominique, H. M. Cooper, A. Hladik, C. M. Hladik, E. Pages, G. F. Pariente, A. Petter-Rousseaux & A. Schilling), pp. 75–95. Academic Press, New York, U.S.A.

Coimbra-Filho, A.F. (1972). Aspectos inéditos do comportamento de sagüis do gênero *Callithrix* (Callitrichidae, Primates). *Revista Brasileira de Biologia*, **32**, 505–512.

Coimbra-Filho, A.F., Aldrighi, A.D. & Martins H.F. (1973). Nova contribuição ao restabclccimento da fauna do Parque Nacional de Tijuca. *Brasil Florestal*, **4**, 7–25.

Coimbra-Filho, A.F. & Mittermeier, R.A. (1976). Exudate-eating and tree-gouging in marmosets. *Nature, London*, **262**, 630.

Coimbra-Filho, A.F. & Mittermeier, R.A. (1977). Tree-gouging, exudate-eating and the 'short-tusked' condition in *Callithrix* and *Cebuella*. *The Biology and Conservation of the Callitrichidae* (Ed. by D. G. Kleiman), pp. 105–115. Smithsonian Institution Press, Washington, D.C., U.S.A.

Coimbra-Filho, A.F., Rocha, N. da C. & Pissinatti, A. (1980). Morfofisiologia do cêco e sua correlação com o tipo odontológico em Callitrichidae (Platyrrhini, Primates). *Revista Brasileira de Biologia*, **40**, 177–185.

Coimbra-Filho, A.F., Mittermeier, R.A. & Constable, I.D. (1981). *Callithrix flaviceps* (Thomas 1903) recorded from Minas Gerais, Brazil (Callitrichidae, Primates). *Revista Brasileira de Biologia*, **41**, 141–147.

Fonseca, G.A.B., Lacher T., Jr, Alves, C., Jr & Magalhães Castro, B. (1980). Some ecological aspects of free-living black tufted-ear marmosets (*Callithrix jacchus penicillata*). *Antropologia Contemporanea*, **3**, 197.

Ford, S.M. (1980). Callitrichids as phyletic dwarfs, and the place of the Callitrichidae in Platyrrhini. *Primates*, **21**, 31–43.

Garber, P.A. (1980). Locomotor behaviour and feeding ecology of the Panamanian tamarin (*Saguinus oedipus geoffroyi*, Callitrichidae, Primates). *International Journal of Primatology*, **1**, 185–201.

Harder, R.N., Fitting, H., Sierp, H. & Karsten, G. (1965). *Textbook of Botany*. Sixth English Edition. (Ed. by P. Bell & D. Combe), London, U.K.

Hershkovitz, P. (1977). *Living New World Monkeys (Platyrrhini) with an Introduction to the Primates.* Vol. I. Chicago University Press, Chicago, U.S.A.

Janson, C.H., Terborgh, J. & Emmons, L.H. (1981). Non-flying mammals as pollinating agents in the amazonian forest. *Biotropica, Supplement-Reproductive Botany.* **13**, 1–6.

Kinzey, W.G., Rosenberger, A.L. & Ramirez, M. (1975). Vertical clinging and leaping in a neotropical anthropoid. *Nature, London*, **255**, 327–328.

Petter, J.J., Schilling, A. & Pariente, G. (1971). Observations eco-éthologiques sur deux lémuriens malgaches nocturnes: *Phaner furcifer* et *Microcebus coquereli. Terre et Vie*, **25**, 287–327.

Ramirez, M., Freese, C.H. & Revilla, J. (1977). Feeding ecology of the pygmy marmoset, *Cebuella pygmaea*, in north-eastern Peru. *The Biology and Conservation of the Callitrichidae* (Ed. by D. G. Kleiman), pp. 91–104. Smithsonian Institution Press, Washington, D.C., U.S.A.

Rizzini, C.T. & Coimbra-Filho, A.F. (1981). Lesões produzidas pelo sagüi, *Callithrix penicillata penicillata* (E. Geoffroy 1812), em árvores do cerrado (Callitrichidae, Primates). *Revista Brasileira de Biologia*, **41**, 579–583.

Rosenberger, A.L. (1978). Loss of incisor enamel in marmosets. *Journal of Mammalogy*, **59**, 207–208.

Rylands, A.B. (1982). The Behaviour and Ecology of Three Species of Marmosets and Tamarins (Callitrichidae, Primates) in Brazil. Doctoral Dissertation, University of Cambridge, U.K.

Smith, A.P. (1982). Diet and feeding strategies of the marsupial sugar glider in temperate Australia. *Journal of Animal Ecology*, **51**, 149–166.

Soini, P. (1982). Ecology and population dynamics of the pygmy marmoset, *Cebuella pygmaea. Folia Primatologica*, **39**, 1–21.

Stevenson M.F. & Rylands, A.B. (in press). The marmosets, genus *Callithrix. The Ecology and Behavior of Neotropical Primates*. II. (Ed. by R. A. Mittermeier & A. F. Coimbra-Filho).

Torres de Assumpção, C. (1983). A Study of the Primates of Southeastern Brazil with emphasis on *Cebus apella*. Doctoral Dissertation, University of Edinburgh, U.K.

Waterman, P.G., Mbi, C.N., Mckey, D.B. & Gartlan, J.S. (1980). African rain forest vegetation and rumen microbes: phenolic compounds and nutrients as correlates of digestibility. *Oecologia, Berl.*, **47**, 22–33.

Wrangham, R.W. & Waterman, P.G. (1981). Feeding behaviour of vervet monkeys on *Acacia tortilis* and *Acacia xanthophlea* with special reference to reproductive strategies and tannin production. *Journal of Animal Ecology*, **50**, 715–731.

Fruit bat niche dynamics: their role in maintaining tropical forest diversity

FRANK J. BONACCORSO* AND STEPHEN R. HUMPHREY
Biology Department, University of Miami, Coral Gables, FL 33124, U.S.A. and Department of Natural Sciences, Florida State Museum, University of Florida, Gainesville, FL 32611, U.S.A.

SUMMARY

1   The abundance and diet of volant phyllostomid fruit bats and the availability of bat-dispersed fruits were monitored for a complete year in four habitats in a tropical moist forest life zone on and around Barro Colorado Island, Panama.

2   Resource levels of bat-dispersed fruits change seasonally and so consequently do the diets of even the most specialized frugivorous bat species.

3   All members of the fruit bat community vary seasonally in abundance and in contribution to species diversity. Some specialized species migrate to unknown habitats or life zones when their staple food resources become scarce.

4   Frugivorous phyllostomid bats are high-quality dispersal agents that promote regeneration of many gap colonizing and forest invading plant species.

INTRODUCTION

Frugivorous bats and fruiting plants are mutualists that have a direct impact on each others' populations in tropical forest ecosystems. As a result of their seed dispersal activities, bats promote plant gene flow, make seeds less obvious to seed predators, reduce parent-offspring competition, and move seeds to sites favourable for seedling colonization (see Heithaus 1982 for a review). In addition to providing bats with nutrients and energy (Morrison 1980; Herbst 1983) the spatio-temporal distribution of fruiting plants and fruit crop biomass may influence bat reproductive timing (Bonaccorso 1979; Racey 1982), roost size and refuging strategy (T. Fleming, pers. comm.), foraging strategy (Bonaccorso & Gush 1982) and, perhaps predation by animals that are attracted to fruiting plants or concentrations of bats (Morrison 1978a; Bonaccorso 1979).

In the Neotropical region, all obligate frugivorous bats belong to the family Phyllostomidae (Phyllostomatidae of Gardner 1977). Obligate frugivores are here defined as dependent on fruits for >90% of the total annual diet. On Barro Colorado Island (BCI), Panama, ten species of obligate frugivorous bats belong to two feeding guilds defined by Bonaccorso (1979). Briefly, the canopy frugivore guild consists of eight species of stenodermine bats that eat mostly small to medium sized fruits (1 to 25 g) growing on canopy trees. An understorey frugivore guild consists of two carolline bats species that mostly eat small fruits (0·5 to 4 g) of understorey shrubs and small sub-canopy trees. *Piper* species (Piperaceae, peppers) are keystone mutualists (*sensu* Gilbert 1980) of bats of the understorey guild on BCI, as are *Ficus* species (Moraceae, figs) for most members of the canopy guild.

*Present address: Lake City Community College, Lake City, Florida 32055 U.S.A.

Previous work has demonstrated that frugivorous bats on BCI disperse the seeds of at least 44 plant species (Bonaccorso 1979) and that bat reproduction coincides with abundant levels of fruit resources (Bonaccorso 1979; Humphrey & Bonaccorso 1979). In this paper we describe additional seasonal patterns in the community-level mutualism between bat-dispersed plants and fruit-eating bats on BCI. We will address the following questions: (1) Is the fruit bat community self-contained or do seasonal dynamics and habitat requirements dictate dependence on several environments? (2) Does the frugivorous bat community promote replacement of parental plant stocks in pioneering and/ or maturing forest habitats? (3) What are the implications of these findings for conservation of tropical forests?

Study Site

The study was conducted on Barro Colorado Island (BCI), Panama, lying within the freshwater Lake Gatun at 9° 10′ N and 79° 51′ W. Dry season months, January–March, each receive less than 60 mm of rain (Smythe 1974). Wet season months, May–November, each receive more than 200 mm of rain. April and December are months of transition between dry-to-wet and wet-to-dry seasons, and they receive rainfall that varies annually. Monthly rainfall for 1973 is shown in Figure 1. During night-time sampling of bats, humidity under the forest canopy never fell below 80%, as determined with a sling psychrometer 2·0 m above the ground. Daily air temperatures at the forest floor fluctuated from a mean minimum of 22·1°C to a mean maximum of 28·0°C with no significant seasonal variation (Smythe 1974).

BCI is in the Tropical Moist Forest life zone of Holdridge (1967) and has been an undisturbed biological preserve since 1923. Half of this 15 km² island is covered with mature forest over 100 years in age (Foster 1973). The other half is second-growth closed canopy forest 60 to 100 years in age. This 'second-growth' forest, however, is very near to the climax condition, the main distinguishing features being a slightly more dense understorey and an abundance of pioneering or subclimax tree species such as *Ficus insipida* and *Spondias mombin*.

MATERIALS AND METHODS

Seventeen sampling stations were located in a 2 km² strip centred in the second-growth forest (Bonaccorso 1979). Each sampling station consisted of four or six 6 × 2 m mist nets and one or two 2 × 2 m harp traps (Tuttle 1974), set perpendicular to permanent trails or creeks. Nets were set in pairs at 100 m intervals, with one of each pair set at 0 to 3 m (shrub layer) and the other at 3 to 12 m (subcanopy) above ground. Harp traps were placed at shrub or sub-canopy levels in narrow tunnel-like passages created by the vegetation and/or trails.

Nets and traps were open from sunset to sunrise on 67 nights between 11 January and 31 December 1973. Sampling took place only on nights between last and first quarter moon, so activity cycles of flying bats were not affected by the lunar phobia described by Morrison (1978b). Total sampling involved 4047 net-hours, 2136 trap-hours, and 2136 bats of 31 species captured in 1973.

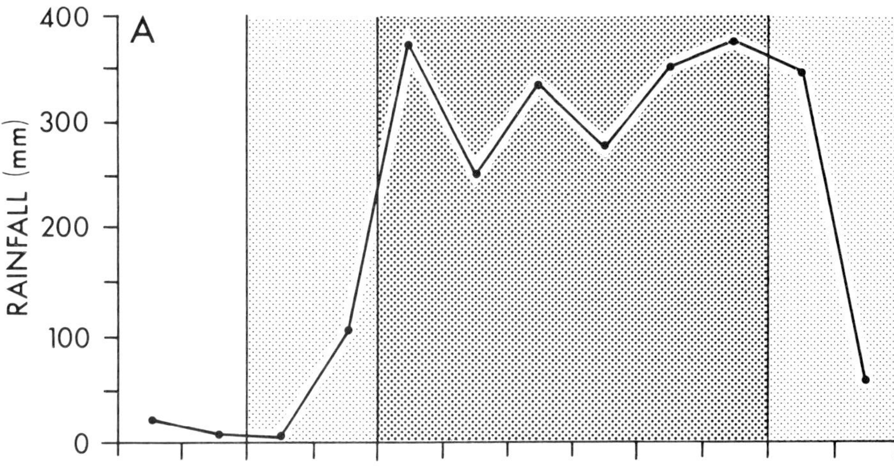

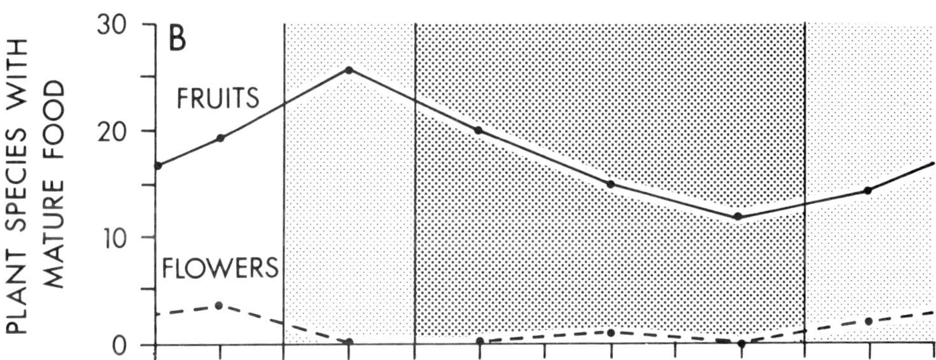

FIG. 1. Seasonal distribution of (A) precipitation and (B) number of plant species serving as food for bats during 1973 on Barro Colorado Island.

Nets were checked at least twice each hour. Each bat was held for about one hour in an individual cloth bag after which food, body size, and reproductive data were collected before banding and releasing the animal near the capture site.

Diversity data were pooled into bimonthly samples coinciding with lunar cycles. Species-individuals discovery curves (not shown) had plateaued for each bimonthly sample, indicating that such samples were adequate for estimating species diversity parameters (see Fleming *et al.* 1972). Species diversity, $H' = -\Sigma p_i \log_e p_1$, and equitability, $E = H'/H'\text{max}$, were calculated according to Shannon and Weaver (1949) and Sheldon (1969). The contribution of certain species to diversity, $H'n$, was calculated after Humphrey (1975). Bat species were treated as members of foraging guilds as defined in Bonaccorso (1979).

RESULTS

Diet and Host Plants

The largest canopy frugivores, *Vampyrodes caraccioloi*, *Artibeus jamaicensis*, and *A. lituratus*, are specialists on large figs and have moderate to low feeding niche breadths (Bonaccorso 1979). *A. jamaicensis* and *A. lituratus* eat figs throughout the year (Fig. 2).

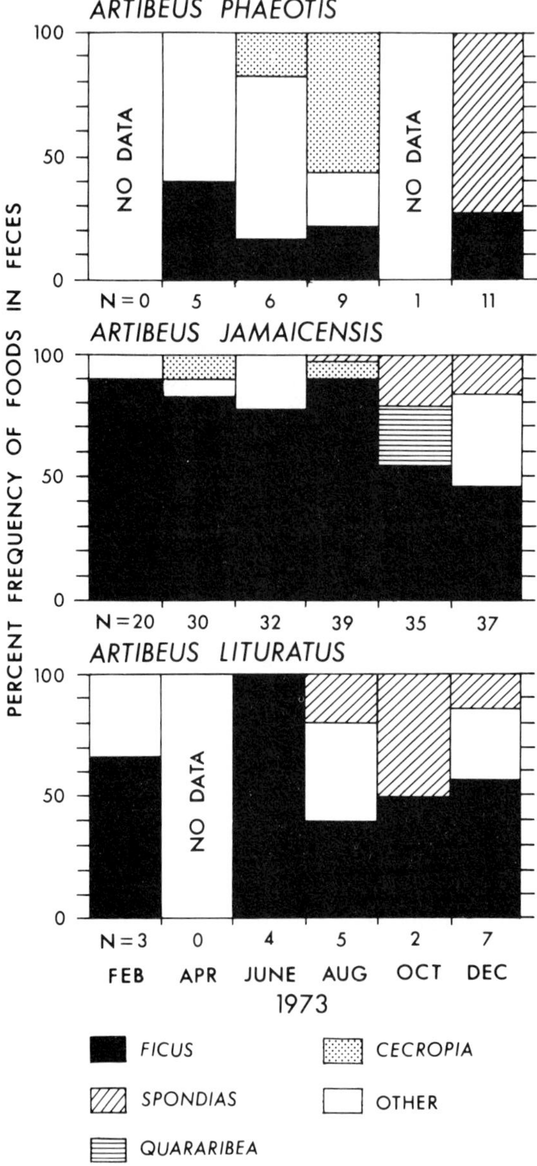

FIG. 2. Diets of the most abundant bat species in the canopy frugivore guild.

However, figs become less prominent in the diet late in the wet season as a result of declining fig crop biomass (Morrison 1978a). At the end of the wet season and during the transition to the dry season, three other large fruits, *Spondias mombin*, *S. radlkoferi*, and *Quararibea asterolepis*, become important dietary components. By January, *Ficus* fruit biomass returns to abundant levels and figs are again a dietary staple until the following September. Data are not sufficient to analyse the diet of *V. caraccioloi* on a seasonal basis.

Artibeus phaeotis is unique among canopy frugivores in being a feeding generalist with a high feeding niche breadth (Bonaccorso 1979). Small figs, primarily *F. yoponensis* and the smallest individual fruits from *F. insipida* and other figs, are important components of the diet through the year, and two species each of *Cecropia* and *Spondias* are seasonally important. A number of other fruits are minor components of the diet when available and include *Clusia odorata*, *Markea panamensis*, *Solanum hayseii* and *Tetrathylacium johansoni*.

Other small canopy guild fruit bats, ranging from 8 to 22 g mean body mass, appear to be fig-specialists from the limited data (see Bonaccorso 1979).

The understorey frugivore guild members, *Carollia castanea* and *C. perspicillata*, have high values of niche breadth (Bonaccorso 1979). Fruits of eleven *Piper* shrub species occur in the diets of these two bat species throughout the year, except in October–November for *C. perspicillata* (Fig. 3). *Piper* fruits are small, 1–3 g in mass for the species eaten by *Carollia* on BCI. These shrubs are common in early successional habitats and along streambeds where they are exposed to bright sunlight for at least part of the day. Only one species, *P. cordulatum*, is abundant under closed-canopy forest.

Carollia castanea is a *Piper* specialist throughout the year and its large food species niche breadth results from eating many *Piper* species. In wet season months *Markea panamensis* fruits additionally form an important dietary item with a small mixture of several other fruiting species.

C. perspicillata is less restricted to pepper fruits than is *C. castanea* and also includes more fruits from small and large trees in its diet. During the transition period from dry to wet season, coinciding with its first period of lactation, *C. perspicillata* diversifies its diet with insects (Bonaccorso 1979). During the lactation period of the year's second reproductive peak, females in our mature forest site rely almost entirely on fruits from sub-canopy and canopy trees (October–November in Fig. 2). At this time, *Quararibea asterolepis* becomes the most important food species. Other canopy trees of seasonal importance in the diet of *C. perspicillata* include *Vismia baccifera*, *Vismia* species, *Solanum hayesii*, *Markea panamensis*, *Dipteryx panamensis*, and *Anacardium excelsum*. Two *C. perspicillata* day roosts on BCI are in hollow *A. excelsum* trees. *Anacardium* fruits are important dietary items in January–March for bats living in *A. excelsum* roost trees as determined by fruits and seed coats dropped inside the roosts. However, *A. excelsum* is not identifiable in the fecal material from volant captures and we are not able to show its importance in Figure 3. When pepper fruits are not abundant on BCI in the late wet season several fruit species are harvested from sub-canopy and canopy trees by *C. perspicillata*. This is reflected in its high capture rate in both high and low mist-nets during that time of year (Bonaccorso 1979).

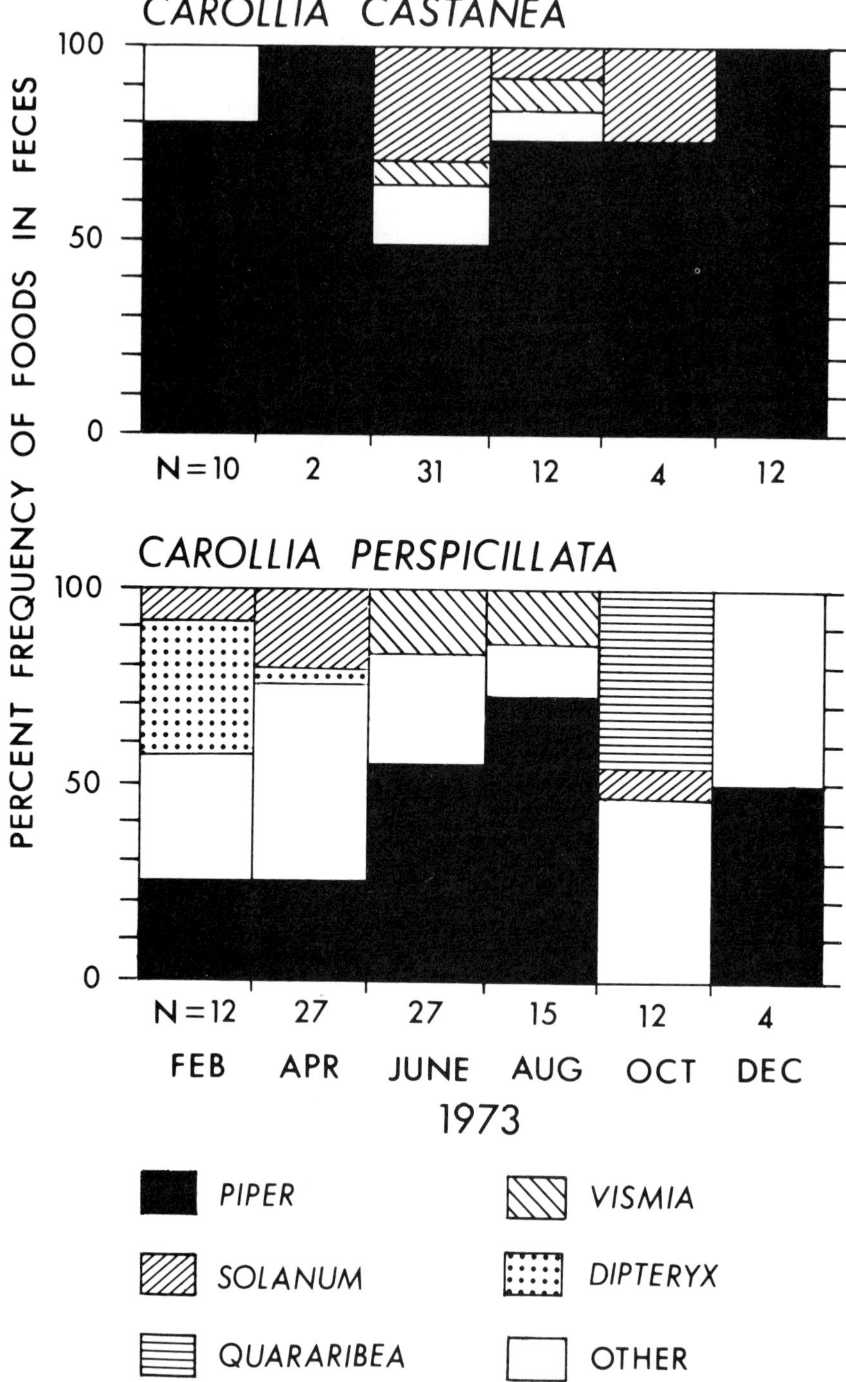

Fig. 3. Diets of the bat species in the understorey frugivore guild.

Seasonality of community diversity and abundance

The seasonal fluctuation in number of ripe bat-dispersed fruits is presented in Figure 1. The number of kinds of bat-dispersed fruits peaks in April, a transition period, when irregular rains marking the prelude to the rainy season occur. The total number of fruiting species available as bat food then declines to a low in October and November. Because fruit bat body mass in the frugivore community on BCI ranges from 8 to 70 g, and because fruit bats select fruits proportional in size to their body mass (Bonaccorso 1979), it is important to determine if a seasonal difference in size of bat fruits occurs as it does for animal-dispersed fruits in general (Smythe 1970).

Figure 4 shows that small-sized bat fruits produced by canopy and understorey trees peak in variety in March and are relatively few in September, November and December. Large canopy fruits are more uniformly available year-round than small canopy fruits. Few kinds of shrub fruits are available to bats from September through November. Except for two species of figs, biomass data for fruit crops are not available.

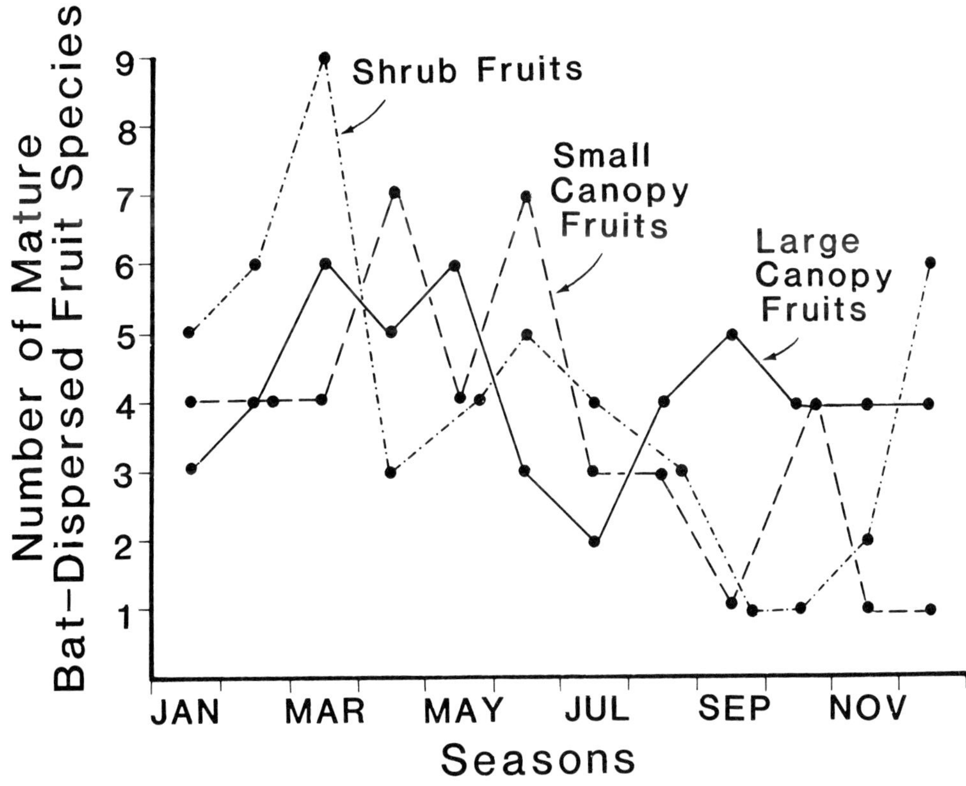

Fig. 4. Seasonal distribution of fruits in bat diets, comparing canopy and shrub species. Few species of small-canopy fruits and shrub fruits are available late in the rainy season.

The dominant food species for small fig-specialist bats, *Ficus yoponensis*, is at an annual low in biomass in September–October, and only a few individual trees produce fruits then (Morrison 1978a). From the low variety and biomass of small canopy/sub-canopy fruits from September to November, one would predict that this would be the most likely time of annual food shortage for small canopy frugivores on BCI.

The least diversity of large fruits (>4 g) is available in June, July and January. However, at these times *Ficus insipida*, a keystone species for large fruit bats, is producing a large fruit biomass (Morrison 1978a). When *F. insipida* trees are producing few fruits in March, eight other species of large bat-dispersed canopy fruits are available. Again when few *F. insipida* fruits are available in October, several kinds of other large, common canopy trees produce large fruit crops on BCI. These tree species are Spondias *mombin, S. radlkoferi* and *Quararibea asterolepis*. Therefore, the two large fruit bats should not have an annual period of fruit scarcity on BCI.

Species number and species diversity in the entire frugivorous bat community are low between July and September (Table 1). Species number is lowered because the entire

TABLE 1. Seasonal variation in diversity of frugivorous bat species on Barro Colorado Island

Seasons; Months:	Dry Jan–Mar	Dry–Wet Mar–May	Early-Wet May–Jul	Mid-Wet Jul–Sept	Late-Wet Sept–Nov	Wet–Dry Nov–Jan
Species diversity (H')	1·698	1·523	1·568	1·338*	1·094*	1·661
Equitability (E)	0·662	0·594	0·630	0·581	0·456	0·693
Species number	13†	13†	12	10	11	11
Total bats sampled	248	360	212	207	261	162

†Species number includes omnivorous bats eating fruit in a given sampling period.
*Significant difference ($P \leq 0.05$) from all other species diversity values by '*t*'-test (Hutcheson 1970).

population of *Vampyressa pusilla* migrates off the study site, because several uncommon species become even less abundant, and because omnivorous species switch to other food types. Species diversity (H') is significantly low (Table 1, 't' test, $P \leq 0.05$) because of reduced species number and equitability. *A. jamaicensis* and *A. lituratus* increase to the point of lowering equitability of the samples. The increase in these two largest species is consistent with the entrance of sub-adult bats into the volant populations and the pattern of large fruit abundance late in the wet season (Fig. 4). Smaller fruit bats, including *Vampyrodes caraccioloi* (36 g), *Chiroderma villosum* (22 g), *Vampyrops helleri* (16 g), *Artibeus phaeotis* (13 g) and especially *Vampyressa pusilla* (8 g), are sensitive to the decline in small canopy fruits between August and November. These bats decrease in abundance during this period (Fig. 5).

The contribution to diversity ($H'n$) of important members of the frugivore guild are plotted in Figs. 5–7. Only *A. jamaicensis* is a consistently dominant species in the community (51% of all bat captures on BCI). The decrease in $H'n$ of *A. jamaicensis* from August to October is a result of lower equitability in the index, though the capture rate of this species is increased on an absolute scale (Fig. 5 and Table 1). $H'n$ values plotted for all other bat species are directly proportional to the number of individuals captured.

The results on the species area relationship for guilds of specialized leaf-mining insects on British trees, presented by Claridge & Wilson (1982), can be interpreted in a similar way. The only significant relationship between host-plant abundance and number of associated species was for the Lepidoptera. It may be significant that this is the only major order of phytophagous insect which is thought to have evolved *after* the diversification of the angiosperms. Colonization of a diverse range of host-plants would have, of necessity, involved a good deal of 'jumping around' between different host-plant lines. By contrast, no significant relationship was demonstrated for the older insect orders Hymenoptera, Diptera and Coleoptera which were extant before the angiosperm explosion and which have evolved *with* the plants. In seeking to present general ecological theories, we are perhaps ignoring the fact that insect groups differ in their evolutionary history and their relationships with the host-plants. Rather than viewing host-plants as islands in evolutionary time it is perhaps more apposite, at least for certain specialized (K-selected?) insect groups such as the Psylloidea, to view the plants as rafts transporting the insects down the river of evolutionary time. As the original raft began to break up (plant diversification) each section drifted apart, carrying its own fauna, which then began to diversify and adapt to its changed environment. Jumping between raft sections may have been an uncommon occurrence.

REFERENCES

Bekker-Migdisova, E.E. (1967). Tertiary Homoptera of Stavropol and a method of reconstruction of continental palaeobiocoenoses. *Palaeontology*, **10**, 542–553.

Bekker-Migdisova, E.E. (1973). Systematics of the Psyllomorpha and the position of the group within the order Homoptera. *Dokalady na dvadzat chetvertom escheghodnom chtenii pamyati* (Ed. by E. P. Narchik), pp. 90–117. A. N. Kholodovskogo 1971 [In Russian, English translation, British Lending Library, Boston Spa, U.K.].

Claridge, M.F. & Wilson, M.R. (1981). Host plant associations, diversity and species-area relationships of mesophyll-feeding leafhoppers of trees and shrubs in Britain. *Ecological Entomology*, **6**, 217–238.

Claridge, M.F. & Wilson, M.R. (1982). Insect herbivore guilds and species-area relationships: leafminers on British trees. *Ecological Entomology*, **7**, 19–30.

Hodkinson, I.D. (1974). The biology of the Psylloidea (Homoptera): a review. *Bulletin of Entomological Research*, **64**, 325–339.

Hodkinson, I.D. (1980). Present-day distribution patterns of the holarctic Psylloidea (Homoptera: Insecta) with particular reference to the origin of the nearctic fauna. *Journal of Biogeography*, **7**, 127–146.

Hodkinson, I.D. (1983). The psyllids (Homoptera: Psylloidea) of the Austro-Oriental, Pacific and Hawaiian zoogeographical realms: an annotated check list. *Journal of Natural History*, **17**, 341–377.

Hodkinson, I.D. & White, I.M. (1981). The Neotropical Psylloidea (Homoptera: Insecta): an annotated check list. *Journal of Natural History*, **15**, 491–523.

Janzen, D.H. (1968). Host-plants as islands in evolutionary and contemporary time. *American Naturalist*, **102**, 592–595.

Janzen, D.H. (1980). Specificity of seed-attacking beetles in a Costa Rican deciduous forest. *Journal of Ecology*, **68**, 929–952.

Lawton, J.H. & Price, P.W. (1979). Species richness of parasites on hosts: Agromyzid flies on the British Umbelliferae. *Journal of Animal Ecology*, **48**, 610–637.

Lawton, J.H. & Schröder, D. (1977). Effects of plant type, size of geographical range and taxonomic isolation on numbers of insect species associated with British plants. *Nature*, **265**, 137–140.

Mathur, R.N. (1975). *Psyllidae of the Indian Subcontinent.* Indian Council of Agricultural Research, New Delhi, India.

Smart, J. & Hughes, N.F. (1973). The insect and the plant: progressive palaeoecological integration. *Insect/Plant Relationships* (Ed. by H. F. van Emden), pp. 143–155. Royal Entomological Society of London, U.K.

Southwood, T.R.E. (1961). The numbers of species of insects associated with various trees. *Journal of Animal Ecology*, **30**, 1–8.

Southwood, T.R.E. (1973). The insect–plant relationship — an evolutionary perspective. *Insect/Plant Relationships* (Ed. by H. F. van Emden), pp. 3–30. Royal Entomological Society of London, U.K.

Strong, D.R. (1979). Biogeographic dynamics of insect-host plant communities. *Annual Review of Entomology*, **24**, 89–119.

White, I.M. (1980). Nymphal taxonomy and systematics of the Psylloidea (Homoptera). Ph.D. thesis (CNAA), Liverpool Polytechnic, U.K.

Tropical Rain-Forest: The Leeds Symposium, pp. 195–204

Extinction as a creative force:
the butterflies of the rain-forest

JOHN R. G. TURNER

Department of Genetics, University of Leeds, Leeds LS2 9JT

SUMMARY

Extinction creates diversity. When a biome is subdivided, the extinction of different species in the various isolated patches causes divergence of the community structures and alteration in the occupancy of ecological niches. As the remaining species adapt to these changes they form diversified geographical races, which probably constitute the basis for adaptive radiation in the long term. Without extinction, a considerable part of evolution would come to a stop.

The whole process is illustrated in some detail and with considerable beauty, by the evolving mimetic patterns of the *Heliconius* butterflies of the South American rain-forests, which have been split, probably repeatedly, into isolated forest refuges during the Quaternary.

Unfortunately the pattern of destruction which we are inflicting on the rain-forest, while it will undoubtedly lead to massive extinction, is unlikely to generate very much diversity by way of compensation.

EXTINCTION AND DESTRUCTION

When we wipe out the world's rain-forests, something will take their place. If we are very clever and very lucky, that 'something' might resemble the farmlands of northern Europe; if we are moderately lucky it might resemble the poor heather moors of the Scottish Highlands; more probably, it will be something like the Sahara. Whatever habitat does replace the forests, it will have its own fauna and flora, probably consisting chiefly of us, our crops and stock, and our indestructable commensals and pests. A very large number of species will be exterminated: the extinction rate over the next thirty years will probably make the destruction of the last hundred and fifty look like a Victorian duck-shoot.

Extinction may rob us of irreplaceable resources; at the least it pains us aesthetically. The exterminated species join the outer portions of the 'Night Watch', the final two movements of Schubert's Eighth Symphony, and Rimbaud's greatest prose poem, 'La Chasse Spirituelle', the unrecoverable beauties that once were and will never be again.

But our belief in extinction as a purely destructive and negative thing is based irrationally in our perception of lost works of art, and our own awareness of death. What should it matter if a species becomes extinct? Why do we concern ourselves with species? Why not populations, or subspecies, or genera, or families? Why does it distress us more that nature is careless of the type, than that she is careless of the single life? If I perish, what does the extinction of *Homo sapiens* mean more or less to me? Indeed, as the extinction of species has been a recurrent event throughout earth history, and as we are the undoubted beneficiaries of the process, in that had certain other species not become extinct we would not ourselves have evolved, we are hardly in a position to complain about it. While most budding zoologists must at one time or another have wanted a pet pterodactyl, or to see a trilobite with all its legs in action, we have to recognize that extinction of one life form is part of the creative process which brings others into being. The more misanthropic, zoophilic of us have no doubt wondered whether the benefits to the planet of the extinction of *Homo sapiens* would not be perhaps, just worth it.

The creative effects of extinction may be seen on a time-scale smaller than those of the mass extinctions which chiefly occupy our attention — of the trilobites, the dinosaurs, or the ammonites. We (Turner 1982; Sheppard, Turner, Brown, Benson and Singer, 1985) have been studying their role in creating diversity in one small group of neotropical butterflies, the Heliconiinae. Several species of *Heliconius* in particular, show a truly delightful diversity of races, as well as a quite astounding degree of mimicry, one of another. Figure 1 shows the most spectacular pair, *Heliconius melpomene* and *Heliconius erato*, which follow each other in strict parallel mimicry through a diversity of some

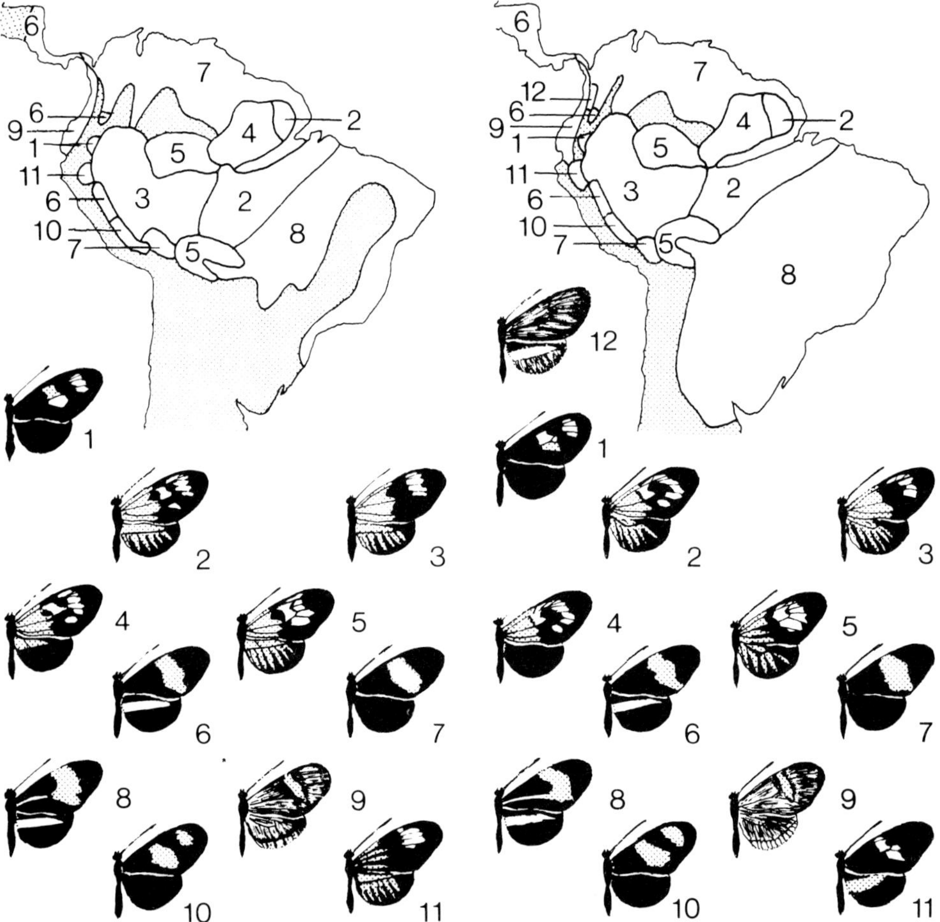

FIG. 1. Parallel variation and mimicry between *Heliconius melpomene* (left) and *Heliconius erato* (right), somewhat simplified. A more detailed map is given by Sheppard *et al.* (1985). From Turner (1981).

twenty-two easily recognizable geographical races (more than the numbers in the figure, as a few have been combined for simplicity, and where a similar pattern occurs in two widely separated places, such as Venezuela and the Peruvian Andes, it has been given the same number). The Belém race of *melpomene* will be familiar to some readers from butterfly houses and wildlife parks, where our breeding stock of it has now become the staple captive butterfly.

Such diversity is, as H. W. Bates put it when he first noted it in Amazonia, calculated to excite our wonder and curiosity to the highest degree. Why should a species diversify to such an extent within itself, and yet maintain so close a resemblance to another, related but not that closely related, species? Our attempts to unravel this problem have led us to the conclusion that one of the major forces generating this diversity has been extinction.

The very close resemblance between *melpomene* and *erato* in any one place (the only major exception is the Valle del Cauca, where *erato* occurs alone), a resemblance which includes, in the central part of the range in Amazonia, some half-dozen other species of *Heliconius*, is undoubtedly an example of Muellerian mimicry, the mutual resemblance of protected species. *Heliconius* synthesize cyanoglucosides (Nahrstedt and Davis 1983), and are known to be distasteful to birds (Brower *et al.* 1963); the resemblance between some of the species is close enough to confuse an experienced entomologist, and an encounter with one species in the mimicry 'ring' undoubtedly deters predators from attacking the other species. It is therefore clear enough why the species resemble each other so closely: deviants from the common protected pattern will be sampled more, as unfamiliar prey, by birds (an effect which has been demonstrated experimentally by the simple expedient of painting *Heliconius* with a different pattern — altered butterflies were recaptured less than controls (Benson 1972)), and species which approximately resemble each other will in the course of time, converge on to a common warning pattern. When the species are fairly closely related, as are *Heliconius*, and likely to use similar developmental systems to produce the mimetic patterns, if not the 'same' genes, the resemblance can be very close indeed.

But this conclusion leaves us with a curious paradox: the development of Muellerian mimicry brings the patterns of diverse species closer together, because deviants from the commonest, and hence best protected, pattern are sampled by predators (as it is easier to learn about something that is common than something that is rare, the rule in warning coloration is that nothing succeeds like being abundant). By the same argument, evolution in such species should be highly conservative: the keynote is presenting to the predator the same bad brand image which it knows to accompany a nasty experience and individuals deviating from the norm of the species will be at a disadvantage. How then have the geographical races of *melpomene* and of *erato* come to diverge to such a degree? The genetic changes needed to start the change of one pattern to another should have been removed from the population soon after they appeared.

At this stage in the argument we must notice another curiosity of Muellerian mimicry. What has just been said leads us to expect that all the warningly coloured species in one area will share the same mimetic pattern, and indeed many of them do. But at any one place in the neotropical forest we can find flying not just one warning pattern among the long-winged butterflies, but five. Each pattern contains many species and all are rather distinct (Papageorgis 1975). One of the patterns is the *melpomene-erato* pattern we have already met, predominantly black, red and yellow; another is black, blue and yellow; a third 'tiger-striped'- the fourth 'transparent' — it contains chiefly ithomiids and only rarely *Heliconius* —; and the fifth, flying over the forest canopy rather than in the shade, is the bright orange colour of the familiar Flambeau butterfly, *Dryas iulia*. This phenomenon, the coexistence of several Muellerian mimicry rings, is widespread, probably world wide: the warningly-coloured butterflies of West Africa fall into five rather distinct rings (Owen 1974), and distinct rings have been noted in the wasps of Hawaii, and the bumble-bees of the Holarctic (Perkins 1912, Plowright and Owen 1980). Now while it is perhaps not too surprising that butterflies have not come to mimic wasps (although of course some moths, particularly ctenuchids, do it magnificently), it is not so obvious why the butterflies, all very similar in morphology, and probably not too dissimilar in behaviour, should not have come to adopt a common pattern. The fact that the phenomenon is so widespread leads us to believe that it is a more or less stable condition, not some kind of temporary evolutionary disequilibrium.

The solution is to be found in the fact that two warning patterns will undergo convergent evolution only if one is on occasion mistaken for the other. Butterflies do not converge to wasps, not merely because this would mean massive restructuring, but because they are so different that no slight variation of a butterfly in the direction of the appearance of a wasp would remind a predator of a wasp. Mutual convergence between two protected species will occur only when small variations in pattern *A*, while still resembling pattern *A* sufficiently to be protected on that account, also remind some predators some of the time of pattern *B*, and conversely, if some of the variants of *B* in the directions of *A* are similarly favoured.

What we must assume about the coexisting mimicry rings is that the patterns are so distinctive that such variants as appear in the normal range of variation of the butterflies simply do not (or very seldom do) remind the predators of the patterns of any of the other mimicry rings. Given that situation, the rings will stay separate indefinitely, and will, like planets forming in a dust cloud, pull into themselves any species with a pattern 'in between'.

Again, we have a situation which, although a little more complicated, is still stable, and not expected to lead to a long-term evolutionary diversification. What should have happened to each species is slow evolutionary convergence into the 'nearest' Muellerian mimicry ring and that is where it should have stayed. But this theory does make one interesting prediction: slow evolution of this kind will be produced by means of the accumulated effects of a fair number of genetic changes, individually of rather small effect, building up the change in pattern.

EVOLUTION IN *HELICONIUS*

We have investigated some half-dozen races in *melpomene* and *erato* genetically and find that the differences between their races are not of this type at all — most of the differences in pattern which separate one race of *melpomene* from another, or one race of *erato* from another (we have not, and probably cannot, hybridize the two species), are produced by a small number of genes of individually large effect: whole parts of the pattern, such as the great red blotch on the forewing or the yellow bar on the hind wing, are taken out or added at a single stroke, by a single genetic change. Whatever process led to the diversification of the races, it was not that they were pulled gradually and gently into different mimicry rings.

The clue as to what is happening was discovered in the populations of the rare and relict species *Heliconius hermathena* along the lower Amazonas (Brown and Benson 1977). This butterfly has a pattern of yellow bars and red splotches, and rather unusually for a *Heliconius*, does not belong to any mimicry ring: its pattern stands quite alone (Fig. 2). Presumably it is so unlike any of the standard mimicry rings that its pattern simply cannot be pulled in: in effect, it forms an independent ring of its own (perhaps having lost other members of the ring by local or general extinction). But in one small area of the lower Amazonas (the black spot in Fig. 2) it flies with the race of *melpomene* that has the black pattern with the single red splotch on the forewing. This is not too unlike the pattern of *hermathena*: all that is required for the two to become Muellerian mimics is that *melpomene* should gain the yellow bars or that *hermathena* should lose them. In fact, it is *hermathena* that has lost the bars, making an excellent, although not perfect, mimic of *melpomene*. Data on the frequency of the yellow bars, a pattern with traces of bars, and one lacking them almost entirely, in the population, indicate that the loss of the bars is produced mostly by a single gene mutation, analagous to those we have discovered which remove yellow bars in *melpomene* and *erato*.

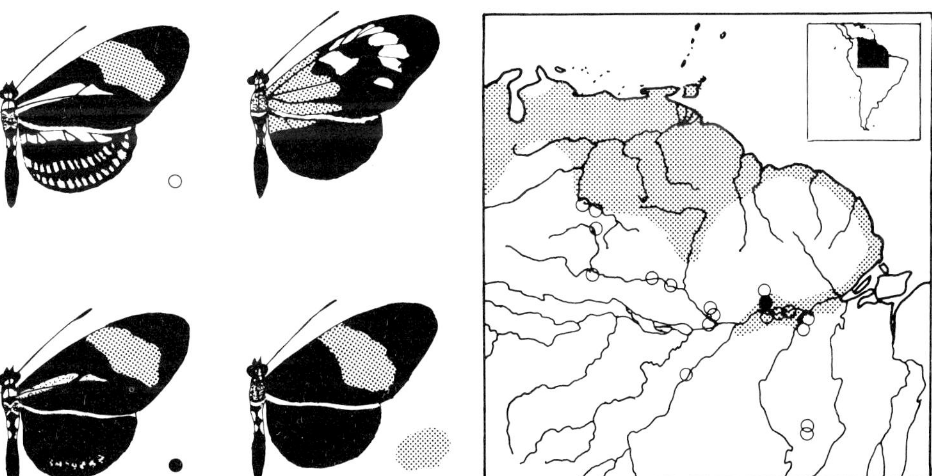

FIG. 2. *Heliconius hermathena*, a species which normally exhibits its own distinctive pattern (open circles) has one population (closed circle) which mimics the local races of *H. melpomene* and *H. erato* (shaded). In most of the area in which *hermathena* keeps its distinctive pattern (open circles) the sympatric populations of *melpomene* and *erato* (butterfly at top right) are so different from *hermathena* that mimicry cannot be achieved. From data of Brown, Benson and Sheppard, in Turner (1984).

The inference is clear: the diverging races of *melpomene* and *erato* (and by using a bit of cladistic wizardry we can reconstruct a good guess at the actual course they have taken — Fig. 3) have been captured in this same way by different, protected species in different parts of South America. They have not in general just been slowly pulled into a particular

'climax' forest? How should such a forest be defined in terms of the ecosystem to which it belongs?

THE ECOLOGICAL AND PALAEOECOLOGICAL SETTING

Aubréville's sweeping concept of a continuous forest belt between the Sahel and the Kalahari before its large-scale destruction by man is, admittedly, both an overgeneralization and an oversimplification (e.g. Adejuwon 1971; Avenard *et al.* 1974; Hamilton 1982; Swaine *et al.* 1976; Wickens 1975). However, by and large, the concept appears to be a valid one according to the vegetation experts (Acocks 1953; Adam 1971; Chapman & White 1970; Guillaumet & Adjanohoun 1971; Keay 1959; Letouzey 1968; Schnell 1952, 1976; Schmitz 1962; Sillans 1958; Werger 1983). This applies particularly when we look at relict forests protected either by man or by natural firebreaks, or at the regenerative power of those man-made Guinean, Sudanian and Zambesian woodlands and savannas where bushfires have been prevented for a number of years (Aubréville 1947; Brookman-Amissah *et al.* 1980; Fanshawe 1960; Hepper 1965; Jaeger 1956; Malaisse 1973; Phillips 1974; Tillon 1961; Werger & Coetzee 1978; van Wyk 1971). Even in the Sahelian belt the existence of relict forests suggests that some kind of low forest-like vegetation must once have been much more widespread than nowadays (Depierre & Gillet 1971; Schnell 1976; Patterson *et al.* 1973).

In spite of all this, tropical Africa harbours, in various climatic zones, a quite rich and diversified woodland, bushland and savanna flora, and an equally rich fauna adapted exclusively to these kinds of habitats, as everyone can see in the national parks and game reserves (e.g. Dorst & Dandelot 1976; Haltenorth & Diller 1977; Kingdon 1971). To illustrate this point, Africa south of the Sahara harbours only 250 typically lowland forest-dwelling breeding bird species, but no less than 887 typically lowland non forest-dwelling breeding bird species, and 344 species adapted to both and/or to other habitats (Moreau 1966). Non-forest habitats must, therefore, have been quite widespread when all these species evolved. Moreover, palaeobotanical data indicate that such habitats have been common in large areas of Africa since the Eocene and Oligocene (from 55 to 23 million years ago), and that they gradually extended their surface in the subsequent Miocene, Pliocene and Pleistocene (Axelrod & Raven 1978; Butzer 1978; Dewey *et al.* 1973; Germeraad *et al.* 1968; Kedves 1971; Kennett 1977; Kortlandt 1980b, 1983, Louvet 1971; Smith & Briden 1979; van Zinderen Bakker 1977/78). Similarly, evidence from fossil vertebrates demonstrates a continuous increase of woodland, bushland and savanna-dwelling species during the Miocene and Pliocene (from 23 to 2 million years ago), at least in East Africa where most of the fossil material has been found (Andrews & Van Couvering 1975; Andrews *et al.* 1979; Kortlandt 1983; and ref. in Cross & Maglio 1975 and Maglio & Cooke 1978). Approximately present-day patterns of climate and vegetation were established 2½ million years ago, just before the Ice Age climatic fluctuations started (Bonnefille 1976).

Thus there is a conspicuous discrepancy between, on the one hand, the forestry evidence suggesting an almost entirely forested tropical belt between the Sahel and the Kalahari before the advent of human interference with vegetation, and, on the other hand, the floristic, faunal and palaeoecological evidence demonstrating a widespread abundance of non-forest habitats within the same zone for millions of years before man evolved. We have to try and account for the lack of fit between the two sets of data.

THE BULLDOZER HERBIVORES

To explain the discrepancy, lightning-kindled fires are too infrequent. Such fires do occur occasionally in tropical Africa (Chapman & White 1970; Lebrun 1947/48; Mitchell 1960; Phillips 1974; Schnell 1971) but too rarely to exert much impact on the overall character of the vegetation. They normally occur only at the onset of the rainy season. They are then, as a rule, soon extinguished by the same thunderstorm that caused the fire.

A much more important factor could be the destructive effect that results from browsing, de-barking, breaking, uprooting, digging and trampling by the large herbivores. Foresters often tend greatly to underestimate the amount of damage to trees that can be inflicted in a natural ecosystem, especially by elephant, and to a lesser degree by buffalo, hippo, rhino, giraffe and certain pigs. The reason is that in forest reserves hunting is usually permitted and most of the game has been largely exterminated. In many national parks and game reserves, however, one can observe that the large pachyderms (if abundant enough) are able locally to convert a closed forest into an open forest, an open forest into a woodland, and a woodland into a savanna or bushland, or even (temporarily) into a semi-desert (Photos 1–8, and Barnes 1979, 1980; Buechner & Dawkins 1961; Croze 1974; Douglas-Hamilton & Douglas-Hamilton 1975; Eggeling 1947; Fayad & Fayad 1980; Harrington & Ross 1974; Jackson 1956; Kortlandt 1972, 1976 and unpubl.; Lamprey *et al.* 1967; Laws *et al.* 1975; Penzhorn *et al.* 1974; Sheldrick 1973; Werger 1977; Wing & Buss 1970). A dramatic example is the surroundings of the famous Treetops Hotel in Kenya. In the 1930s this was a small cabin built in the top of a tall tree at the side of a drinking and wallowing place in an undisturbed forest. Since then both the pond and the hotel have been greatly enlarged, and the animals have been strictly protected against any disturbance. Nowadays nothing is left of the forest around the waterhole. The tourists see instead a plain almost as large as a football field, with a few dying trees still standing, and many fallen logs lying around and rotting away. Conversely, after the onslaught on elephant in the Ugandese national parks in the 1970s, many areas that until then were open grasslands have now become *Acacia* woodlands (Eltringham, pers. comm.).

Elephant can break off tree trunks having a diameter of up to 40 cm, push over and deroot trunks of up to 60 cm, kill even bigger trees by girdling them and crush baobab trees of any size (e.g. Barnes 1980; Buechner & Dawkins 1961; Caughley 1976). Equally damaging is their preference for foraging on young and half-grown trees, because this prevents regeneration of those species which are palatable to their taste. They also destroy trees in what has been called 'mischief', 'display' or 'weeding' behaviour. Furthermore, some species of tree are killed by de-barking. Others (in forests) die due to damage to the soil and to the root system as a result of trampling and/or loss of shade when the surrounding vegetation is consumed (e.g. Buechner & Dawkins 1961). However, the ultimate effect is not always destructive. In open forests and in woodlands,

FIGS 1A & B. Foraging elephant can kill and destroy even quite large trees by uprooting or debarking them, by breaking off the trees' branches with their trunks, and/or (in soft wood) by using their tusks as crowbars. (A baobab tree in Tsavo West National Park, location 2° 59′ S 38° 14′ E, altitude 900 m, estimated long-term annual rainfall ~550 mm, original vetetation *Commiphora-Acacia* woodland largely destroyed by elephant, photo 1975.) (Photos © A. Kortlandt).

browsing and grazing will decrease the heat of bushfires and may even prevent their spread (e.g. Kortlandt 1965, 1968; Mitchell 1960; Vesey-FitzGerald 1973).

As to the other species of large herbivore, the destructiveness of their action is much less conspicuous than that of elephant, partly because the larger ravage eclipses the smaller. However, the amount of damage they cause should not be underrated (ref. below). Moreover, in regions inhabited by pastoralists one can observe how much damage is being done in woodland habitats by the ecological equivalents of the wild game, i.e. the cattle, sheep and goats. They provide an additional measure of what, in past times, the wild game might have brought about, especially in Sahelian and Sudanian landscapes.

THE INTERACTION PROCESS BETWEEN HERBIVORES AND VEGETATION

In spite of all these easily observable and unequivocal data, we are still far from understanding the ultimate effect of the interaction between herbivores and vegetation. The following aspects deserve consideration:

(1) During the last few centuries the large game have been intensively hunted for their meat and ivory (Corfield 1974; Fosbrooke 1968; Spinage 1973). Thus we have no accurate historical data about their former population densities in various habitats. In recent decades, agricultural expansion has led to the expulsion of the remaining game from many areas and consequently to overpopulation in national parks and game reserves. Again, we do not know what the natural equilibrium would have been (e.g. Cobb 1976; Corfield 1973; Lamprey *et al.* 1967).

(2) In a tall forest with a closed canopy, little daylight reaches the lower strata. Consequently the biomass production of food within reach of the ground-dwelling herbivores is quite low, even when the elephant break or topple the small and medium-sized trees. Thus the population density of game animals is also low and they would be expected to be unable seriously to harm the upper-stratum trees, even by de-barking (e.g. Laws *et al.* 1975; Merz 1981; Short 1981). However, they would be able to consume many or most of those young trees which are edible to them (i.e. non-poisonous), so that eventually, after a century or so, due to such selection, the local forest would become largely inedible (ref. below). They then would move out to another area, and the edible tree species would get a new chance to flourish in the area.

We know that such interaction processes with an in-built time-lag usually lead to oscillating population dynamics, as has been described in various mathematical models since Lotka's, Volterra's and d'Ancona's work in the 1930s. Consequently the forest would develop a floristic mosaic structure on a local scale. The existence of such mosaic patterns has been noticed by botanists but they were unable to explain them by differences in topography and soil (Aubréville 1938; Letouzey 1968; see however Hall & Swaine 1976). In many cases the phenomenon may have resulted from shifting cultivation whose traces have disappeared. In other cases, however, the large game in past times could perhaps provide the clue, even if dynamic mechanisms within the vegetation may also have played a role (see also Jones 1955; Short 1981).

Figs 2A & B. Rabongo Forest, a small semi-deciduous *Cynometra-Holoptelea* relict rain forest surrounded by savanna in Kabalega National Park (formerly Murchison Falls National Park) in Uganda. A dense population of both elephant and hippo has greatly thinned out and secondarized the forest vegetation. Many of the largest trees have been killed by debarking. Before the slaughter of elephant in the 1970s this forest was expected eventually to be entirely destroyed (2° 04′ N 31° 52′ E, altitude 940 m, estimated long-term rainfall 1200–1300 mm, photo 1964). (Photos © A. Kortlandt).

FIGS 3A & B. In the montane forest of Aberdare National Park, Kenya, the amount of damage caused by elephant (and to a much lesser extent by buffalo, rhino, pigs and antelopes) depends primarily on the relief. (Photos © A. Kortlandt).

FIG. 3A. Background left, behind the valley: Aberdare Forest Reserve, where elephant are shot or driven away by firecrackers. The tree trunks are visible owing to selective felling of some of the trees but for the rest the forest has remained intact. Middleground: A V-shaped promontory between two deep and steep valleys coming together on the left, located within the National Park but hardly accessible to elephant. The forest here is virtually intact. Foreground before the valley: Remaining forest vegetation within the National Park, heavily secondarized by elephant. Bottom right: Forest destroyed, with two dead tree trunks still standing (0° 23′ S 36° 48′ E, view SSW-ward, altitude 2400 m, 18-year mean rainfall 1438 mm, photo 1981).

FIG. 3B. A view in the National Park, 2 or 3 km east of the above picture and looking NNE. Most of the forest has been destroyed, bush encroachment has followed and the landscape has been 'parklandized'. A few surviving tall forest trees are still visible. However, I have been unable to assess whether wood-cutting and shifting agriculture before the establishment of the Park in 1950 could also have contributed to the secondarization of the vegetation. (0° 23′ S 36° 49′ E, altitude 2350 m, 18-year mean rainfall 1438 mm, photo 1981.)

the present paper I am indebted to Dr M. S. Boyce, Professor F. Bultot, Dr M. Coe, Dr S. K. Eltringham, Ms I. Isheim, Mr W. Kerkhof, Dr J. Phillipson, Mr R. J. Prickett, Ms C. Schamhardt, Mr B. J. Shorter, Mrs J. Watts and Dr W. van Wijngaarden.

REFERENCES

Acocks, J.P.H. (1953). Veld types of South Africa. Department of Agriculture, Botanical Survey Memoir, **28.** Government Printer, Petoria, South Africa.

Adam, J.G. (1971). Le milieu biologique. In: Dupuy, A. R., *Le Niokolo-Koba*, 43–62. Dakar, G.I.A.

Adejuwon, J.O. (1971). Savanna patches within forest areas in western Nigeria: a study of the dynamics of forest savanna boundary. *Bulletin de l'Institute Francais d'Afrique Noire, serie A. Sciences naturelles,* **33,** A, 327–344.

Agnew, A.D.Q. (1968). Observations on the changing vegetation of Tsavo National Park (East). *East African Wildlife Journal,* **6,** 75–80.

Alexandre, D.-Y. (1978). Le rôle disséminateur des éléphants en forêt de Taï, Côte-d'Ivoire. *La Terre et la Vie,* **32,** 47–72.

Andrews, P. & Couvering, J.A.H. Van (1975). Palaeoenvironments in the East African Miocene. In: Szalay, F. S. (ed.), *Approaches to primate paleobiology. Contributions to Primatology,* **5,** 62–103. Karger, Basel, Switzerland.

Andrews, P., Lord, J.M. & Evans Nesbit E.M. (1979). Patterns of ecological diversity in fossil and modern mammalian faunas. *Biological Journal of the Linnaean Society of London,* **11,** 177–205.

Aubréville, A. (1938). La forêt coloniale. *Annales, Académie des Sciences Coloniales,* **9.** Société d'Editions Géographiques, Maritimes et Coloniales, Paris, France.

Aubréville, A. (1947). Les brousses secondaires en Afrique Equatoriale. *Bois et Forêts des Tropiques,* **2,** 24–49.

Aubréville, A. (1948). *Etude sur les forêts de l'Afrique Equatoriale Française et du Cameroun.* Ministère de la France d'Outre Mer, Direction de l'Agriculture de l'Elevage et des Forêts, Paris, France.

Aubréville, A. (1949). *Climats, forêts et désertification de l'Afrique tropicale.* Société d'Editions Géographiques, Maritimes et Coloniales, Paris, France.

Avenard, J.-M., Bonvallot, J., Latham, M., Renard-Dugerdil, M. & Richard, J. (1974). Aspects du contact forêt-savane. (*Travaux et Documents de l'O.R.S.T.O.M.*) O.R.S.T.O.M., Paris, France.

Axelrod, D.I. & Raven, P.H. (1978). Late Cretaceous and Tertiary vegetation history of Africa. In: Werger, M. J. A. (ed.), *Biogeography and ecology of southern Africa* (Monographiae biologicae 31), 77–130. Junk, The Hague.

Bakker, E.M. van Zinderen (1977/78). Late-Mesozoic and Tertiary palaeoenvironments of the Sahara region. In: Bakker, E. M. van Zinderen (ed.), *Antartic glacial history and world palaeoenvironments,* 129–135. Balkema, Rotterdam, The Netherlands.

Barnes, R.F.W. (1979). *Elephant ecology in Ruaha National Park, Tanzania.* (Ph.D. thesis) Cambridge, U.K.

Barnes, R.F.W. (1980). The decline of the baobab tree in Ruaha National Park, Tanzania. *African Journal of Ecology,* **18,** 243–252.

Bonnefille, R. (1976). Palynological evidence for an important change in the vegetation of the Omo Basin between 2·5 and 2 million years ago. In: Coppens, Y., *et al.* (eds), *Earliest man and environments in the Lake Rudolf Basin,* 421–431. University Press, Chicago, U.S.A.

Bourlière, F. (1963). Observations on the ecology of some large African mammals. In: Howell, F. C. & Bourlière, F. (eds), *African ecology and human evolution,* 43–54. Aldine, Chicago, U.S.A.

Bourlière, F. & Verschuren, J. (1960). *Introduction à l'écologie des ongulés du Parc National Albert.* Institut des Parcs Nationaux du Congo Belge, Bruxelles, Belgium.

Brookman-Amissah, J., Hall, J.B., Swaine, M.D. & Attakorah, J.Y. (1980). A re-assessment of a fire protection experiment in north-eastern Ghana savanna. *Journal of Applied Ecology,* **17,** 85–99.

Buechner, H.K. & Dawkins, H.C. (1961). Vegetation change induced by elephants and fire in Murchison Falls National Park, Uganda. *Ecology,* **42,** 752–766.

Butzer, K.W. (1978). Geoecological perspectives on early hominid evolution. In: Jolly, C. (ed.), *Early hominids of Africa,* 191–217. Duckworth, London, U.K.

Caughley, G. (1976). The elephant problem — an alternative hypothesis. *East African Wildlife Journal*, **14**, 265–283.

Chapman, J.D. & White F. (1970). *The evergreen forests of Malawi*. Commonwealth Forestry Institute, Oxford, U.K.

Cobb, S. (1976). *The distribution and abundance of the large herbivore community of Tsavo National Park, Kenya*. (Ph.D. Thesis). University of Oxford, U.K.

Coe, M. (1981). Body size and the extinction of the Pleistocene megafauna. In: Coetzee, J. A. & van Zinderen Bakker Sr, E. M. (eds), *Palaeoecology of Africa*, **13**, 139–145. Balkema, Rotterdam, The Netherlands.

Cooke, H.B.S. (1978). Faunal evidence for the biotic setting of early African hominids. In: Jolly, C. (ed.), *Early hominids of Africa*, 267–281. Duckworth, London, U.K.

Corfield, M. (1974). *Historical notes on Tsavo*. Kenya National Parks, Nairobi, Kenya.

Corfield, T.F. (1973). Elephant mortality in Tsavo National Park, Kenya. *East African Wildlife Journal*, **11**, 339–368.

Cross, M.W. & Maglio, V.J. (1975). *A bibliography of the fossil mammals of Africa, 1950–1972*. Dept. of Geological and Geophysical Sciences, Princeton, U.S.A.

Croze, H. (1974). The Seronera bull problem. *East African Wildlife Journal*, **12**, 1–27 & 29–47.

Depierre, D. & Gillet, H. (1971). Désertification de la zone sahélienne au Tchad. *Bois et Forêts des Tropiques*, **139**, 3–25.

Dewey, J.F., Pitman, W.C., Ryan, W.B.F. & Bonnin, J. (1973). Plate tectonics and the evolution of the Alpine system. *Geological Society of America Bulletin*, **84**, 3137–3180.

Dorst, J. & Dandelot, P. (1976). *A field guide to the larger mammals of Africa*. Collins, London, U.K.

Douglas-Hamilton, I. & Douglas-Hamilton, O. (1975). *Among the elephants*. Collins, London, U.K.

Douglas-Hamilton, O., 1980. Africa's elephants. Can they survive? National Geographic Magazine **158**, 568–603.

Eggeling, W.J. (1947). Observations on the ecology of the Budongo rain forest, Uganda. *Journal of Ecology*, **34**, 20–67.

Eltringham, S.K. & Woodford, M.H. (1973). The numbers and distribution of buffalo in the Ruwenzori National Park, Uganda. *East African Wildlife Journal*, **11**, 151–164.

Evrard, C. (1968). *Recherches écologiques sur le peuplement forestier des sols hydromorphes de la Cuvette centrale congolaise*. Publication de l'Institut National pour l'Étude Agronomique du Congo Belge, Série scientifique, 110, Bruxelles, Belgium.

Ewer, R.F. (1973). *The carnivores*. Weidenfeld & Nicolson, London, U.K.

Fanshawe, D.B. (1960). Evergreen forest relics in Northern Rhodesia. *Kirkia*, **1**, 20–24.

Fayad, V.C. & Fayad, C. (1980). *An ecological survey of the Nguruman Forest, Kenya*. (Unpublished report to AWLF, Nairobi).

Field, C.R. (1970). A study of the feeding habits of the hippopotamus (*Hippopotamus amphibius* Linn.) in the Queen Elizabeth National Park, Uganda, with some management implications. *Zoologica Africana*, **5**, 71–86.

Fosbrooke, H.A. (1968). Elephants in the Serengeti National Park: an early record. *East African Wildlife Journal*, **6**, 150–152.

Gadow, K. von (1973). Observations on the utilization of indigenous trees by the Knysna elephants. *Forestry in South Africa*, **14**, 13–17.

Germain, R. & Evrard, C. (1956). *Etude écologique et phytosociologique de la forêt à Brachystegia laurentii*. Publication de l'Institut National pour l'Étude Agronomique du Congo Belge, Série scientifique, 67, Bruxelles, Belgium.

Germeraad, J.H., Hopping, C.A. & Muller, J. (1968). Palynology of Tertiary sediments from tropical areas. *Review of Palaeobotany and Palynology*, **6**, 189–348.

Guillaumet, J.-L. (1967). *Recherches sur la végétation et la flore de la région du Bas-Cavally (Côte-d'Ivoire)*. O.R.S.T.O.M., Paris, France.

Guillaumet, J.-L. & Adjanohoun, E. (1971). La végétation de la Côte d'Ivoire. In: Avenard, J. M. (ed.), *Le milieu naturel de la Côte d'Ivoire*, 157–263. Mémoires ORSTOM 50.

Hall, J.B. & Swaine, M.D. (1976). Classification and ecology of closed-canopy forest in Ghana. *Journal of Ecology*, **64**, 913–951.

Hall, J.B. & Swaine, M.D. (1980). Seed stocks in Ghanaian forest soils. *Biotropica*, **12**, 256–263.

Haltenorth, Th. & Diller, H. (1977). *Säugetiere Afrikas und Madagaskars.* BLV, München, F.R.G.

Hamilton, A.C. (1982). *Environmental history of East Africa.* Academic Press, London, U.K.

Harrington, G.N. & Ross, I.C. (1974). The savanna ecology of Kidepo Valley National Park, I. The effects of burning and browsing on the vegetation. *East African Wildlife Journal,* **12,** 93–105.

Harris, J.M. (1975). Evolution of feeding mechanisms in the family Deinotheriidae (Mammalia: Proboscidea). *Zoological Journal of the Linnaean Society,* **56,** 331–362.

Harris, L.D. & Fowler, N.K. (1975). Ecosystems analysis and simulation of the Mkomazi Reserve, Tanzania. *East African Wildlife Journal,* **13,** 325–346.

Hepper, F.N. (1965). The vegetation and flora of the Vogel Peak Massif, Northern Nigeria. *Bulletin de l'Institut Français d'Afrique Noire, Série A. Sciences Naturelles,* **27,** A, 413–513.

Jackson, J.K. (1956). The vegetation of the Imatong Mountains. *Journal of Ecology,* **44,** 341–374.

Jaeger, P. (1956). Contribution à l'étude des forêts reliques du Soudan occidental. *Bulletin de l'Institut Français d'Afrique Noire, Série A. Sciences Naturelles,* **18,** A, 993–1053.

Janzen, D.H. & Martin, P.S. (1982). Neotropical anachronisms: the fruits the gomphotheres ate. *Science,* **215,** 19–27.

Jones, E.W. (1955/56). Ecological studies on the rain forest of Southern Nigeria IV. The plateau forest of the Okomu Forest Reserve. *Journal of Ecology,* **43,** 564–594, **44,** 83–117.

Keay, R.W.J. (1959). *An outline of Nigerian vegetation.* 3rd ed. Federal Government Printer, Lagos, Nigeria.

Kedves, M. (1971). Présence de types sporomorphes importants dans les sédiments préquaternaires égyptiens. *Acta Botanica Acadamiae Scientarum Hungaricae,* **17,** 371–378.

Kennett, J.P. (1977). Cenozoic evolution of Antarctic glaciation, the Circum-Antarctic Ocean, and their impact on global paleoceanography. *Journal of Geophysical Research,* **82,** 3843–3860.

Kingdon, J. (1971). *East African mammals 1.* Academic Press, London, U.K.

Kortlandt, A. (1965). *Some results of a pilot study on chimpanzee ecology.* Zoologisch Laboratorium, Amsterdam, the Netherlands.

Kortlandt, A. (1968). Handgebrauch bei freilebenden Schimpansen. In: Rensch, B. (ed.), *Handgebrauch und Verständigung bei Affen und Frühmenschen,* 59–102. Huber, Bern, Switzerland.

Kortlandt, A. (1972). *New perspectives on ape and human evolution,* Amsterdam, the Netherlands. Stichting voor Psychobiologie.

Kortlandt, A. (1976). Tree destruction by elephants in Tsavo National Park and the role of man in African ecosystems. *Netherlands Journal of Zoology,* **26,** 449–451.

Kortlandt, A. (1980a). How might early hominids have defended themselves against large predators and food competitors: *Journal of Human Evolution,* **9,** 79–112.

Kortlandt, A. (1980b). The Fayum primate forest: did it exist? *Journal of Human Evolution,* **9,** 277–297.

Kortlandt, A. (1983). Facts and fallacies concerning Miocene ape habitats. In: Ciochon, R. L. & Corruccini, R. S. (eds), *New interpretations of ape and human ancestry,* 465–514. Plenum, New York, U.S.A.

Kortlandt, A. (1984). Habitat richness, foraging range and diet in chimpanzees and some other primates. In: Chivers, D. J., Wood, B. A., & Bilsborough, A. (eds), *Food acquisition and processing in primates,* 119–159. Plenum, New York, U.S.A.

Kurtén, B. (1971). *The age of mammals.* Weidenfeld & Nicolson, London, U.K.

Lamprey, H.F., Glover, P.E., Turner, M.I.M. & Bell, R.H.V. (1967). Invasion of the Serengeti National Park by elephants. *East African Wildlife Journal,* **5,** 151–166.

Laws, R.M., Parker, I.S.C. & Johnstone, R.C.B. (1975). *Elephants and their habitats.* Clarendon, Oxford, U.K.

Leakey, L.S.B. (1969). *Animals of East Africa.* National Geographic Society, Washington, D.C., U.S.A.

Lebrun, J. (1947/48). *Végétation de la plaine alluviale au sud du Lac Édouard.* Exploration du Parc National Albert, Mission J. Lebrun (1937–1938). Institut des Parcs Nationaux du Congo Belge, Bruxelles, Belgium.

Lebrun, J. (1960). Sur la richesse de la flore de divers territoires africains. *Académie Royale des Sciences d'Outre Mer, Bulletin des Séances.* N.s. **6** (4), 669–690.

Letouzey, R. (1968). *Etude phytogéographique du Cameroun.* Lechevalier, Paris, France.

Leuthold, W. (1977). Changes in tree populations of Tsavo East National Park, Kenya. *East African Wildlife Journal,* **15,** 61–69.

Leuthold, W. & Sale, J.B. (1973). Movements and patterns of habitat utilization of elephants in Tsavo National Park, Kenya. *East African Wildlife Journal*, **11**, 369–384.

Louvet, P. (1971). *Sur l'évolution des flores tertiaires de l'Afrique nord-équatoriale.* (Thèse.) Université de Paris VI, Paris, France.

Maglio, V.J. (1978). Patterns of faunal evolution. In: Maglio, V. J. & Cooke, H.B.S. (eds), *Evolution of African mammals*, 603–619. Harvard University Press, Cambridge, Mass., U.S.A.

Maglio, V.J. & Cooke, H.B.S. (eds) (1978). *Evolution of African mammals.* Harvard University Press, Cambridge, Mass., U.S.A.

Malaisse, F. (1973). Contribution à l'étude de l'ecosystème forêt claire (miombo). *Annales de l'Université d'Abidjan, E,* **6**, 227–250.

Martin, P.S. (1966). Africa and Pleistocene overkill. *Nature,* **212**, 339–342.

Merz, G. (1981). Recherches sur la biologie de nutrition et les habitats préférés de l'éléphant de forêt, *Loxodonta africana cyclotis* Matschie, 1900. *Mammalia,* **45**, 299–312.

Mitchell, B.L. (1960). Ecological aspects of game control measures in African wilderness and forested areas. *Kirkia,* **1**, 120–128.

Moreau, R.E. (1966). *The bird faunas of Africa and its islands.* Academic Press, New York, U.S.A.

Norton-Griffiths, M. (1979). The influence of grazing, browsing, and fire on the vegetation dynamics of the Serengeti. In: Sinclair, A. R. E. & Norton-Griffiths, M. (eds), *Serengeti, dynamics of an ecosystem*, 310–349. University of Chicago Press, Chicago, U.S.A.

Olivier, R.C.D. & Laurie, W.A. (1974). Habitat utilization by hippopotamus in the Mara River. *East African Wildlife Journal*, **12**, 249–271.

Patterson, J.R., Collier, F.S., Dundas, J., Jones, B., Aubréville, A., Mathey, J., Bachelier, R. (1973). Rapport de la mission forestière anglo-française Nigeria-Niger. *Bois et Forêts des Tropiques*, **148**, 3–26.

Pellew, R.A.P. (1983). The impact of elephant, giraffe and fire upon the *Acacia tortilis* woodlands of the Serengeti. *African Journal of Ecology*, **21**, 41–74.

Penzhorn, B.L., Robbertse, P.J. & Olivier, M.C. (1974). The influence of the African elephant on the vegetation of the Addo Elephant National Park. *Koedoe,* **17**, 137–158.

Petrides, G.A. (1974). The overgrazing cycle as a characteristic of tropical savannas and grasslands in Africa. *Proceedings of the First International Congress of Ecology*, 86–91. Centre for Agricultural Publishing and Documentation, Wageningen, the Netherlands.

Phillips, J. (1974). Effects of fire in forest and savanna ecosystems of Sub-Saharan Africa. In: Kozlowski, T.T. & Ahlgren, C.E. (eds), *Fire and ecosystems*, 435–481. Academic Press, New York, U.S.A.

Piveteau, J. (1958/61). *Traité de paléontologie 6 (1 & 2). Mammifères.* Masson, Paris, France.

Romer, A.S. (1966). *Vertebrate paleontology.* 3rd ed. University Press, Chicago, U.S.A.

Ross, I.C., Field, C.R. & Harrington, G.N. (1976). The savanna ecology of Kidepo Valley National Park, Uganda. III. Animal populations and park management recommendations. *East African Wildlife Journal*, **14**, 35–48.

Schmitz, A. (1962). Les muhulu du Haut-Katanga méridional. *Bulletin du Jardin Botanique de l'Etat, Bruxelles*, **32**, 221–299.

Schnell, R. (1952). Contribution à une étude phytosociologique et phytogéographique de l'Afrique occidentale: les groupements et les unités géobotaniques de la région guinéenne. *Mélanges botaniques, Mémoires de l'Institut Français d'Afrique Noire*, **18**, 41–234.

Schnell, R. (1970/71/76/77). *Introduction à la phytogéographie des pays tropicaux. (1: Les flores — les structures, 1970; 2: Les milieux — les groupements végétaux, 1971; 3: La flore et la végétation de l'Afrique tropicale, 1re partie, 1976; 4: La flore et la végétation de l'Afrique tropicale, 2e partie, 1977.)* Gauthier-Villars, Paris, France.

Sheldrick, D. (1973). *The Tsavo story.* Collins, London, U.K.

Short, J. (1981). Diet and feeding behaviour of the forest elephant. *Mammalia,* **45**, 177–185.

Sillans, R. (1958). *Les savanes de l'Afrique centrale.* Lechevalier, Paris, France.

Smith, A.G. & Briden, J.C. (1979). *Mesozoic and Cenozoic paleocontinental maps.* Cambridge University Press, Cambridge, U.K.

Spinage, C.A. (1973). A review of ivory exploitation and elephant population trends in Africa. *East African Wildlife Journal*, **11**, 281–289.

Swaine, M.D., Hall, J.B. & Lock, J.M. (1976). The forest–savanna boundary in West-Central Ghana. *Ghana Journal of Science*, **16,** 35–52.

Tillon, R. (1961). Etude d'une parcelle de savane mise en défens. *Bois et Forêts des Tropiques*, **77,** 13–21.

Vesey-FitzGerald, D.F. (1969). Utilization of the habitat by buffalo in Lake Manyara National Park. *East African Wildlife Journal*, **7,** 131–145.

Vesey-FitzGerald, D.F. (1973). Animal impact on vegetation and plant succession in Lake Manyara National Park, Tanzania. *Oikos*, **24,** 314–325.

Walter, H. (1973). *Die Vegetation der Erde 1. Die tropischen und subtropischen Zonen*, Fischer, Jena, G.D.R.

Werger, M.J.A. (1977). Effects of game and domestic livestock on vegetation in East and Southern Africa. In: Krause, W. (ed.), *Handbook of vegetation science*, **13,** 149–159. Junk, The Hague, the Netherlands.

Werger, M.J.A. (1983). Tropical grasslands, savannas, woodlands: natural and manmade. In: Holzner, W., Werger, M.J.A. & Ikusima, I. (eds), *Man's impact on vegetation*, 107–137. Junk, The Hague, the Netherlands.

Werger, M.J.A. & Coetzee, B.J. (1978). The Sudano–Zambesian Region. In: Werger, M. J. A. (ed.), *Biogeography and ecology of Southern Africa* (Monographiae biologicae, 31), 301–462. Junk, The Hague, the Netherlands.

Wickens, G.E. (1975). Changes in the climate and vegetation of the Sudan since 20 000 B.P. *Boissiera*, **24a,** 43–65.

Wing, L.D. & Buss, I.O. (1970). Elephants and forests. *Wildlife Monographs*, **19.**

Wyk, P. van (1971). Veld burnings in the Kruger National Park, an interim report of some aspects of research. *Proceedings Annual Tall Timbers Fire Ecology Conference*.

SECTION IV
RESOURCE MANAGEMENT

Protected areas monitoring by the International Union for Conservation of Nature and Natural Resources

J. HARRISON

Protected Areas Data Unit, Herbarium, Royal Botanic Gardens, Kew, Richmond, Surrey, U.K.

SUMMARY

1   The Protected Areas Data Unit is the data management arm of IUCN responsible for collecting information on the world's protected areas. As part of the IUCN Conservation Monitoring Centre, PADU operates within the auspices of the United Nations Environment Programme's Global Environment Monitoring System.

2   Information is collected from a wide variety of sources and is maintained both on computer files and manually in such a way that it can be used to answer a wide variety of questions on protected areas. Close links with other parts of IUCN and with other conservation agencies are being made and this is improving the ability of IUCN to respond to the growing number of questions on the value, design and management of protected areas.

INTRODUCTION

IUCN, the International Union for Conservation of Nature and Natural Resources, has been collecting information on protected areas worldwide since 1959 when a resolution was passed by the United Nations Economic and Social Council charging IUCN with the task of forming and maintaining an up-to-date list of the world's national parks and equivalent reserves (United Nations 1959). This data collection is the responsibility of IUCN's Commission on National Parks and Protected Areas (CNPPA) and some of the information has been published over the years in the *UN List* (e.g. IUCN 1967, 1971, 1980), and in the *World Directory of National Parks and Other Protected Areas* (IUCN 1975 & 1977).

In 1979 CNPPA began to collect data in a more systematic way with the appointment of 'coordinators' to compile detailed information about protected areas in their parts of the world. Since then, at meetings in Costa Rica, the U.K. (Scotland), Cameroon, Peru, New Zealand, Canada and the U.S.A., and Indonesia, the coordinators and other commission members have presented data sheets on the protected areas in their parts of the world and basic information has now been gathered for a large percentage of the world's protected areas (although the quality and completeness of coverage is still widely variable). Other material such as maps, management plans, species lists, scientific papers, brochures etc. are also being collected.

Any increase in available information would, of course, be of limited use without an improved system for handling the data. For this reason the Protected Areas Data Unit (PADU) was inaugurated in May 1981 as part of IUCN's Conservation Monitoring

Centre (CMC). CMC, which has offices at Kew Gardens and in Cambridge (both within the United Kingdom), operates under the auspices of the United Nations Environment Programme as a part of the Global Environment Monitoring System (GEMS). There are computer facilities at Kew, used to the full by PADU.

DATA COLLECTION

PADU is responsible for the day-to-day collection of information on protected areas for IUCN and for disseminating that information as and when required and in the format required. The information that goes into the PADU files is initially compiled by CNPPA members and correspondents in all parts of the world. These are frequently the government officials responsible for the protected area system of a country, but can also be academics, members of local NGO's, or employees of international organizations. In most cases a 'Protected Areas Information Sheet' is completed for each area by the CNPPA member who is most familiar with it, the sheets being reviewed by appropriate peers.

The information on these sheets is collected under a number of specific headings (Table 1). The biogeographical coding of realm, province and biome is after the system devised for IUCN by Udvardy (1975). The management categories are defined in an IUCN report (IUCN 1978) and are devised to indicate the actual protection a site enjoys

TABLE 1. Headings under which information is collected on the
protected areas information sheets

Name of Protected Area	Vegetation
Management Category	Noteworthy fauna
Biogeographic Province	Zoning
Legal Protection	Disturbances and deficiencies
Date Established	Scientific research
Geographical Location	Special scientific facilities
Altitude	Principle reference material
Area	Staff
Land Tenure	Budget
Physical Features	Local administration

(which may not be reflected by its definition as National Park or Nature Reserve). As was mentioned above, materials such as management plans, maps, field guides and leaflets are also collected. This information may then be updated, corrected and added to, using material from a variety of other sources including published papers, expedition reports and so on.

In general a three-year cycle is being developed for updating the information, based on the biogeographical classification of terrestrial biomes mentioned above. The world is seen as being divided into six units, with the information from two units being updated each year in conjunction with CNPPA working sessions in those units. In 1982, for example, meetings were held in North America and in South-east Asia and in the previous year in Latin America and New Zealand. Updating consists of reviewing the existing sheets, making any changes required and adding new or more complete

information for certain data categories. This does not mean to say that the other regions
are ignored in the intervening years but that information is dealt with as it is received or as
it is needed — there being no complete revision of the region's data.

THE STORAGE AND USE OF THE INFORMATION

Information is stored in the computer in both data processing and word processing files.
The data files contain the basic information and the word processing files contain the
more detailed information. Data fields from the former can be sorted and selected using
any combination of characters or groups of characters within the file. Lists could be
produced, for example, of sites over 100 000 ha in Latin America, or on the National
Parks created since 1945. These lists could be laid out by political unit, or by biogeographical unit, in alphabetic order, by order of size and so on, by appropriate sorting
and reformatting. In October 1982, for example, PADU compiled the 1982 *United
Nations List of National Parks and Protected Areas* (IUCN 1982a). This involved
selection of data from the main data file, sorting it by country, then by management
category within country, size within management category and then arranging the
resulting list into a readable and understandable text.

The data files are in fact quite flexible and can be reformatted and extended as
required. In the near future codes for habitat will be added, so that areas sharing a
particular habitat type can be selected out (this can only be done rather crudely for biome
type at the moment). Codes will also be given which signify the accepted international
importance of the site. At present World Heritage Sites and Biosphere Reserves are
coded within the main file, but this coding is being extended to include sites listed under
the Ramsar Convention, sites within the European Biogenetic Network, sites holding the
European Diploma and so on.

PADU is being used by IUCN and its Commission on National Parks and Protected
Areas to help monitor the protected areas of the world (IUCN 1982a). By carefully
assessing the coverage by protected areas of each biogeographical province on land
(Udvardy 1975) CNPPA will be able to identify gaps in the world-wide system of reserves
(Harrison *et al.* 1982). A parallel classification system, based on both biogeographical
and biophysical criteria has been developed for coastal and marine protected areas
(Hayden *et al.* 1984) and will be used in the same way as the terrestrial system. Using
these two systems it will then be much easier to chart the development of new areas year
by year and to focus attention where it is most required.

PADU is also being used to develop publications of a more detailed sort for IUCN/
CNPPA. Initially it is planned to produce volumes on each of the eight Biogeographical
Realms, serving as handbooks for the protected areas of each major land mass. The first
volume (on the Neotropical Realm) was published earlier this year (IUCN 1982b), and
the Afrotropical Realm is now in preparation. It is also possible to produce publications
on request; a volume on a particular country for example, or on the protected areas of
tropical rain forest around the world, or all the protected areas containing tigers,
bowerbirds, or coco de mer, or on those areas set up to protect important watersheds.

The unit does not work in isolation and close collaboration with the other components of IUCN's Conservation Monitoring Centre, who deal with information on threatened plants and animals, is beginning to produce useful information on the distribution of threatened species within protected areas and in many cases on the effectiveness of the protection afforded. The International Council for Bird Preservation is looking at centres of endemism, particularly in Africa and information on how these centres are covered by protected areas can be found on the PADU files. Further research and comparison of protected area cover, with information on centres of diversity or endemism may bring to light gaps in the system of protected areas not previously seen. Working with the IUCN Commission on Ecology, areas and species can be given more accurate habitat codings rather than the cruder amalgam of classifications at present in use.

Information is also available to those outside IUCN/WWF/UNEP who need it but because of the need to cover costs and to maintain and develop the data handling capabilities, there may be a charge for it. Major users, such as development banks, technical assistance agencies and large NGO's could have access to the data on a paid subscription basis and similarly, anyone wanting the information for commercial purposes would be expected to pay reasonable rates. Students or scientists requesting limited information would, on the other hand, be charged only a nominal fee, while government agencies and others who are contributing protected area information would have reasonable access to the service free of charge.

THE NEED FOR AN INTERNATIONAL PROTECTED AREAS DATA UNIT

It is clear that each individual country has far more information on its own protected areas than could ever be handled by one small unit and that many countries have the capacity to establish computer systems and to maintain their own information in ways that meet their own needs. There are, however, several good reasons for having an international information system, some of which have already been touched on.

Many international agencies would be able to design their projects to enhance sustainable development and to avoid adversely affecting particularly sensitive areas if they could be provided with quick, large-scale, 'overviews' of certain protected areas questions, and with details of the protected areas of the region in which they are working.

IUCN, the World Wildlife Fund and other international conservation agencies need comparative information to help evaluate priority areas for allocation of scarce international conservation funds. UNESCO's 'Man and the Biosphere' Programme and the World Heritage Convention require global information on protected areas, the former in order to ensure that representative areas of all biogeographical provinces are established as biosphere reserves, the latter in order to ensure that sites nominated to the World Heritage List are of truly 'outstanding universal significance'.

There are also numerous examples of the value of a centralized source of information in the field of genetic resource conservation; plant breeders, for example, may need to know where wild ancestors of domestic agricultural crops could be found in protected areas, in order to locate sources of genetic diversity for improving crop breeds, or developing better drugs. Scientists may need information for their research, information that may be on animals or plants, habitats, species ranges, or just lists of the addresses of protected area administrations. In a similar way a centralized source of information for publications, requests from journalists, and other promotional and publicity uses is required by the international effort to promote protected areas.

Governments and protected areas' managers need to know what is being done in the field of protected areas' management in other countries, in order to enhance their own efforts and to avoid repeating mistakes.

Manipulating conservation data by computer is still relatively new and it may be some time before governments develop their own information systems. IUCN is developing a strong capability in the use of computers in conservation, and this expertise is available to those needing assistance in setting up their own systems, including any governments who are interested.

CONCLUSIONS

PADU, and indeed the Conservation Monitoring Centre as a whole, is still developing and is not yet in a position to do all we would like it to, partly because the funds are not there to employ more staff. We are, for example, now able to say only which protected areas have a marine component, and we are not yet in a position to sort the information by habitat type (as opposed to biome type). This is because to do so requires time to sort through the files manually and assign habitat codes for each protected area, which we can then put into the computer files.

Although PADU is a unit in its own right it is an integral part of the IUCN programme, and of the IUCN Conservation Monitoring Centre. Work is currently in progress to link the different components of the centre more closely by more effectively linking the computer files of plant, animal and protected area data, and linking these more efficiently with the files of country/area names and with bibliography and project files (Mackinder, 1984). The closer these links become, the more comprehensive the data available becomes and the more valuable to IUCN and to conservation.

PADU will produce nothing that could not have been produced by members of the IUCN/CNPPA, given sufficient time and energy. The unit will provide only what is fed into it but it will be able to produce the data very quickly and in many different configurations. It will not replace any of the human element in protected area management, but it will allow managers to be more efficient by providing the data needed, when it is needed and in the form required.

More importantly, the collection and presentation of protected-area information in a professional and competent manner demonstrates to governments, development agencies and individuals around the world that national parks and reserves are valuable land-use tools for managing areas which should, for various reasons, be kept in a natural or semi-natural state. Making protected areas data more accessible will help to ensure that the reserves can play their proper role in the process of socio-economic development.

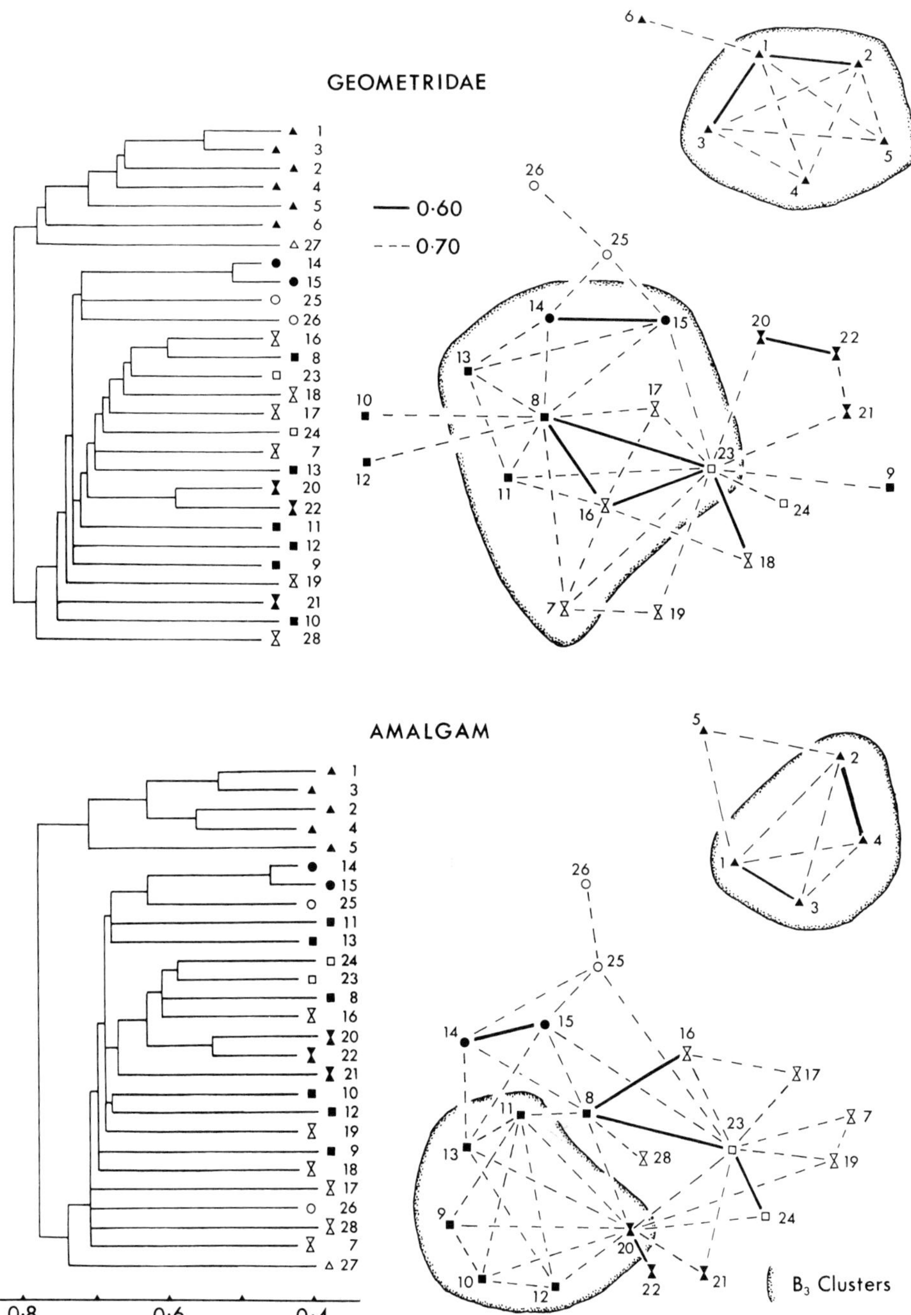

Fig. 3. Single-link dendrograms and linkage diagrams for samples of the Geometridae and an amalgam of various families and subfamilies as discussed in the text. Conventions as for Fig. 1.

with the lower montane trio. Lowland limestone samples are paired as are the two from the kerangas. Pairing in the upper montane cluster is of an understorey pair versus a pair overlooking the canopy. In the linkage diagram there is a distinct association of Mulu lowland understorey samples with the largest kerangas one, and also a trend from these and the lower montane samples to those from the lowland limestone and alluvial forest.

General observations

The proportion of abundant versus rare species in a sample is reflected in the overall level of clustering; the localization of the species is indicated by the strength of the clustering structure. Primary distinctions are between upper montane samples and the rest, the lower montane samples usually being distinguished within the latter.

A general trend from lower montane and Mulu lowland samples to lowland limestone and alluvial ones is evident in the three analyses with the best discrimination. The kerangas samples associate with the former in two analyses and with the lowland limestone in one. The analysis of the amalgam of groups that are well represented in the understorey gives the best discrimination of lowland forest types.

DISCUSSION

The analyses presented here are only the first stage in the process of selecting indicator species and associations for rain forest studies. The next stage is to obtain a classification of species according to their distribution amongst the samples in order to identify significant associations of species that might be related to a particular forest type. Understorey versus canopy specialists may also be identified by this process. A higher proportion of habitat-specific species would be expected in those groups shown to be good discriminators.

In studies of disturbance during various forestry practices and of regeneration processes, the analyses suggest that attention should be focused on the Arctiidae as good discriminants concentrated in the canopy and on the groups in the amalgamated selection for understorey discriminants. For montane forest types the Geometridae as a whole might also be considered, as the subfamily Larentiinae is most diverse at high altitudes.

Noctuidae and Sphingidae, containing numerous ecologically widespread and mobile species, are poor discriminants as a rule, though the Chloephorinae and Hypeninae of the former are exceptions. However, both families contain many species most characteristic of open habitats and secondary growth whose presence might be taken to indicate to some extent the degree of disturbance or degradation of rain forest. These second-growth species are opportunist r-strategists, therefore dispersive and often represented in canopy samples from undisturbed forest, particularly ridge and peak montane forest samples where they may congregate in 'hill-topping' behaviour (Holloway 1977). Their presence in samples must be interpreted with care.

It is perhaps too early to say whether insect sampling provides a viable, useful, readily applicable method of categorizing and monitoring rain-forest. Comparative work in disturbed and regenerating forests has yet to be undertaken. It is not known whether the

17

observations on the various families made in Borneo will prove to be general throughout the tropics. From a consideration of taxonomic parameters one might predict a degree of similarity. The reader must judge whether the goal is worthy of pursuit.

ACKNOWLEDGMENTS

I would like to thank the Sarawak State Government and the Royal Geographical Society for the opportunity to undertake the sampling programme in the Gunung Mulu National Park. My gratitude also goes to the organizers and sponsors of the Leeds Rain Forest Symposium for a generous grant enabling my attendance.

REFERENCES

Holloway, J.D. (1977). *The Lepidoptera of Norfolk Island, their Biogeography and Ecology.* Series Entomologica 13. W. Junk, The Hague.

Holloway, J.D. (1979). *A Survey of the Lepidoptera, Biogeography and Ecology of New Caledonia.* Series Entomologica 15. W. Junk, The Hague.

Holloway, J.D. (1983). Insect surveys: an approach to environmental monitoring. *Atti XII Congr. naz. Ital. Entomol., Roma, 1980,* **1:** 239–261.

Holloway, J.D. (in press). The larger moths of the Gunung Mulu National Park; a preliminary assessment of their distribution, ecology and potential as environmental indicators. In A. C. Jermy and K. P. Kavanagh (eds), *Gunung Mulu National Park, Sarawak.* Part II. *Sarawak Museum Journal,* **30:** Special Issue 2.

Jardine, N. & Sibson, R. (1968). The construction of hierarchic and non-hierarchic classifications. *Comput. J.,* **11,** 177–184.

Preston, F.W. (1962). The canonical distribution of commonness and rarity. *Ecology,* **43,** 185–215, 410–432.

Wolda, H. (1981). Similarity indices, sample size and diversity. *Oecologia (Berl),* **50,** 296–302.

Heterogeneity in early tropical rain-forest regeneration after cutting and burning: ARBOCEL, French Guiana

H. de FORESTA

Laboratoire de Botanique, 163 rue A. Broussonet, 34000 Montpellier, France

SUMMARY

1   In July to September 1976, a 25 ha parcel of primary tropical evergreen rain forest was experimentally cut under conditions simulating those of cutting for paper pulp. One month later two accidental fires crossed the parcel, creating a mosaic of strongly burned and slightly burned areas, following the pattern of branches and trunks lying on the ground.

2   The natural regeneration, studied three and a half years after cutting and burning, was made up of a mosaic of small units, which could be related to ten types of vegetation. The main structural and floristical characteristics of these vegetation types are described, showing important differences already existing between these contemporary or nearly so associations. Above ground phytomass varies up to sevenfold (dry matter).

3   Study of the environmental factors which influenced the synchronous regrowth of vegetation reveals the importance of soil compaction (very little regeneration on the vehicle tracks), soil hydromorphy (herbaceous associations on permanently inundated sites), and intense burning (regeneration drastically delayed on strongly burned areas).

4   The discussion includes consideration of heterogeneity associated with the initial conditions in early natural regeneration of tropical rain forest.

INTRODUCTION

French Guiana represents an area of about $90\,000\,\mathrm{km}^2$, of which more than 90% is occupied by Lowland Evergreen Tropical Rain-forest (de Granville 1979). Up until now logging activities have been of trifling significance, a fact associated with a very small population density ($0.6\,\mathrm{inh./km}^2$). This explains why nearly all Guianese forest is at the present time undisturbed — 'primary', within the meaning of a forest which has not supported any major perturbation for at least the last few centuries.

In 1975 large projects for a paper pulp industry were planned, based upon the utilization of nearly all the forest trees. Therefore, in 1976 a 25 ha parcel of primary forest was cut (ARBOCEL, from the name of the working company) for the purpose of estimating the expenses of the proposed undertaking.

In April 1980, three and a half years after this cutting, the study of natural regeneration on the parcel shows the existence of ten types of vegetation (de Foresta 1981). The aim of the present paper is first to describe the main structural and floristical characteristics of these vegetation types, second to try to explain this heterogeneity in relation to environmental factors and third to look into some of the consequences which arise from theoretical and practical points of view.

ANALYSIS OF THE HETEROGENEITY

Methods

Two perpendicular transects have been studied using 4 m^2 (2m × 2m) elementary plots, the total length being 912 m, representing an area of 1824 m^2. Within these transects, each stem with a D.B.H. diameter at 1·30 m of 1 cm and more was numbered (2243 trees), mapped (ground plan and structural profile), measured (D.B.H., total height, and height of the lower part of the leafy volume) and identified if possible (at the Herbarium of O.R.S.T.O.M. centre in Cayenne). Finally, above ground phytomass of each vegetation type was estimated by sampling ten selected 25 m^2 (5 m × 5 m) plots.

The criteria used to divide the vegetation into physiognomically homogeneous units (Gounot 1956) are as follows (Fig. 1):

(a) respective cover proportions of herbs and trees;

(b) horizontal arrangement of vegetation: all vegetation types are 'closed' except A (very little regeneration on bare ground) and F (dense clusters of trees separated by bare ground) which are 'open';

(c) vertical stratification; the word 'stratum' is used here with the meaning of a leafy volume with definite vertical limits.

These three physiognomical criteria allow the differentiation of ten vegetation types (Fig. 1) to which each sample element cut by the transects can be related.

Structural and floristical relationships

The survey of the main structural characteristics of each vegetation type (Table 1) reveals strong differences in density and basal area as well as in above ground phytomass. The considerable variation in amplitude of the latter parameter should be noticed: three and a half years after cutting, the phytomass varies in proportion of 1 to 7!

The relationships between structure and floristical composition are obvious for the two herbaceous associations (the latter word is used here synonymous with vegetation type): B (one herb stratum: low) is characterized by the abundance of *Pityrogramma calomelanos (L.) Link. (Pteridaceae)*, and C (one herb stratum: high) by the importance of another fern, *Acrostichum aureum L. (Adiantaceae)*.

The floristical differentiation of the associations dominated by trees is a more complex problem. The inclusive analysis of the two transects shows that fifteen tree species clearly dominate the regrowth, with 85% of all trees (Table 2). In addition, no other species represents a contribution higher than 2% to any vegetation type. Therefore, in the woody associations, the floristical keys of the structural and physiognomical diversity must be searched in the quantitative variations of the distribution of the above mentioned fifteen species.

In the following analysis, 5 parameters are used, namely Density, Basal Area, Absolute Frequency, Relative Frequency, and a composed parameter introduced by Sarukhan (1968), the Dominance Index (D.I. = R.F. × D. × B.A.). This composed parameter is considered by Sarukhan (op. cit.) to give a synthetic image of the ecological importance of one species in one type of vegetation; in the present study, the D.I. showed itself an interesting comparative parameter, amplifying the tendencies revealed by the others, therefore reproducing these tendencies in a more perceptible way.

FIG. 1. Physiognomical characterization of vegetation types found on the parcel 'ARBOCEL' (3·5 years after cutting)

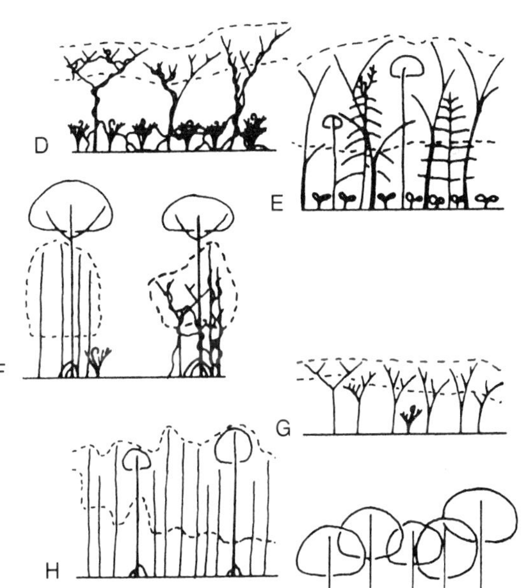

Very scant ground cover (vehicle tracks)

Herbs dominant
   One stratum: low (1 m): B
   One stratum: high (2 m): C

One herb stratum/one tree stratum
   Tree stratum: low (2·5 m): D
   Tree stratum: medium height (5 m): E

Trees dominant
   Open vegetation: F
   Closed vegetation
     One stratum:
       low (2·5 m): G
       medium (5 m): H
     Two strata:
       lower stratum: medium height (5 m): I
       lower stratum: high (7–8 m): J

TABLE 1. Main structural characteristics of the vegetation types found on the parcel 'ARBOCEL' three and a half years after cutting and burning

Vegetation Types		Density trees/ha	Basal area m²/ha	Herbs	Woody Lianas	Trees	Total
Herbaceous Herb stratum: low	B	1470	ε	6100	0	0	6100
Herbaceous Herb stratum: high	C	2500	ε	7500	0	3300	10 800
Herbaceous-woody Tree stratum: low	D	7900	2·39	6100	0	4700	10 800
Herbaceous/woody Tree stratum: medium	E	13 100	8·78	4300	500	29 200	34 000
Woody Open	F	9500	11·74	300	1680	15 930	17 980
Woody One stratum: low	G	8400	3·56	1200	0	4700	5900
Woody One stratum: medium	H	17 000	11·19	900	700	25 700	27 300
Woody, two strata Lower stratum: medium	I	17 400	13·94	170	370	32 240	32 780
Woody, two strata Lower stratum: high	J	19 900	21·12	700	500	38 500	39 700

TABLE 2. Main tree species of the parcel 'ARBOCEL' (3·5 years after cutting)

Sample area (2 transects): 1824 m²
Total number of trees (D.B.H. 1 cm): 2244
Total number of tree species: 124

Species	Family	Frequency	Relative Frequency
Cecropia obtusa Tréc.	Moraceae	458	20·4%
Goupia glabra Aubl.	Celastraceae	178	7·9%
Vismia sessilifolia (Aubl.) D.C.	Hypericaceae	166	7·4%
Solanum subinerme Jacq.	Solanaceae	163	7·3%
Cecropia sciadophylla Mart.	Moraceae	154	6·9%
Laetia procera (P.&E.) Eichl.	Flacourtiaceae	126	5·6%
Isertia spiciformis D.C.	Rubiaceae	118	5·3%
Palicourea guyanensis Aubl.	Rubiaceae	111	4·9%
Vismia guyanensis (Aubl.) Choisy	Hypericaceae	110	4·9%
Solanum rugosum Dun.	Solanaceae	86	3·8%
Xylopia nitida Dun.	Annonaceae	68	3·0%
Loreya mespiloides Miq.	Melastomaceae	59	2·6%
Solanum salviaefolium Lam.	Solanaceae	45	2·0%
Miconia fragilis Naud.	Melastomaceae	34	1·5%
Vismia latifolia (Aubl.) Choisy	Hyperioaceae	19	0·8%
Others (109 species)	at least 34 families 7 trees undetermined to the family level	349	15·6%
Total number of trees	at least 35 families	2244	100·0%

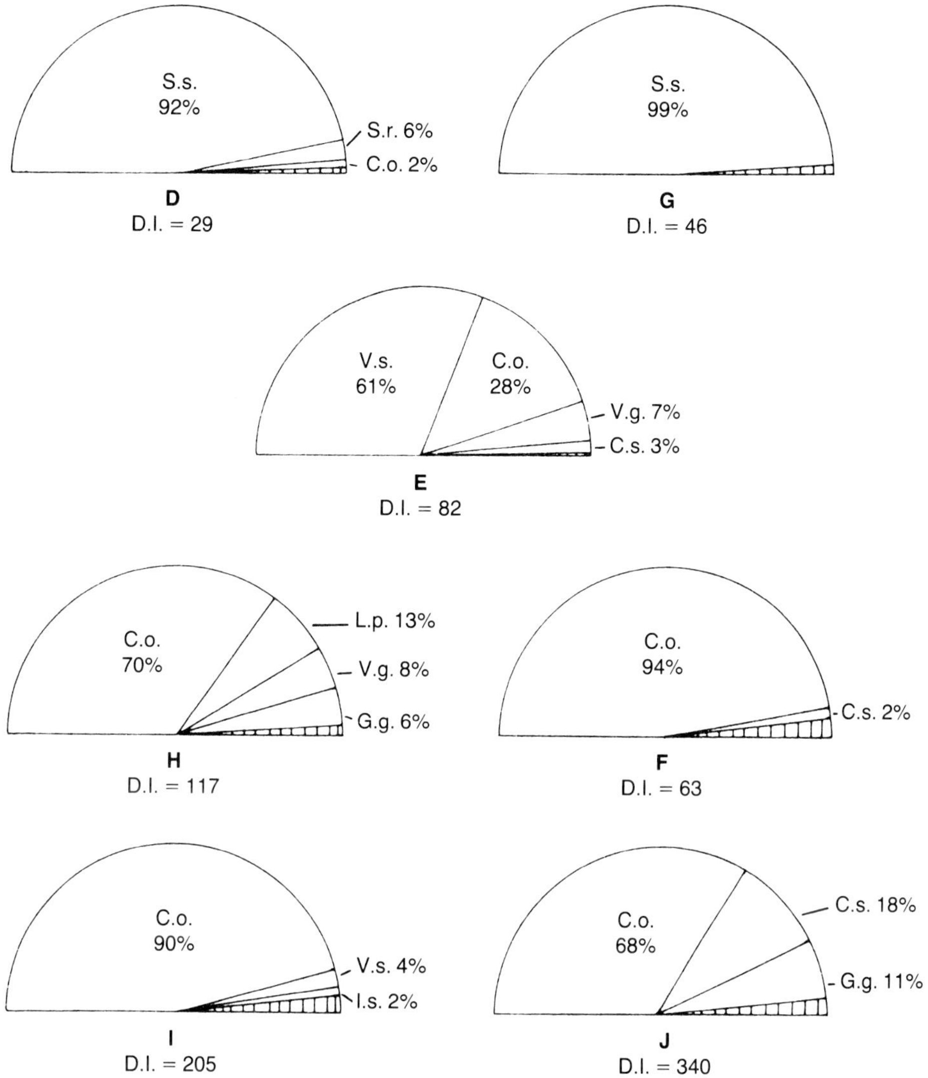

Fig. 2. Diagrams summarizing the relative contributions of the 15 main tree species to the 7 woody vegetation types. 'ARBOCEL', 3·5 years after cutting. Parameter used: Dominance Index (for each association, the total Dominance Index, D.I. is also given)

Species code

C.o. = Cecropia obtusa Tréc.
G.g. = Goupia glabra Aubl.
V.s. = Vismia sessilifolia (Aubl.) D.C.
S.s. = Solanum subinerme Jacq.
C.s. = Cecropia sciadophylla Mart.

L.p. = Laetia procera (P. & E.) Eichl.
I.s. = Isertia spiciformis D.C.
P.g. = Palicourea guyanensis Aubl.
V.g. = Vismia guyanensis (Aubl.) Choisy
S.r. = Solanum rugosum Dun.

X.n. = Xylopia nitida Dun.
L.m. = Loreya mespiloides Miq.
S.f. = Solanum salviaefolium Lam.
M.f. = Miconia fragilis Naud.
V.l. = Vismia latifolia (Aubl.) Choisy

The synthetic diagrams presented on Figure 2 show that three tree associations are floristically clearly different from the others:

D (one herb stratum/one tree stratum: low) recognizable by its herb stratum dominated by *Pityrogramma calomelanos*.

G (one tree stratum: low). D and G can be put together considering the importance of *Solanum subinerme* and the quasi absence of *Cecropia obtusa*.

E (one herb stratum/one tree stratum: medium) is characterized by the dominance of *Vismia sessilifolia* among the tree stratum; the herb stratum is dominated by *Rapatea paludosa Aubl.*

The four other vegetation types can be put together because of the dominance of *Cecropia obtusa*. 'Reciprocal Ordering' (Orloci 1975) made on a 2 × 2 table joining the fifteen main tree species on the one hand and the 27 sample elements (with an area of more than 20 m^2) of E, F, H, I and J, on the other hand, confirms the above conclusion and allows us to determine the internal variability of the four remaining associations (Figs 3 and 4):

J (two tree strata, lower stratum: high), characterized by the importance of *Cecropia sciadophylla* in the higher stratum and of *Goupia glabra* in the lower.

H (one tree stratum: medium height) associated with a relatively small contribution of *Cecropia spp.* and with the importance of *Laetia procera* and *Vismia guyanensis*.

I (two tree strata, lower stratum: medium height), related to the exclusive presence of *Cecropia obtusa* in the higher stratum and to the importance of *Vismia sessilifolia* associated with one or other of the four species *Isertia spiciformis*, *Loreya mespiloides*, *Miconia fragilis*, and *Solanum salviaefolium*.

F (open vegetation type) appearing as a structural variation of H, I, or J, depending on the sample element considered.

A few recent studies (Boerboom 1974; de Foresta 1981; Uhl *et al.* 1981; Zwetsloot 1981) show that, on the one hand, colonization of tropical rain forest-clearings by pioneer tree species is very fast (a few weeks) and that, on the other hand, the number of pioneer trees entering the vegetation during the first few years following this fast colonization is very small. These facts, associated with the small number of saplings observed in the parcel, allow us to conclude that the vegetation types met with are contemporary in origin or nearly so.

This means that the understanding of the heterogeneity of regeneration three and a half years after cutting must rely heavily on a knowledge of the initial conditions in which each vegetation type was established.

ENVIRONMENTAL FACTORS DETERMINING HETEROGENEITY

Soil

In the region studied the soil is a ferrallitic one (bedrock = schist), characterized by a low fertility (Blancaneaux 1979) and by the existence of two types of water dynamics (Boulet

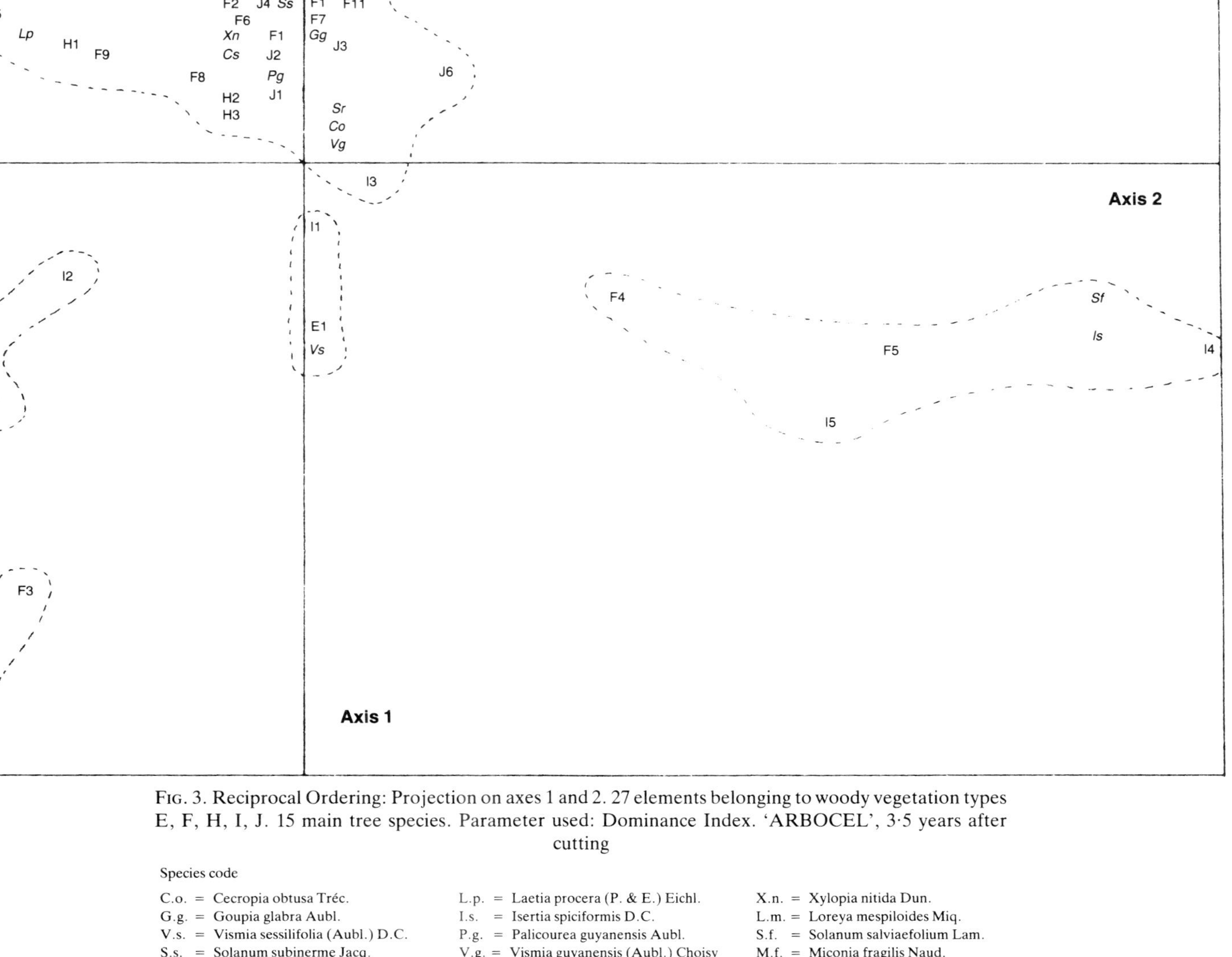

FIG. 3. Reciprocal Ordering: Projection on axes 1 and 2. 27 elements belonging to woody vegetation types E, F, H, I, J. 15 main tree species. Parameter used: Dominance Index. 'ARBOCEL', 3·5 years after cutting

Species code

C.o. = Cecropia obtusa Tréc.	L.p. = Laetia procera (P. & E.) Eichl.	X.n. = Xylopia nitida Dun.
G.g. = Goupia glabra Aubl.	I.s. = Isertia spiciformis D.C.	L.m. = Loreya mespiloides Miq.
V.s. = Vismia sessilifolia (Aubl.) D.C.	P.g. = Palicourea guyanensis Aubl.	S.f. = Solanum salviaefolium Lam.
S.s. = Solanum subinerme Jacq.	V.g. = Vismia guyanensis (Aubl.) Choisy	M.f. = Miconia fragilis Naud.
C.s. = Cecropia sciadophylla Mart.	S.r. = Solanum rugosum Dun.	V.l. = Vismia latifolia (Aubl.) Choisy

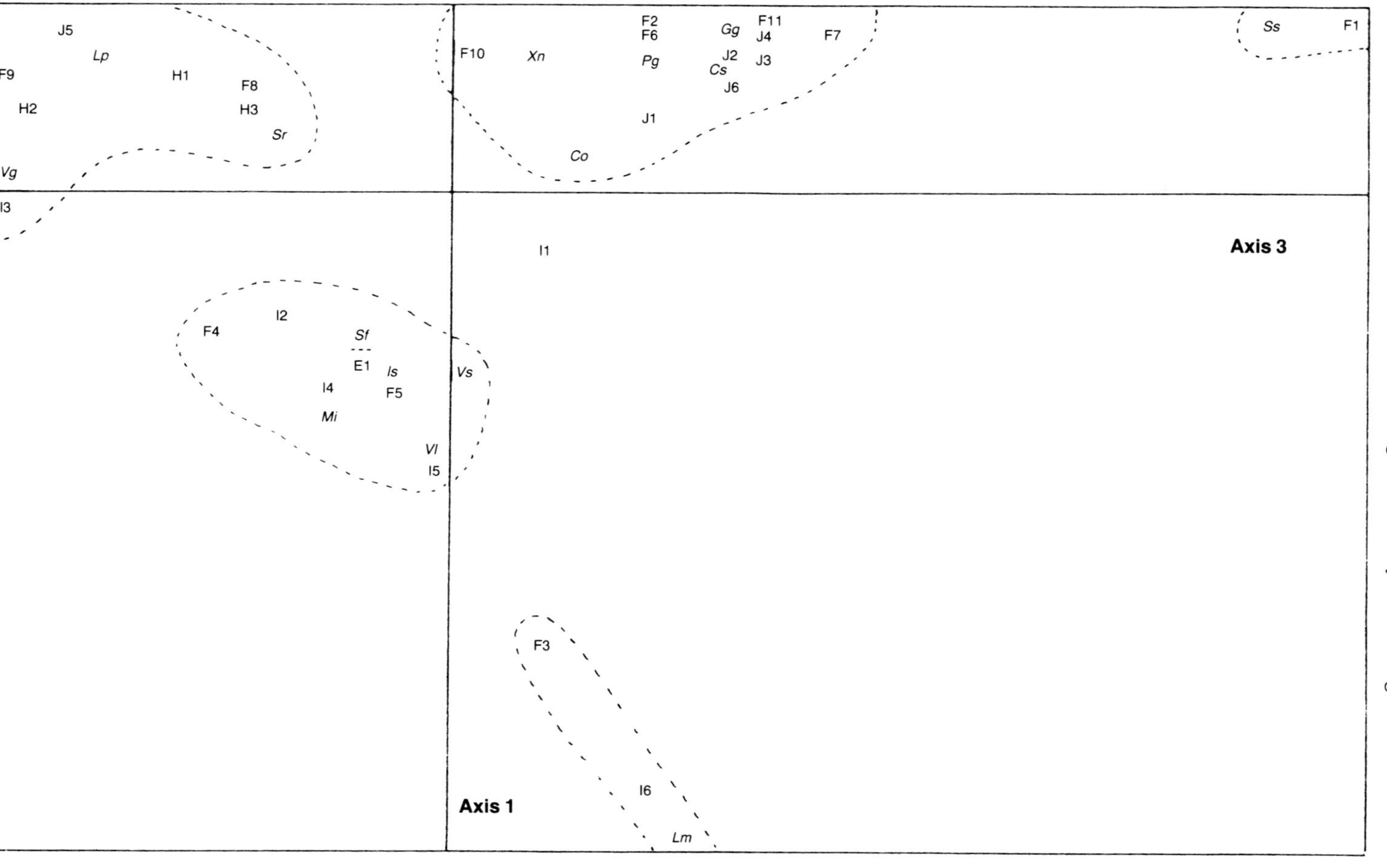

FIG. 4. Reciprocal Ordering: Projection on axes 1 and 3. (same characteristics as in Fig. 3)

Species code

C.o. = Cecropia obtusa Tréc.	L.p. = Laetia procera (P. & E.) Eichl.	X.n. = Xylopia nitida Dun.
G.g. = Goupia glabra Aubl.	I.s. = Isertia spiciformis D.C.	L.m. = Loreya mespiloides Miq.
V.s. = Vismia sessilifolia (Aubl.) D.C.	P.g. = Palicourea guyanensis Aubl.	S.f. = Solanum salviaefolium Lam.
S.s. = Solanum subinerme Jacq.	V.g. = Vismia guyanensis (Aubl.) Choisy	M.f. = Miconia fragilis Naud.

1978) — factors which seems to be important for the development of vegetation (Humbel 1978; Lescure, pers. com.) and which are free vertical drainage on the one hand and superficial and lateral drainage on the other. On ARBOCEL, all the soil samples show that the soil is of the latter type along both transects except in a few swampy places, where it is typically hydromorphic (de Foresta 1981).

Logging conditions

Three stages can be distinguished:

(1) in July to August (beginning of the dry season) 1976, all trees — except the *Chrysobalanaceae* the wood of which was not considered useful for paper pulp making — were cut with chain-saws and removed from a 10 ha area.

(2) in August to September 1976, the *Chrysobalanaceae* still standing and all trees within a 100 m width strip around the 10 ha already cleared (forming therefore a 500 m × 500 m square) were cut with chain-saws and left *in situ*.

(3) finally, in October 1976, two 'accidental' fires crossed the parcel, being the last disturbance before the beginning of natural regeneration.

All things considered, the logging operations caused relatively little indirect damage, with soil compaction, the negative impact of which on regeneration already having been underlined for this soil type (Boulet *et al.* 1979), limited to the tracks used in removing the timber (about 5% from the 25 ha parcel).

Relationship between environmental factors and vegetation type

An analysis of the spatial distribution of vegetation type according to the above-mentioned factors revealed the following.

On the vehicle tracks heavy disturbance resulted in the destruction of all pre-existant seeds, seedlings and saplings. All the very slight recolonization arose from the arrival of diaspores belonging to species able to develop on this damaged soil.

On the hydromorphic soil fire probably did not have a great impact on colonization. Vegetation types C and E appear to be related to the degree of inundation (C on permanently inundated areas, E on temporary ones). The abundance of the Mangrove fern *Acrostichum aureum* in C should be noticed (the nearest potential parent plants growing at a distance of about 20 km).

Elsewhere the dominant factor clearly was fire. Because of the patchiness of its intensity (depending on the characteristics of the ligneous material still lying on the ground), fire created a mosaic of strongly and slightly burned areas. Thus, where fire was slight, vegetation types can be considered to be a result of the competition between individuals of pioneer species arising from the forest soil seed-bank (the existence of such a seed-bank had been established in the neighbouring primary forest by Prevost 1981). Local variations in the composition of this seed-bank could explain the differences between H, I and J.

The main effect of the high temperatures associated with intense burning in such primary tropical rain-forest clearings is the destruction of nearly all the seedlings, saplings, and resprouts (Kartawinata *et al.* 1981; Uhl *et al.* 1981), as well as the destruction of soil embedded seeds, either of forest species (Brinkman & Vieira 1971) or of pioneer species (Lopez-Quiles & Vazquez-Yanes 1976; Uhl *et al.* 1981). Thus, where fire was intense, vegetation types are the result of colonization by diaspores of pioneer species coming from outside the parcel after the fires. Associations B, D, and G seem to be three phases of one successional series, as can be inferred from the presence of saplings of *Solanum subinerme* in the elements of B where some *Pityrogramma calomelanos* have begun to die, and from the presence of dead *Pityrogramma* under the *Solanum* stratum in G–D being the intermediate, with one herb stratum dominated by *Pityrogramma calomelanos* and one tree stratum dominated by *Solanum subinerme*. The last vegetation type, F, a structural variation floristically related to H, I and J, could be explained by local protection of the seed-bank under the piling of trunks (or a preferential dissemination in the immediate vicinity of lying trunks, related to the behaviour of dispersing animals, which could be another hypothesis (de Foresta 1983); present state of knowledge does not allow us to choose between these two hypotheses).

CONCLUSION: THEORETICAL AND PRACTICAL CONSEQUENCES

The analysis of heterogeneity in pioneer vegetation on the 'ARBOCEL' parcel of land three and a half years after cutting and burning suggests the following considerations:

(1)   Whilst the efficiency of the indirect method (i.e. the comparison of plots of different age at one and the same time) in the study of tropical rain-forest regeneration cannot be denied, the present study supports the conclusions of Uhl *et al.* (1981) and Zwetsloot (1981) among others as to the limitations of the method, at least when the first few years of regrowth are considered.

(2)   A completely mechanized clearing using heavy machinery creates very unfavourable conditions for the development of vegetation, as is shown here by the very poor recolonization occurring on the vehicle tracks.

(3)   Intense burning involves a considerable decline in successional dynamics, as is shown by comparing vegetation types established on strongly burned areas (B, D, G, F) and on slightly burned areas (E, H, I, J). Therefore, fire must be avoided when natural regeneration is desired. On the other hand, if plantations of fast growing species are planned after the logging of a primary forest area, burning could have a positive effect, by reducing the competition due to pioneer species during the first few years of plant growth by destroying pre-existing seedlings, saplings and soil embedded seeds.

(4)   When natural regeneration is desired, the colonization characteristics of the primary forest species which will relay pioneer vegetation statistically, progression from the periphery to the centre of the clearing proceeds at a speed inversely correlated with the dimensions of the cleared area — provide strong arguments in support of a limitation in area of elementary clearings.

(5)   Finally, a survey of the abundance of seedlings in the parcel seems to indicate that all the vegetation types unaffected by previous fires (E, H, I and J) show favourable microclimatic conditions for the installation of primary forest species. This important fact suggests that enrichment and acceleration of sequential natural regeneration could be

achieved by planting valuable primary forest tree species under the cover of pioneer vegetation. Testing the conditions for the success (species to be planted, time of planting, density of planting, etc . . .) of such a sylvicultural suggestion could be a fascinating field of research for any ecologist concerned by the rapid regression of tropical rain-forest and the correlated progression of secondary vegetation.

ACKNOWLEDGMENTS

My thanks go to the Museum National d'Histoire Naturelle de Paris, which gave me the opportunity to go to French Guiana and to carry out this study; to all the staff of the O.R.S.T.O.M. Centre in Cayenne for their important material and personal assistance, and to the staff of the Laboratoire de Botanique in Montpellier for their assistance during my thesis work.

Finally, I wish to express my gratitude to Professor F. Halle to whom I owe so much, and to R. Tjon Lim Sang who agreed to correct my English.

REFERENCES

Blancaneaux, P. (1979). Les facteurs de la pédogenèse in: *Atlas de la Guyane.* Eds. C.N.R.S.–O.R.S.T.O.M.

Boerboom, J.H.A. (1974). Succession studies in the humid tropical lowlands of Surinam. In: *Proceedings of the First National Congress of Ecology.* The Hague, Netherlands, pp. 343–347.

Boulet, R. (1978). Existence de systèmes à forte différenciation latérale en milieu ferrallitique guyanais: un nouvel exemple de couverture pédologique en déséquilibre. *Science du sol; Bulletin de l'A.F.E.S.*, **2**, 75–82.

Boulet, R., Brugiere, J.M. & Humbel, F.X. (1979). Relations entre organisation des sols et dynamique de l'eau en Guyane française septentrionale. *Sciences du sol; Bulletin de l'A.F.E.S.*, **1**, 3–18.

Brinkman, W.L.F. & Vieira, A.N. (1971). The effect of burning on germination of seeds, at different soil depth, of various tropical tree species. *Turrialba*, **21**(1), 77–82.

de Foresta, H. (1981). *Premier temps de la régénération naturelle après exploitation papetière en forêt tropicale humide; ARBOCEL — Guyane française.* Thèse de 3ᵉ cycle, Montpellier, 114 pp.

de Foresta, H. (1983). Agriculture sur brulis en forêt tropicale humide: à propos du rôle du feu dans la compétition entre espèces cultivées et espèces pionnières. In Press (Turrialba).

de Granville, J.J. (1979). Végétation. In: *Atlas de la Guyane.* Eds. C.N.R.S.–O.R.S.T.O.M.

Gounot, M. (1956). A propos de l'homogénéité et du choix des surfaces de relevés. *Bulletin du Service de la Carte Phytogéographique Ser. B*, **1**(1), 7–17.

Humbel, F.X. (1978). Caractérisation, par des mesures physiques, hydriques et d'enracinement, des sols de Guyane française à dynamique de l'eau superficielle. *Sciences du sol; Bulletin de l'A.F.E.S.*, **2**, 83–93.

Kartawinata, K., Riswan, J. & Soedjito, H. (1980). The floristic changes after disturbances in lowland Dipterocarp forest in East Kalimantan, Indonesia. In: *Proceedings of the Fifth International Symposium of Tropical Ecology*, Furtado, Ed., 47–54.

Lopez-Quiles, M. & Vazquez-Yanes, C. (1976). Estudio sobre la germinacion de semillas en condiciones naturales controladas. In: *Regeneracion de Selvas.* Gomez-Pompa *et al.* Eds. Mexico, 250–261.

Orloci, L. (1975). *Multivariate analysis in vegetation research.* W. Junk, The Hague, Netherlands.

Prevost, M.F. (1981). Mise en évidence de graines d'espèces pionnières dans le sol de forêt primaire en Guyane. *Turrialba*, **31**(2), 121–127.

Sarukhan, J.K. (1968). *Analisis sinecologico de las selvas de Terminalia amazonia.* Tesis. Chapingo, Mexico.

Uhl, C., Clark, K., Clark, H. & Murphy, P. (1981). Early plant succession after cutting and burning in the upper Rio Negro region of the Amazon Basin. *Journal of Ecology*, **69**, 631–649.

Zwetsloot, H. (1981). Forest succession on a deforested area in Suriname. *Turrialba*, **31**(4), 369–379.

Land clearing behaviour in small farmer settlement schemes in the Brazilian Amazon and its relation to human carrying capacity

PHILIP M. FEARNSIDE

Department of Ecology,
National Institute for Research in the Amazon (INPA), C.P. 478, 69.000 Manaus, Amazonas, Brazil

SUMMARY

1   The behaviour of colonists on Brazil's Transamazon Highway with respect to felling virgin forest and clearing second growth is modelled as a part of a computer simulation designed to estimate human carrying capacity.

2   Areas cleared are limited by the resources available to the colonists: land, labour and capital. Input parameters for the simulation are based on interviews conducted with colonists in a study area located 50 km west of Altamira, in the State of Pará. Data from the Ouro Preto Colonization Project in the State of Rondônia show many similarities with the patterns observed in Altamira. For purposes of simulation, areas available to colonists in their lots are classed by age of second growth, with a separate class for virgin forest (not previously felled by colonists).

3   The probability of clearing within each class is calculated from the proportion of lot-years in which the class was present and was cleared. The probabilities are for clearing some part of the area of the class in question; these 'clearings' are preparations of land for crops other than pasture (pasture is calculated separately).

4   In Rondônia, cleared areas in lots occupied by a single owner increase linearly for about six years, after which a plateau is reached. Lot sales to newcomers lead to renewed periods of rapid clearing.

5   The effects of clearing behaviour on carrying capacity include: (a) the lack of a fallowing schedule with uncultivated periods sufficient to restore soil quality, such as those in traditional systems of shifting cultivation, can potentially lead to degradation and lowering of carrying capacity, (b) rapid deforestation leads to the planting of pasture, which is linked to low human carrying capacity, and (c) exceeding a maximum limit for felling can be taken as one of the criteria for determining carrying capacity.

INTRODUCTION

Deforestation in the Brazilian Amazon, and in tropical rain-forest areas generally, is increasing steadily and is a cause of both local and global concern (Brazil, Presidência da República, INPA 1979; United States, Department of State 1978, United States Inter-agency Task Force on Tropical Forests 1980; Myers 1980). Lack of adequate ground truth data for specific areas is often a hinderance to deforestation studies using remote sensing technologies, adding to the difficulty of assessing the extent and dynamics of this process.

Understanding the process of deforestation in the Amazon, and the eventual formulation of adequate governmental policies to bring this process under control, requires better knowledge of the causes of deforestation (Fearnside 1979a, 1982). One of these causes is the clearing of land by small farmers for agriculture, although most clearing in Amazonia occurs on large cattle ranches. Deforestation rates are affected by the decisions of farmers in choosing between clearing virgin forest and the re-use of areas in second growth of different ages. These decisions also affect the sustainability of the farmers' agricultural operations over the long term (Nye & Greenland 1960; Ahn 1979). Land clearing behaviour therefore affects human carrying capacity, or the density of the human population that can be supported in an area indefinitely given appropriate assumptions concerning living standards, technology, and consumptive habits (Allan 1949, 1965; Street 1969).

The present paper forms a part of a larger study dealing with the effects of different factors on human carrying capacity in colonization areas on Brazil's Transamazon Highway in Pará (Fearnside 1978, 1979b, 1983a, 1984a), and Cuiabá-Porto Velho Highway in Rondônia. Carrying capacity is operationally defined in terms of a gradient of increasing probability of colonist failure with increasing population density within a limited range of densities. 'Failures' are defined in terms of individual families falling below any one of a series of different criteria, most of which are measures of consumption levels. Environmental quality criteria can also be applied, such as the requirement that a certain fraction of the land remain uncleared. Brazilian law requires that 50% of the forest in each colonist's lot be left intact (Decree Law 4771, 15/ix/65), although this law is not enforced in actual practice (Fearnside 1979a). Carrying capacity is considered to be exceeded when the probability of failure over a long period of time surpasses a maximum acceptable level.

MATERIALS AND METHODS

Data Collection

Information on land clearing and agricultural practices was obtained from colonists settled in the Brazilian government's planned colonization area near Altamira, in the State of Pará and Ouro Preto d'Oeste, in the State of Rondônia (Fig. 1). In the first area, an intensive study area was delimited which includes 236 lots (100 ha each) centred on Agrovila Grande Esperança, located in the Municipio of Prainha at 3° 22′ S. latitude, 52° 38′ W. longitude, 50 km west of Altamira on the Transamazon Highway. The study area includes the roadside lots from km 43 to 58, and the full length of three lateral roads (15/17, 16/18 and 17/19). Colonization began in the Altamira area in 1970, and in the intensive study area in 1971. Most of the information presented here comes from interviews conducted while residing in the study area (1974–76) and during seven subsequent visits (1978–80). Some of the data from 1976 onwards were collected by field assistants. Questionnaires applied are of two types, one related to the clearing and land use decisions for the lot as a whole, and another for information related to individual field histories. Most of the area information is taken from colonist responses, although a few fields were measured using a rangefinder with a 500 m measure range (Topcon model DM-500). Rough visual confirmation was possible for many other areas, since soil samples were taken in most lots. Some of the larger clearings had been measured by the colonists themselves, since hired labour on a per-area contract basis is often used for clearing by financed colonists. Data on cleared areas collected by government agencies can sometimes be in error if clearing loans have been granted and the areas reported by colonists misrepresented (usually inflated) to conform to the areas specified by loan terms. As more colonists pass the legally allowed maximum cleared area of 50%, the sign of the bias in official records can be expected to reverse. No government data on land clearing were used in the present study, and the data are believed to be free of any major biases.

Data collection in the second study area was undertaken between September 1980 and February 1982 in 182 lots scattered over approximately 300 000 ha of the Ouro Preto

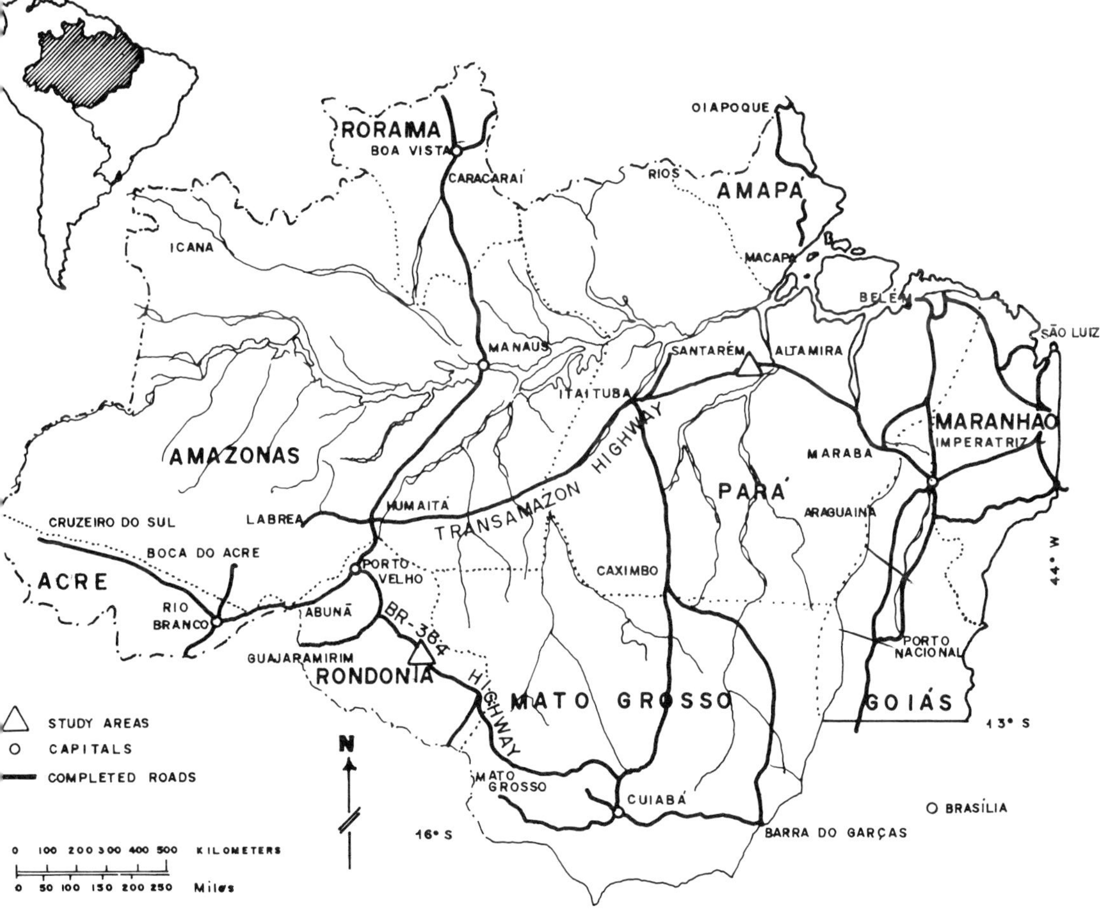

FIG. 1. Map of Brazil's Legal Amazon, showing study areas on the Transamazon Highway in Pará and the BR-364 Highway in Rondônia

Integrated Colonization Project, centred on the town of Ouro Preto d'Oeste (10° 44′ 17″ S latitude; 62° 13′ 30″ W. longitude). Older establishments are over-represented, as most sampled lots are within 20 km of the Cuiabá–Porto Velho Highway (BR-364), although a few are more than twice this distance. Data collection relies on responses to interviews using questionnaires similar to those used on the Transamazon Highway, plus one which traces the history of each cleared area forward in time from the year of virgin forest felling. Most of the interviews in Rondônia were performed by research assistants.

Simulation Procedure

Computer simulations were run for the Transamazon Highway agricultural system using a FORTRAN program called 'KPROG2', which was written for estimating human carrying capacity under conditions prevailing in the area, and under those conditions as altered by various alternative assumptions (Fearnside 1979b). Both deterministic and stochastic runs were made. Stochastic runs include the probability distributions about the means for a number of parameters. In deterministic runs a single lot is simulated, while in stochastic runs calculations are based on 10 simulated lots of 25 ha each (one-quarter the size of actual lots on the Transamazon Highway). Colonist family size is frozen at six persons, all types of colonist are included (Fearnside 1980a). Simulated clearing and land use allocations are made for hypothetical 'patches' of land 0·25 ha in area.

Land clearing decisions are a part of the resource allocation sector of the model. The patches of land available for allocation in the lot are 'cleared', or prepared for planting, in an order which is guided by the preference of the simulated colonist for the different categories of land available to him for clearing.

Patches to be cleared are chosen from those which are not occupied by a crop which would preclude the use of the patch for another crop. Excluded are patches planted in perennial crops or pasture, or in manioc (sweet or bitter) that has not completed its growth cycle. Patches are also excluded which have been under continuous cultivation for the maximum number of years permitted before weeds make the planting of a new crop impossible without an intervening fallow period. Here 'continuous cultivation' includes annual crops, perennial crops, pasture, and 'bare or weeds' (less than 240 days old). The intervening fallow period must be at least to the 'second growth' (over 240 days) stage. The maximum number of years permitted in continuous cultivation is an input parameter, a value of two years being used to reflect the usual practice on the Transamazon Highway.

Each available patch is assigned to a clearing category depending on the age of the secondary vegetation, with a separate category for virgin forest (forest not previously cleared by colonists).

Financing for clearing operations is determined (Fearnside 1980a), and financed virgin felling is carried out before other types of clearing. For patches not influenced by virgin clearing financing, the clearing category of the patch to be cleared is chosen from among the categories for which there are some patches available in the lot. This is done based on clearing probabilities, which represent the probability of clearing some of the land of the class in question, given both the existence of virgin land and the presence of land of the category in the simulated lot. These probabilities are only for clearing land for uses other than pasture, pasture being planted after other uses (Fearnside 1980a). Clearing, and the associated land use allocations, continue until the simulated colonist's resources of land, labour, or capital have been exhausted.

RESULTS

Colonist Land Clearing

Transamazon Highway

The probabilities of clearing within the different land categories, as found by questionnaire response, are given in Figure 2. These were used in simulating colonist decisions on the Transamazon Highway. The probabilities that a field is burned following clearing were 0·271 ($n = 48$) for land less than eight months fallow, and 1·0 in the cases of land

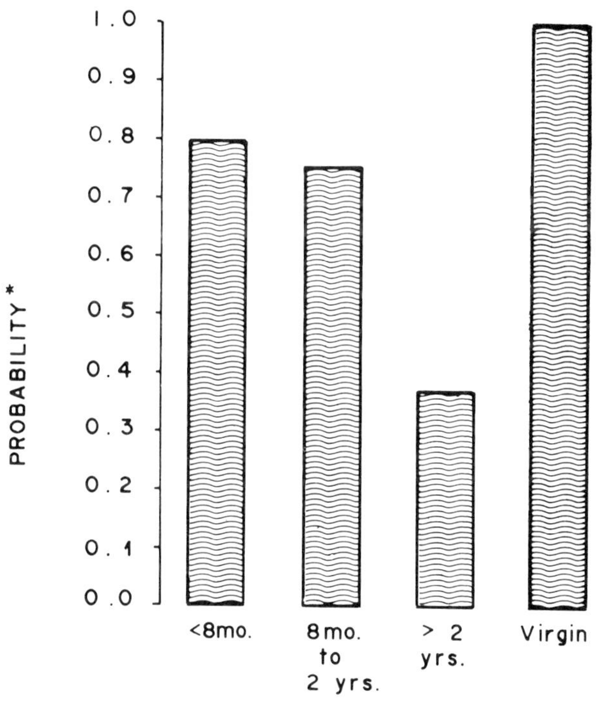

FIG. 2. Clearing probabilities on the Transamazon Highway. Land category times are age of regrowth

fallow for from 8 months to 2 years ($n = 20$), for over 2 years ($n = 5$) and for virgin forest ($n = 247$). The probabilities that older second growth than the field in question was present in the lot and left uncleared were 0·295 ($n = 17$) in the case of land fallow less than 8 months and 0·077 ($n = 13$) in the case of land fallow 8 months to 2 years.

The probabilities in Figure 2 refer only to land cleared for uses other than pasture. For land cleared for use as pasture the probability is 1·0 ($n = 22$) that some land of category 'bare or weeds' (or land which has been uncultivated for less than eight months) is cleared for this use, given both the availability of land of the category and the fact that pasture was planted somewhere on the lot in the year in question. Of 24 fields cleared for pasture, four were burned (16·7%). Six of the 24 fields (25%) belonged to colonists who had cattle; it should be noted that this applies to the 1973–76 period, and a substantially higher proportion of colonists have subsequently obtained cattle. None of the colonists with cattle at the time of pasture planting burned the fields as a part of the clearing procedure: the probability of burning may therefore be lower at present, at least for fields planted to pastures immediately following annual crops. It should be noted that all but one of the 24 fields in the sample planted to pasture were in the 'bare or weeds' category (<8 months uncultivated), the one exception being a virgin field in which the burn was so poor that annual crops could not be planted. The greatly increased number of cattle in the area since the sample, as well as the ranching orientation of many of the wealthier newcomer colonists, may be leading to more pasture being planted in fields cleared of older second growths or of virgin forest, thus necessitating burning as a part of land preparation.

The number of years that a field has been under continuous cultivation could be expected to influence (reduce) the frequency with which a field in the 'bare or weeds' condition following a crop will be cleared (prepared) for replanting. This should be especially true if the crop to be planted is other than pasture, as weeds and other problems will result in lower yields. For clearing in the 'bare or weeds' category for crops other than pasture, the probability of clearing a field that has been under continuous cultivation for one year is 0·804 ($n = 51$), and for two years is 0·750 ($n = 8$). For three years the one case available was cleared; if this case is lumped with the two-year-old fields the probability becomes 0·778 ($n = 9$). In the case of pasture as the next crop, the probability is 1·0 for both one-year-old fields ($n = 16$) and two-year-old fields ($n = 6$). The mean time under continuous cultivation for land planted to pasture is 1·27 years (SD = 0·46, $n = 22$), while the mean for fields planted to other crops is 1·17 years (SD = 0·42, $n = 60$).

The clearing rates of virgin forest on the Transamazon Highway for all uses are presented in Table 1. Cumulative areas cleared, expressed as percentages of the lot area, are shown in Figure 3 ($n = 60$ lots).

Rondonia

Colonists' decisions to clear second growth rather than primary forest are closely tied to the intended land use (Fig. 4). Cattle pasture is much more likely to be planted on land in second growth or in weeds following the harvest of an annual crop, while virgin forest is

TABLE 1. Rain-forest clearing rates in
colonist lots on the Transamazon
Highway

Year of felling	Mean area cleared/lot during year (ha)	SD (ha)	n (lots)
1971	2·29	4·25	122
1972	4·29	4·43	120
1973	5·44	4·50	122
1974	2·77	4·40	124
1975	3·23	3·22	34

usually felled if perennial crops are to be planted. Secondary and primary vegetation have equally high probabilities of being cleared for planting annual crops.

The turnover in the colonist population accelerates the expansion of cleared areas, as virgin forest felling is greater among newcomer colonists in the first four years after arrival than among original lot owners (Fig. 5). The amounts cleared are highly variable among colonists, and for different years for the same colonist. When a newcomer colonist buys a lot, he often spends a year or two clearing second growth left by the previous lot owner before the increased level of clearing activity is reflected in virgin forest felling (Fig. 6). Even after the backlog of second growth has been reduced or eliminated, colonists often continue to fell in pulses, clearing a large amount one year followed by a year without clearing. Averaging felling over a four-year period, these irregularities tend to disappear (Fig. 6).

The pattern of felling in a lot during the tenancy of any given owner shows a linear increase for about six years, followed by a plateau when felling levels off. The trend in

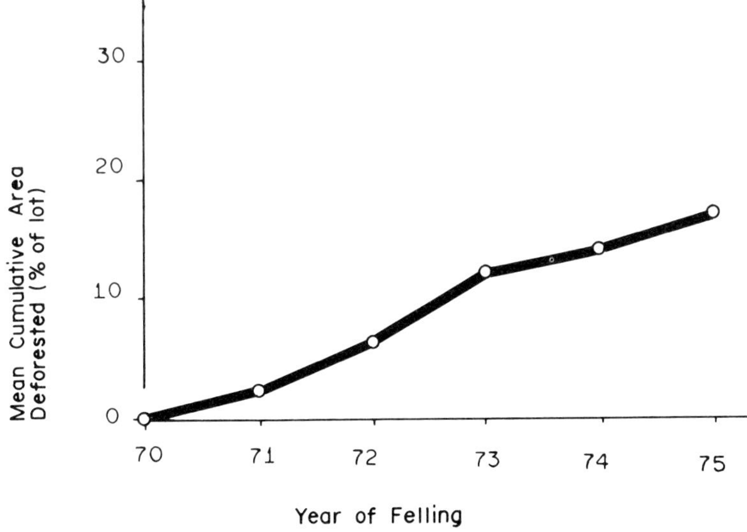

FIG. 3. Observed cumulative felling on the Transamazon Highway

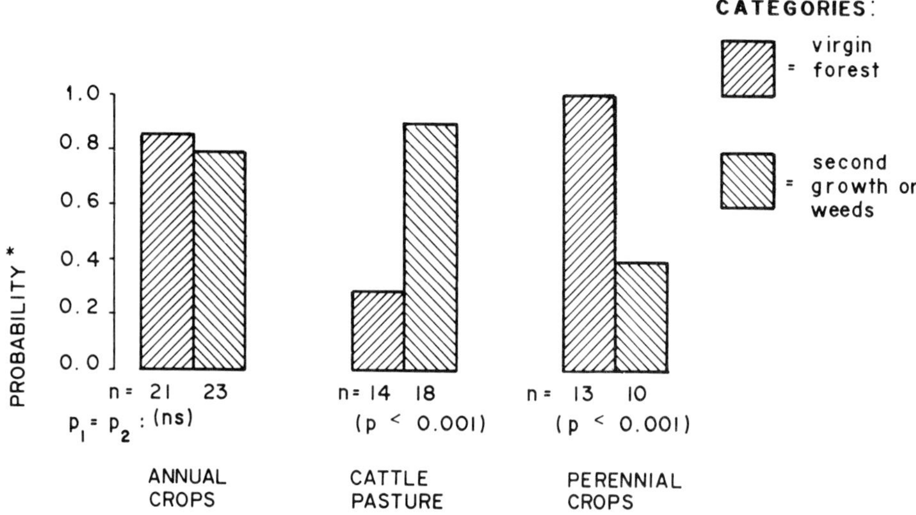

Fig. 4. Effect of intended land use on clearing choices in Rondônia

cumulative felling by original lot owners up to the tenth year of occupation, shown in Figure 7 ($n = 18$ lots), is identical to the trend for a larger sample size to nine years of occupancy ($n = 30$ lots).

Simulated Land Clearing

Simulated land clearing from the KPROG2 carrying capacity estimation program is shown in Figure 8. The clearing probabilities from Figure 2 have been used as input parameters.

DISCUSSION

Observed Felling Patterns

Transamazon Highway

The observed colonist clearing choices (Fig. 2) indicate very high probabilities for clearing weeds or young second growth. This leads to the conclusion that the colonists are

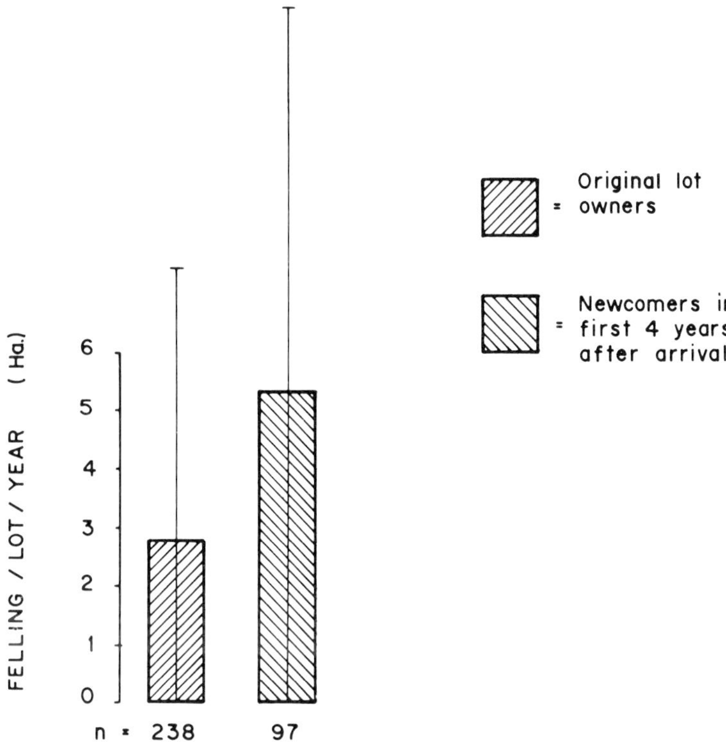

Fig. 5. Effect of colonist turnover on felling rates in Rondônia

not following the pattern of traditional shifting agriculturalists in allowing land to lie fallow for sufficient time to permit regeneration of its former productive potential by regenerating soil fertility, restoring soil structure to the uncompacted state characterizing forest soils, and reducing losses from weeds, pests and plant diseases. The areas converted to perennial crops, such as cacao (*Theobroma cacao*) and black pepper (*Piper nigrum*), do not account for more than a tiny fraction of the area cleared, the bulk of the land being planted in either annual crops (mostly upland rice) or Guinea grass (*Panicum maximum*) pasture. Annual crops cannot be expected to produce on a sustainable basis without either adequate fallows or the supply of a wide array of the nutritional needs of the plants through fertilization (Sánchez 1977; Sánchez *et al.* 1982), which is currently not economic (Fearnside 1984b). The most common result is for an ever larger portion of the land to be converted to cattle pasture as time progresses.

It should be noted that it is the height rather than the age of a stand of second growth which serves as the trigger for clearing by traditional farmers in most of Amazonia. The

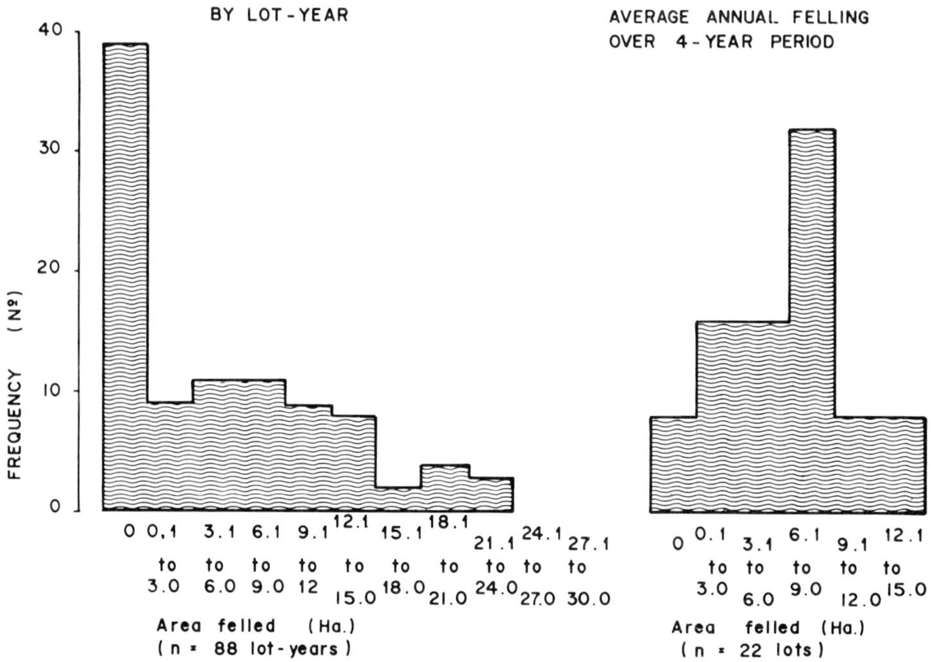

FIG. 6. Frequency distribution of areas felled by newcomer colonists in Rondônia

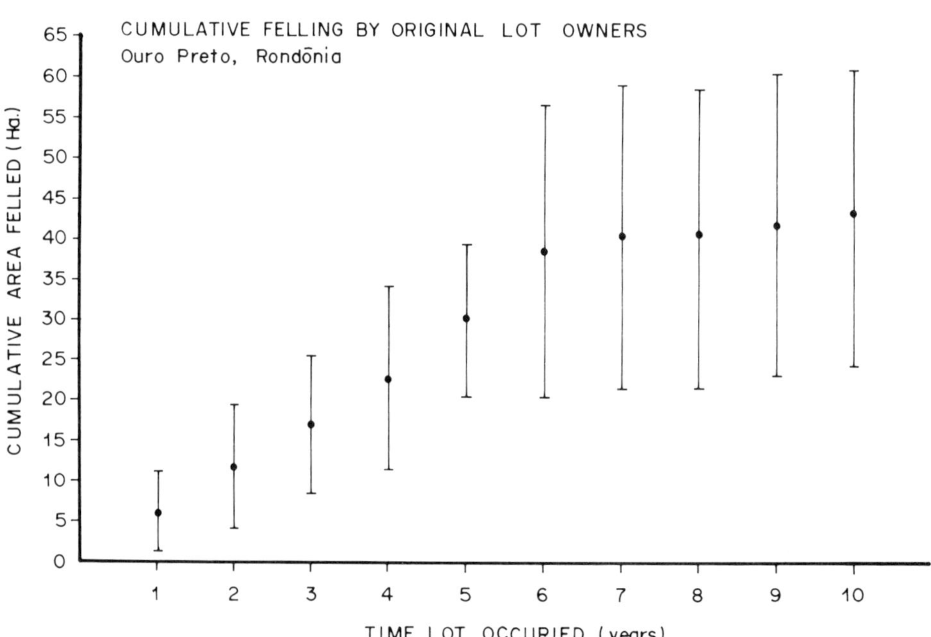

FIG. 7. Observed felling in Rondônia in a cohort of lots occupied by their original owners

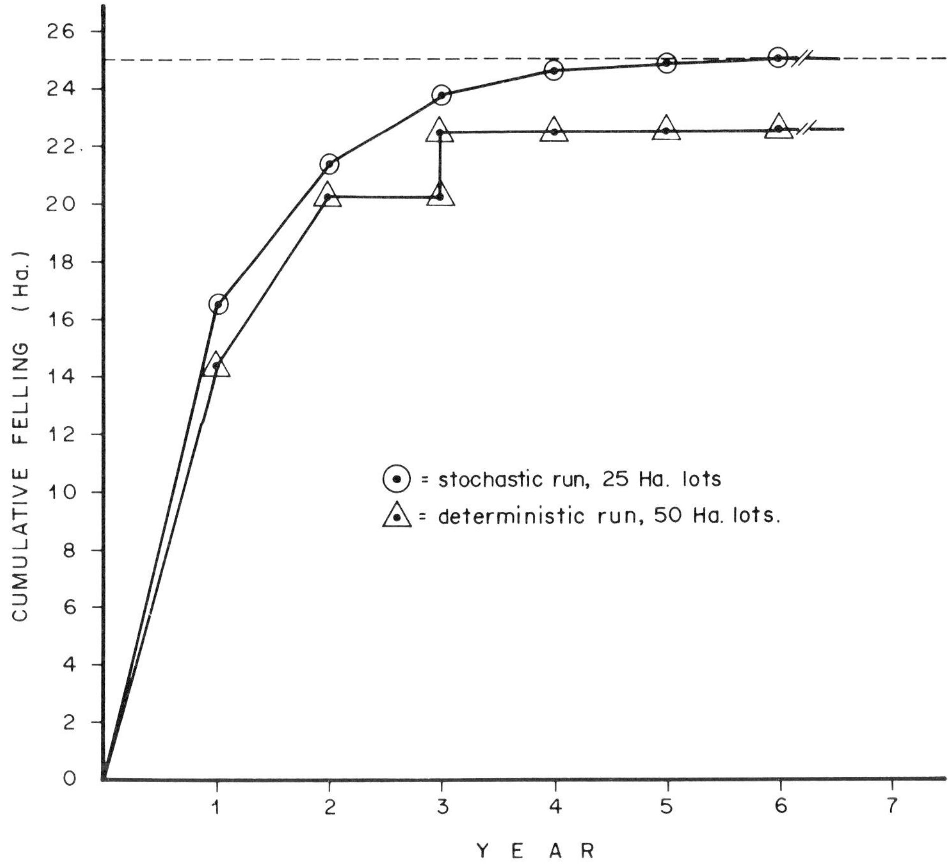

FIG. 8. Simulated felling on the Transamazon Highway

rate of growth of secondary vegetation is probably related to various soil properties which deteriorate with repeated or prolonged cultivation. In the colonization area of the Transamazon Highway, the regrowth is still quite rapid, stands of *Cecropia* reaching approximately 3 m in height after one year, 5–7 m after two years, and 9–12 m after three years. The agricultural activities in the Transamazon Highway study area were too recent at the time of data collection for the computation of the clearing probabilities for stands of second growth to be available in the older categories.

The observed virgin forest clearing rates (Table 1) are higher in the years 1972 and 1973 than in other years. There are several possible reasons for this. The availability of financing is a key factor. In contrast to later years, during this period there was more promotion of financed clearing by the government agricultural extension agency, and fewer of the colonists had been disqualified from receiving further financing by failure to repay past loans. The terms of virgin clearing loans were also more favourable than in later years: beginning in 1974 the granting of loans with grace periods of three years, terms of eight years, and interest rates of 7%/year was discontinued and replaced by a programme of loans with no grace periods, terms of one year, and interest rates of 10%/

Agrisylviculture from the standpoint of the management and conservation of forest resources*

François GRISON

Institute for Agronomic Research, Centre for Forestry Research, B.P. 2102 Yaounde, United Republic of Cameroon

SUMMARY

1   Traditional and changing ways in which the tropical forests have been used by man and effects on forest regrowth are outlined.

2   The possibilities of combining agricultural production and forestry are considered.

3   Agroforestry, integrating subsistence agriculture with the retention of a certain number of trees, could contribute to the conservation of extensive forest cover.

INTRODUCTION

In the traditional way of life in dense forest, that is, before the development of means of communication and before international trade in wood, man found in the forest around him satisfaction for all his principal needs: wood, food, medicines and cultivable soils produced by forest regeneration over sufficiently long time scale. This system of shifting cultivation could survive indefinitely in the same area of forest if the forest 'fallow' phase lasted a sufficiently long time, which was possible subject to two conditions:

(1)   that the population be of low density so that every family had at its disposal a sufficient space: the area 'occupied' by each family was, in effect, extended in proportion to the length of time needed for forest fallow;

(2)   that the population retained a certain mobility which permitted it to re-locate its villages from time to time to retain proximity to its cultivated plots.

Thus, in the traditional way of life, the sound knowledge man had concerning the forest permitted him to find the satisfaction of the greatest part of his needs without damaging the long-term viability of the forest — his interests lay in conserving it in its entirety and in its diversity.

The development of means of communications, of commerce, of individual needs and expectations, and the emergence of what one might call 'a modern way of life', has provoked an upset in the relationship between man and the forest.

Populations have become concentrated along the road networks, for reasons of convenience (easier access to schools, hospitals, shops . . .), and villages have become permanent. Fields and plots must not be far away in the absence of transport. The area available for each person has become less than on the traditional system, resulting in a reduction of the duration of the fallow phase and in a progressive drop in fertility of the soil as well as a disappearance of the forest all along the road network.

Industrial cultivars (coffee, cocoa, rubber, oil palms . . .) as they develop, occupy a greater and greater amount of land and contribute to the reduction in the area forested.

*translated by A. C. Chadwick

273

Wood has acquired a monetary value: formerly limited to obtaining a few species, exploitation for forestry has affected a greater and greater area, an ever-greater volume of timber and an ever-increasing number of species. The removal of trees has built up to such an extent over many tens of years that measures have had to be taken with a view to conserving the heritage of the forester.

The traditional solution to the problem of maintaining productivity for forestry is to place the forests under the control of the State, which then undertakes a programme of sylviculture, usually by creating plantations after the destruction of the forest which formerly existed.

This control is necessary with a view to:

(1)   the conservation of natural forest and

(2)   the production under intensive sylviculture of timber having moderate or long term turnover characteristics. The State, more than anyone else, can envisage long-term growth and returns in forestry.

But this activity, albeit indispensible, is insufficient to ensure the conservation of the patrimony, for two reasons:

(1)   Even major reforestation programmes are not extensive enough to produce a quantity of timber equivalent to that extracted from the forest each year and, despite the fact that there is a natural regrowth in forest conserved after selective exploitation, the heritage of useful trees diminishes, e.g. for certain species which occur only rarely.

(2)   The forests placed under the control of the State do not cover a sufficient area to exert on their own an ecological buffer such that one can envisage with complacency the destruction of the remaining forest cover.

These two reasons, economic and ecological, require that to State sylviculture of the dominant forest areas must be added conservation activity and an augmentation of the value placed on these forests which are not State owned, which could be undertaken by private individuals.

Before seeing how world agriculture could be associated with, and interest itself in conservation and in augmenting the value of forestry activities, a recap of the effect of agriculture on the forest is necessary.

IMPACT OF AGRICULTURE ON THE FOREST

Traditional shifting cultivations leave behind them areas of between about 0·5 ha to a few hectares, which are quickly recolonized by forest, notably by encroachment from the forest edges. It is thus that one can explain the progress of the Okume (*Aucoumea klaineana Pierre*) across Gabon (Aubréville 1948) and the existence of few populations pure and uncontaminated by this type. Young populations thus established subsequently constitute a secondary forest beneath which a second level of slow growing types can succeed in developing (Donis 1956). Shifting cultivation whilst conserving the forest, nevertheless favours its replacement and selective enrichment by types having rapid growth, which today are greatly increased in number through this effect. Furthermore, certain species (e.g. *Baillonella toxisperma Pierre, Chlorophora excelsa Bentham and Hooker F.*) and other species either useful or difficult to destroy have been treated with respect at the time of felling and the diversity of the forest preserved thereby in large part.

The redistribution of the human population and its increased density, together with the curtailment of the fallow period which has resulted, has caused the disappearance of the forest along the routes of communication. By the same token, forest situated far from these routes is no longer cleared. It evolves and returns progressively to a climatic climax state even given exploitation for forestry which, in abstracting some choice trees of certain species (1 to 3 per hectare most frequently), introduces a further evolutionary factor. Subsequent to exploitation, the forest cover is conserved in its entirety, apart from a few gaps which will probably encourage perimeter species and perhaps some seedlings. The growth and progressive changes in plant distribution provoked by exploitation for forestry constitute a difficult but exciting research theme, on which rigorous scientific studies are currently in progress.

THE POSSIBILITIES FOR ASSOCIATING AGRICULTURE PRODUCTION WITH FORESTRY

Though the State can (and must) envisage forest exploitation and sylviculture in the long term, this is not the same for individuals, who do not normally have access to the financial means for such investments and who frequently are preoccupied with the short term. Nevertheless, it does happen that private individuals do undertake such planting for quick turnover (e.g. production of poles) but this so far only affects a small area.

We are concerned rather with the circumstances where it is in the interest of the agriculturalists to integrate trees with his crops and to carry out what is called agro-forestry: examples will be presented and then we can demonstrate what is the impact of the agroforestry on forestry resources in general.

The cultivation of trees in association with subsistence agriculture in order to maintain the fertility of the soil constitutes a research theme under active investigation in Cameroon and in Nigeria. The underlying principle is to maintain the richness of the soil and humus content by utilizing species of trees in which the deeper roots will intercept mineral elements leached into the lower layers of the soil and bring about their recycling. In addition one should choose species capable of enriching the soil in nitrogen as a result of their possession of nodules of nitrogen fixing bacteria on their roots. Furthermore it is necessary that the species utilized should have a root system which is active at deeper levels (which is not always the case in the forest) and that the nitrogenous enrichment should be effective.

The shade offered in forestry production can provide the opportunity to grow certain crops. Thus the cultivation of cocoa (*Theobroma cacao L.*) is carried out traditionally in the shade of trees which have been retained during the initial clearing of the natural forest. The practise of cocoa cultivation has subsequently evolved towards total exposure, which permits a greater productivity but necessitates more frequent applica-tions of plant protectants and a perfect mastery of the cultivation technique. One is moving now towards a less intensive cultivation procedure for cocoa in order to liberate oneself to some extent from the heavy constraints imposed by these treatments (both in cost and in time), by utilizing the shade of cultivated trees of which the wood itself will be an appreciable element of complementary productivity. In Cameroon it is envisaged to use for this purpose terminalias (*Terminalia superba Engl. & Diels and Terminalia ivorensis A. Chev.*), which will be planted at the same time as the young plants of cocoa and also bananas. The latter will offer shade initially to the cocoa before being superseded by the terminalias and from which the harvests will be welcome before the entry into production of the cocoa towards the fourth season.

The sylviculture of fallow ground could, finally, constitute an adaption by shifting cultivations to modern exigencies of productivity, fallow both restoring the fertility of the soil and producing wood in commercial quantities.

The taungya method permits the agriculturalists to establish fields in the lands which the State is re-afforesting. At the same time, one can envisage that in his fields of subsistence agriculture the agriculturalist could plant forest trees, which he would cultivate at the same time as his own crops and which would no longer be much trouble to look after when he quitted his fields after the third year as they would already be sufficiently grown soon to constitute and significant forestry element.

This method offers the advantage of a considerable augmentation of forestry production for minimum effort. It presupposes that it is possible to guarantee the ownership of the trees to whoever has planted them and that the population is of a sufficiently low density to be able to envisage fallows lasting the thirty years or so necessary for certain species of useful timber trees.

THE IMPACT OF THIS SORT OF AGRICULTURE ON FOREST RESOURCES

Returning to the theme of the tropical forest symposium: what contribution can agroforestry make towards the management of the tropical forest?

Development in areas of dense forest and increase in agricultural production necessitates the clearing of part of the forest. The special interest of the associations we have described is that they permit the development of agricultural production whilst at the same time contributing to the safeguarding of the forest heritage. In effect, the integration of trees into subsistence agriculture, whilst maintaining the fertility of the soil, sedenterizes agriculture and breaks the vicious circle of fallows becoming shorter and shorter in duration whilst the forest becomes more and more degraded. Along the routes of communication there would be a zone of permanent cultivation and, further away from these routes, a zone of forestry. Here the practice of shifting cultivation could be followed, with fallows of a sufficient length which could also produce commercial timber products.

Plantations of cocoa utilizing the shade of forest trees throughout the large area devoted to cacao production would have a double impact, both economic and ecological.

As far as economics are concerned, the plantations would produce significant quantities of timber which could be turned to commercial advantage: the forest would thus contribute directly to the enrichment of the itinerant population through the sale of wood of which they were the proprietors by virtue of having produced it.

As far as ecology is concerned, the production of timber from cultivated trees could bring about a reduction in the exploitation pressure on the natural forest. Furthermore, the light but continuous covering of shade trees would give the cocoa plantation a beneficial forest character.

Thus, from a practical point of view, cocoa cultivation appears to be one of those rare instances of economic growth which permits the simultaneous development of forestry and permanent agriculture in one and the same place, reconciling the concern for developing agricultural production with the necessity of conserving extensive forest cover.

CONCLUSION

Agroforestry arose out of necessity a long time ago in the savannah zone from the need of the population to cultivate trees for the production of posts and poles as much as for firewood.

The development of agriculture and the redistribution of populations along the highways provides, together with agroforestry in the forest interior, a real opportunity from the point of view of conservation of forest soils and of the heritage of the forest.

The possibilities offered by agroforestry must be understood and used to maximum effect by those responsible for forest development and for land management in countries which still possess this inestimably rich resource, the diverse rain forest.

REFERENCES

Aubréville, A. (1948). Etude sur les forêts de l'Afrique équatoriale française et du Cameroun — (In: Ministère de la France d'Outre-Mer, Bulletin scientifique n° 2, mai 1948).

Donis, C. (1956). La forêt dense congolaise et l'état actuel de sa sylviculture (In: Bulletin agricole du Congo Belge XLVII (1956), **2**, 261–320).

present and future food production but also, in this case, there is an apparent trade-off between present food production and return from labour.

Two further comments can be made on Figs 4 and 5. The first concerns the large benefit of higher soil fertility, not only in terms of yields, which are increased 'by definition', but also of labour efficiency (Fig. 5). The second comment concerns the apparent remarkable similarity of labour efficiencies between systems with $t_f = 10$ and 5. Food production apparently expands at about the same rate as labour requirement. However, it should be pointed out that the system with the shorter fallow has a cycle length of 5 years less and, since it leaves the soil less fertile, during the first 5 years of the next cycle it will then be operating at a lower labour efficiency than the other system. Taken over the duration of the longer cycle, the labour efficiency of the more intensive system will therefore be lower. Although further analysis is needed to clarify how a similar argument would apply to systems differing in nt_c, the conclusion of the last paragraph can probably be broadened to include changes in food production due to manipulation of either of the two management variables, nt_c or t_f.

DISCUSSION

In what appears to be a first attempt to model a shifting cultivation system, ruthless simplifications of detail have led to a simple mathematical description of the behaviour of a single plot through a rotational cycle. Making the naive assumption that this plot is representative of other plots in the system when they are at the same stage in their cycle, the effects of various durations of cropping and fallow phases have been estimated. This approach avoids the complications of treating each plot individually, but thereby it raises unresolved questions about how representative is the reference plot of all the other plots. However, using criteria given above, the least reliable estimates of whole system behaviour are when soil fertility is changing rapidly between cycles and when the number of crops taken is not small relative to the duration of the fallow. Such estimates are found in the top right-hand corner of the square parameter space explored in Fig. 3 and in the points referring to $nt_c = 10$ in Figs 4 and 5. Although this casts doubt on the reality of the productivity maxima at $nt_c = 4$, $t_f = 5$ (shown for $F_{oc} = 2$ t/ha in Fig. 3a and for $F_{oc} = 2$ and 3 t/ha in Figs 4 and 5), the same maximum in the $F_{oc} = 1$ t/ha results (Figs 4 and 5) seems credible, since systems in that region ($4 < nt_c < 10$, $t_f = 5$) all lie within 5% of zero fertility change. With soil fertility nearly stationary over cycles and with management in an assumed steady state, all plots will return to a very similar F_{oc} for the start of a new cycle wherever that start may fall within the modelled cycle of the reference plot. In this case at least, the reference plot is almost perfectly representative of all the other plots with respect to the characters calculated and the productivity maximum is real.

Among the approximations and simplifications made in the model, that of regarding falling yields in a cropping sequence as being due to a decline in 'soil fertility' may seem the least defensible. The increase in competition from weeds is in many cases equally or more important (Nakano 1978; Lambert & Arnason 1982). Accumulation of pests and erosion of soil may also contribute to yield decline. Nevertheless, if 'soil fertility' is understood as a composite concept embracing all such effects, the use of the term may be more acceptable. The restoration of fertility during the fallow phase can similarly be seen as involving processes such as suppression of weeds by taller vegetation and decline of pest populations due to the absence of hosts. Again concerning weeds, a lack of consideration of the extra labour needed to control weeds in the later stages of cropping is possibly a fault of the model. Although it would not be hard to remedy this, it might be pointed out that sometimes no extra labour is involved. For instance, in the $nt_c = 4$, $t_f = 15$ system in Belize, simple burning may be the only measure used against weeds in the cropping phase (Lambert & Arnason 1982).

Since widespread intensification of shifting cultivation is occurring as increasing numbers of familes are obliged to seek subsistence in forest and uplands (UNESCO 1978; PESAM 1982), it seems important to ask whether the model can suggest any insights into the implications of this intensification. Intensification takes the form of a lengthening of cropping phases and/or a shortening of the fallows. Such changes in nt_c and t_f involve a shift across the square parameter space of Fig. 3 to the right and upwards. As an instance of the kinds of change to be considered, Karen farmers in Northern Thailand tradition-ally preferred to have at least a 10-year fallow, but even by 1969 shortage of land led to 84% of plots in one village having a fallow shorter than this; for these plots, the average t_f became 6·4 years (Hinton 1978). Similarly, in Cuzco, Peru, in the 25 years up to 1971 a predominantly $nt_c = 1$, $t_f = 10$ system changed to one approximating $nt_c = 3$, $t_f = 3$ (Watters 1971).

To provide an example of the effects of intensification, we may consider the implications of a shift from $nt_c = 1$, $t_f = 10$ to $nt_c = 5$, $t_f = 5$. According to the results of Fig. 3, the original system with $F_{oc} = 2$ t/ha would provide subsistence for 3·5 ME from a labour input of 0·6 ME. The loss of fertility and yields per cycle would be just below 4% so that such a system is essentially sustainable; it will reach a stable equilibrium at a slightly lower fertility level. This matches well the ecological sustainability inferred by Sabhasri (1978) for an $nt_c = 1$, $t_f = 10$ Lua system in Northern Thailand. In the original hypothetical system the labour efficiency, measured as the ratio food produced (ME)/ labour input (ME), is estimated to be 6·2. Commenting on the variation in the labour efficiency of such systems, Godelier (1974, in UNESCO 1978) quotes a 'high' figure of 16[2] for an ancient Mayan system of the same type; a low figure for Karen farmers in Northern Thailand is 1·05 (data of Hinton 1978. In contrast with the original system, Fig. 3 indicates that the new system would provide subsistence for three-times more people (10·7 ME) from a labour input which is 4·5-times greater. The fertility loss in the first cycle is, however, estimated to be 45% so that F_{oc} and hence yields for the second cycle would be only about half of what they were in the first. Results from the model run with an initial fertility level ($F_{oc} = 1$ t/ha) near this new level suggest that, if the new system were continued, it would be very close to stationary with respect to fertility. In this final state, the system would provide for only 1·6-times the original number of people but continuing with a labour input of 4·5-times the original. The labour efficiency would thus be 2·1, one-third of the original level.

---

[2]Assuming that the 'family of five' contained 4 ME and that a working year contains 261 days.

The results of this comparison of the intensified system with the traditional one exemplify several well-known development dilemmas. The advantages of using a model to generate them are that the source of relationships between variables can be readily identified, at least in the hypothetical system and that analysis or gaming with the model can suggest feasible ways of avoiding undesirable future states. A first dilemma is that when an urgent need for higher productivity is answered with an increase of effort or other inputs, the resulting higher productivity is often not sustained. This effect is here seen in the trade-off between short- and long-term productivity. The source of this trade-off has been shown to lie in the dynamics of soil fertility. An alternative way of stating this dilemma is that agricultural intensification has environmental costs. This is seen in the trade-off between productivity and the conservation of soil fertility (Fig. 4); environmental damage rebounds after a time lag.

A second dilemma is that returns from a unit amount of input fall as more units are put in. In shifting cultivation systems the main input is labour and the trade-off between labour efficiency and productivity is very evident in Fig. 5. Since low labour efficiency leads to impoverishment of farmers through depriving them of surplus production, efforts to increase production lead to a poverty trap: intensification in a first cycle provides extra production at a similar level of labour efficiency, but in the following cycle the lower soil fertilities lock the farmers into systems with much lower labour efficiencies (Fig. 5). If, in the real world, further intensification is then undertaken to offset the effect of lowered efficiency, the model indicates that this will lead to a steeply declining standard of living. Associated with this will be effectively irreversible changes in the environment and collapse of the system. Zinke *et al.* (1978) suggest that this process may explain the abandonment of the ancient settlements around Angkor Wat, Cambodia, in Northern Thailand and in Central America.

Possible uses of the model include the assessing of various ways to control the undesirable processes that intensification promotes. For instance, by setting the equation for fertility change to zero, the necessary values of K_F can be found for any system which will theoretically make it ecologically sustainable. As K_F data become available on fertility increase rates under 'improved' fallows (Thiagalingam & Famy 1981), a preliminary assessment of their potential for this purpose could be made. In another sort of application, a suitable calibrated model could be used in conjunction with serial aerial photographs (or high-resolution satellite data), soil maps and limited ground survey to estimate rates of fertility depletion and thus likely trends of future yields. Programmed for a hand calculator, a simple model of this kind could even find use in extension field work. However, for more detailed ecological work its limitations would immediately become apparent. A more complex approach is already being developed which is able to take account of the type of 'instant' collapse that occurs over large areas in South-east Asia when forest regeneration suddenly fails and the plot becomes an *Imperata* grassland.

ACKNOWLEDGMENTS

I am grateful to Kenneth Jackson, Benjamin Samson, Soedarsono and David Lamb for helpful discussions and views on parameter values, to the Program on Environmental

Science and Management, University of the Philippines at Los Baños and to the Multiple Cropping Program, Chiang Mai University, Thailand, for opportunities to visit field sites, to Janet Davis for technical help, and to Maureen Robinson for typing the manuscript. The work was partly supported by the U.K. Department of the Environment.

REFERENCES

Arnason, T., Lambert, J.D.H., Gale, J., Cal, J. & Vernon, H. (1982). Decline of soil fertility due to intensification of land use by shifting agriculturalists in Belize, Central America. *Agro-ecosystems*, **8,** 27–37.

Aweto, A.O. (1981). Secondary succession and soil fertility restoration in south-western Nigeria. 2. Soil fertility restoration. *Journal of Ecology*, **69,** 609–614.

Crocker, R.L. & Major, J. (1955). Soil development in relation to vegetation and surface age in Glacier Bay, Alaska. *Journal of Ecology*, **43,** 427–448.

Greenland, D.J. & Okigbo, B.D. (In press). Crop production under shifting cultivation, and the maintenance of soil fertility. In: *Symposium on Potential Productivity of Field Crops Under Different Environments*. 22–26 September 1980, I.R.R.I., Los Banos, Philippines. International Rice Research Institute.

Hinton, P. (1978). Declining production among sedentary swidden cultivators: the case of Pwo Karen. In: *Farmers in the forest* (Ed. by P. Kunstadter, E. C. Chapman & S. Sabhasri). University Press of Hawaii, Honolulu. pp. 185–198.

Hoare, P., Nuglar, S. & Panichporn, S. (unpublished manuscript). *A Subsistence Rice Model for Northern Thailand.*

Jenkinson, D.S. (1981). The nitrogen cycle in long-term field experiments. Philosophical Transactions of the Royal Society, London, Series B, **296,** 563–571.

Kunstadter, P. (1978). Subsistence agricultural economies of Lua' and Karen hill farmers, Mae Sariang District, North-western Thailand. In: *Farmers in the forest* (Ed. by P. Kunstadter, E. C. Chapman & S. Sabhasri). University Press of Hawaii, Honolulu. pp. 74–130.

Lamb, D. (1980). Soil nitrogen mineralization in a secondary rain forest succession. *Oecologia (Berl.)*, **47,** 257–263.

Lambert, J.D.H. & Arnason, J.T. (1982). *Traditional Milpa Agriculture in Belize.* Discussion paper 824, Institute for International Co-operation, University of Ottawa, Ontario, Canada.

Major, R. (1974). Nitrogen accumulation in successions. In: *Handbook of vegetation science. Part VIII. Vegetation dynamics* (Ed. by R. Knapp) W. Junk, Hague. pp. 217–223.

Nakano, K. (1978). An Ecological Study of Swidden Agriculture at a village in Northern Thailand. *South East Asian Studies*, **16**(3), 411–446.

Nguu, N.V. & Corpuz, E.B. (1979). *Resources, production activities and financial status of a Kaingin farm.* Paper presented at the Vth International Symposium on Tropical Ecology, 16–21 April 1979, University of Malaysia, Kuala Lumpur.

PESAM (1982). *Buhi Lalo's Partners in Upland Development.* PESAM Bulletin II, Program on Environmental Science and Management, U.P. Los Banos, Philippines. pp. 6–7.

Ruthenberg, H. (1976). *Farming systems in the tropics.* Clarendon Press, Oxford.

Sabhasri, S. (1978). Effects of forest fallow cultivation on forest production and soil. In: *Farmers in the forest* (Ed. by P. Kunstadter, E. C. Chapman & S. Sabhasri). University of Hawaii, Honolulu. pp. 160–184.

Sanchez, P. (1976). *Properties and management of soils in the tropics.* Wiley, Chichester and New York.

Sanchez, P.A. (1977). *Advances in the management of oxisols and ultisols in tropical South America.* Proc. Int. Seminar on Soil Environment and Fertility Management in Intensive Agriculture. Soc. Sci. Soil and Manure, Tokyo, Japan. pp. 535–566.

Thiagalingam, K. & Famy, F.N. (1981). The role of *Casuarina* under shifting cultivation — a preliminary study. In: *Nitrogen Cycling in South-East Asian Wet Monsoonal Ecosystems* (Ed. by R. Wetselaar, J. R. Simpson & T. Rosswall). Australian Academy of Science, Canberra. pp. 154–155.

UNESCO/UNEP/FAO (1978). *Tropical forest ecosystems: a state-of-knowledge report.* Natural Resources Research XIV. UNESCO, Paris.
Watson, E.R. (1969). The influence of subterranean clover pastures on soil fertility. III. The effect of applied phosphorus and sulphur. Australian Journal of Agricultural Research, **20,** 447–456.
Watters, R.F. (1971). *Shifting Cultivation in Latin America.* Food and Agriculture Organization, Rome.
Zinke, P.J., Sabhasri, S. & Kunstadter, P. (1978). Soil fertility aspects of the Lua' forest fallow system of shifting cultivation. In: Farmers in the forest (Ed. by P. Kunstadter, E. C. Chapman & S. Sabhasri). University Press of Hawaii, Honolulu. pp. 134–159.

POSTER ABSTRACTS

1

Observations on a variety of habitats in Brunei and their relationship with the environment.
Benedict Allen, Pollards, Whiteleaf, Aylesbury, Bucks., U.K.

This work was carried out as a member of the Ulu Temburong Expedition 1981, when observations were made at a variety of invertebrate study sites concerning the nature of the invertebrates present and their relationship with the environment.

Differences in environmental processes operating at the sites (in Lowland Heath, Lower and Upper Diptercarp, and 'Moss Forest' Formations) emerge clearly when the sites are placed in relationship to each other. Changes with altitude are particularly apparent and the effects on soil and flora are shown to be very strong with increased depth of organic matter accumulation and occurrence of Moss Forest species with altitude being cited an example of this.

2

The Saturniidae of Borneo — moths of the primary rain-forest. Lt Col M. G. Allen,
33 Bridgefield, Farnham, Surrey, U.K.

Twenty species of Saturniidae which have been recorded in Borneo are illustrated, together with photographs of their habitat. All but one (*Attacus atlas*) appear to be dependent on primary rain-forest and are not usually found in secondary forest in Borneo.

3

The vertical distribution of flying insects in a lowland forest site in Panama. Caroline Ash[1]
and Stephen Sutton[2]; [1]Molteno Institute, University of Cambridge, CB2 3EE, and
[2]Department of Pure and Applied Zoology, University of Leeds, LS2 9JT, U.K.

A survey of the distribution of small flying insects in lowland primary forest was undertaken in relation to forest structure at several tropical sites. Results from Panama (08° 48′N, 77° 40′W) are described. Four ultra-violet light traps were suspended from an emergent tree, at 28, 18, 9 and 1 metres and operated from 21 January to 2 February 1979 at 1900 to 0700 hours.

The numbers of insects caught at each level were summarized as a total and analysed by taxonomic order and by family for a selection of representative groups. In most cases there was significant stratification ($p < 0.001$) although there was also high heterogeneity from night to night. Generally distributions concentrated in the upper canopy and were most clearly seen in the Lepidoptera Homoptera and Orthoptera. The Diptera and Trichoptera showed a marked abundance at ground level and the Ephemeroptera had an intermediate distribution, possibly a reflection of a riverine site. Other groups had a bimodal distribution, peaking in the canopy and near ground level, for example the Coleoptera. However, other groups did not conform to this pattern and it cannot be simply predicted that the bulk of flying insects will occur in the upper canopy since their distributions are influenced by forest structure and diversity and by climatic variation.

4

Offspring recruitment around neotropical trees: influence of fungal pathogens and light-gaps. Carol K. Augspurger, University of Illinois, Urbana, Illinois, U.S.A.

The spatial pattern of dispersed seeds and subsequent mortality of offspring determine recruitment distance relative to the parent tree. For isolated parents of the Panamanian tree, *Platypodium elegans* (Leguminosae), the distributions of wind-dispersed seeds were strongly skewed downwind. After 15–20 m the number of seeds declined steeply with increasing distance from the parent tree. The distribution of germinated seeds was concordant with that of dispersed seeds.

Damping-off by fungal pathogens caused the majority of seedling mortality. The incidence of damping-off was inversely correlated with distance from the parent tree and positively correlated with density of seedlings. Irrespective of density, a lower incidence of damping-off occurred in the light-gaps than in the shaded understorey. After three months the median distance of surviving seedlings was greater than that of germinated seeds. After one year the median distance either increased or decreased, depending on the location of light-gaps in which survival and growth were greatly enhanced. Saplings were further from the parent than either dispersed seeds or one-year-old seedlings. The results demonstrate the combined importance of fungal pathogens and light-gaps as factors contributing to the non-clumped distribution of adult trees of this species.

5

Seed predation by neotropical primates. J. M. C. Ayres and M. van Roosmalen, Sub-Department of Veterinary Anatomy, University of Cambridge, U.K.

Studies conducted on *Chiropotes albinasus* (in Aripuana River–Mt. Brazil), *Chiropotes satanas* and *Pithecia pithecia* (Northern Manaus, Brazil and Voltzberg Park, Surinam) have shown that these three species of the subfamily Pitheciinae have a considerable proportion on their diet consisting of young seeds and nuts mainly from plants of Sapotaceae, Lecythidaceae, Moraceae and Bignoniaceae. For occupying this niche they developed a distinctive dentition with well-developed canines, for opening the hard cover of immature fruits.

Chiropotes lives in multimale troops ranging from 15 to 30 individuals which forage as a unit in the upper and emergent levels of the undisturbed lowland forests in the Amazon basin. Its diet is complemented by mesocarps of mature fruits. *Pithecia* lives in monogamous groups, ranging from 2 to 4 individuals and foraging in lower and middle levels of lowland forest as well several other vegetation types within Amazonia. Its diet is supplemented by flowers, mature mesocarps and leaves.

Chiropotes and *Ateles* are both frugivores, having a similar group size and home range. As *Chiropotes* is a seed predator it can feed on fruits of different fruiting stages and that allows foraging as a unit. Although *Ateles* has similar basic ecological features they feed on ripe fruits which are not always available at the same time and that results in the peculiar 'fission–fusion' foraging pattern common to this genus which is an important seed disperser.

6

The 1981–82 Hull University Cameroon Expedition. R. G. Baker, S. G. Compton,
D. Newsome, K. Richards and C. Rimes (Hull University Departments of Geography
and Plant Biology) and S. Edwards (University Museum, Manchester), U.K.

Six main projects were undertaken during this three-month expedition which lasted from
November 1981 to January 1982.

1. A twelve-metre sediment core was extracted at Lake Mooandong and will be
analysed for it pollen contents.

2. Flowers were collected to augment modern pollen collections.

3. Mosses were obtained in order to assist in the preparation of the forthcoming
'Generic Moss Flora of West Africa'.

4. Fig wasps and associated insects were reared from *Ficus* species.

5. A study of soil micromorphology in the Bamenda Highlands.

6. Live epiphytic orchids were collected from montane regions for the Royal
Botanic Gardens, Kew.

7

Insect exploitation of ephemeral habitats. R. A. Beaver, School of Natural Resources,
The University of the South Pacific, P.O. Box 1168, Suva, Fiji.

Three types of ephemeral habitat — carrion, dung and dead wood — and the insect
communities that live in them, are compared in tropical and temperate regions. Many
similarities are evident both among habitats and regions, and differences tend to be
quantitative rather than qualitative. The habitats form more or less discrete units
characterized by patchiness, transience and changeability, characters which cause problems for the exploiting insects, particularly in the tropics where heterogeneity is greater
and decay faster.

The communities are dominated by Diptera (carrion), Coleoptera (dead wood) or
both (dung), and are rich in species, but each habitat unit contains only a small fraction of
them. Species richness on a regional scale increases (*c.* 2×) in the tropics, but less than
the number of species providing habitat units. Colonization of the units and successional
changes within them are faster in the tropics. A regular succession of guilds usually
occurs, but detailed successional paths depend on a variety of factors including a
stochastic element in colonization. The communities can never reach equilibrium on the
scale of the habitat unit.

The coexistence of numerous species in habitats in which competition is both frequent
and intense can be related in part to resource partitioning in several habitat dimensions,
but habitat patchiness, aggregative behaviour and priority effects also seem to be
important. There seems to be no limiting similarity between species.

Life history strategies are related in the adult stage to the need to find and colonize
patchily distributed, transient, habitat units. Adaptations which help to reduce the
environmental heterogeneity apparent to the insect are particularly evident in tropical
insects, and include polyphagy, spanandry, phoresy on dung producers, and the use of
more regularly renewed habitat units such as *Nepenthes* pitchers or fallen leafstalks.

(during The Royal Geographical Society/Sarawak Government Gn. Mulu Expedition). The material consists of *c.* 170 species and 21 700 individuals. Species richness was highest in the alluvial forest and the mixed dipterocarp forest below 200 m; kerangas (heath forest) and limestone forest had species-poor communities; and species richness decreased steadily with increasing altitude on the sandstone mountain Mulu. Very few species were caught from the summit (2376 m). The lowland and montane communities were distinct in their species composition, and the lower montane community was intermediate, though some species occurred exclusively in the LMF. Species turn-over amongst the 22 abundant montane species included more elevational replacements by congeners (10) than one would have expected by chance ($4\cdot5\pm1\cdot5$, mean$\pm$SD), which suggests some form of interspecific interaction (both exploitative competition and problems in species recognition probably played a role). Species number out of the 22 abundant ones remained constant at 7–8 between 500 and 2000 m, although in the total material species richness decreased with altitude.

30

Treefall gap frequency in two co-occuring tropical forests and its impact on species diversity. Terese and John Hart, Epulu Project, Zaïre, P.O. Box 21285, Nairobi, Kenya.

In the Ituri region of Zaïre two forest types co-occur without edaphic boundaries. The mixed forest, which has a higher species diversity, also has a higher rate of treefall gap formation. The average gap size is also larger in mixed forest than in the single species dominant 'Mbau' forest.

Species diversity is maintained through natural disturbance by:

(a) differential survival of shade intolerant 'pioneer' species,

(b) release of tree seedlings of limited shade tolerance.

Although the same array of about ten pioneer tree species germinate in the gaps of both forests, only the quickest growing of these species mature in the Mbau Forest. Also, a greater abundance of slow growing, partially shade tolerant, species are able to mature in mixed forest, presumably due to the more frequent canopy openings.

31

Species diversity patterns in moth communities of Papua New Guinea. Paul D. N. Herbert[1] and Rudolf Harmsen[2]; [1]Biology Department, University of Windsor, Windsor, N9B 3P4, and [2]Biology Department, Queen's University, Kingston, Ontario, Canada.

Macrolepidopterans have been sampled using UV light at a number of undisturbed sites from sea level to 3400 m in Papua New Guinea. Species diversities peak at approximately 1000 m and decline with altitudinal increase or decrease. Repeated sampling of one transect indicated that, at least in the montane zone (2000–3000 m), species diversities are stable seasonally and that there is little change in species assemblages during the year. Furthermore, the altitudinal ranges of individual moth species are well defined: hill-topping seems unimportant. Comparative studies reveal that the diversity statistic α provides a better indication of diversity shifts than the Shannon-Weaver or Simpson indices. At the sites with highest diversity more than 1500 species of moths fly in a single evening. Diversity analysis indicates that the abundance of species in these very diverse communities are more equitable than expected on the basis of Preston's canonical hypothesis.

32

Floral biology of Brownea rosa-de-monte. *P. J. Hudson[1] and A. M. Sugden[2]; [1]Mews House, Askrigg, Wensleydayle, Yorkshire, U.K., and [2]Botany School, Downing Street, Cambridge, U.K.

The floral biology of *Brownea rosa-de-monte* (Leguminosae), an understorey tree, was studied in the San Blas region of Panama. Trees produce red capitate inflorescences which survive for just one day. Production of inflorescences tends to be synchronized within localized groups. Detailed observations were conducted to determine how flower presentation influences the number of visits made by the hummingbird *Phaethornis superciliosus*. Large inflorescences were visited more than small ones but the number of visits per flower was greatest when there were approximately 25 flowers per inflorescence and this corresponds to the mean size. Nectar flow decreased during the day and was influenced by interference from stingless bees and lepidopteran larvae.
*See also Ibis 1984 Vol. 126 no. 3.

33

Effects of habitat disturbance on a Malayan forest community. A. D. Jones, E. B. M. Barrett and D. J. Chivers, Sub-Department of Veterinary Anatomy, University of Cambridge, U.K.

Commercial logging affects all members of a forest community. Drastic habitat alteration to provide land for agricultural use or for plantation forestry is normally incompatible with rain-forest conservation. Selective removal of timber trees, however, seems to permit the survival of a forest community, if in a somewhat altered form. Alterations in forest structure and tree species composition are reflected in the range of niches available to animal species. There is variation in survival rates and adaptation to these changes: different species may not survive in logged forest, may remain in reduced numbers, or may increase in numbers.

34

Chorisia speciosa *St Hill. (Bombacaceae) an example of the complexity of the flooding tolerance mechanisms in tropical trees.* C. A. Joly and R. M. M. Crawford, Botany Department, University of St Andrews, Fife, Scotland, U.K.

Chorisia speciosa does not occur naturally in flood prone areas of Brazil. Nevertheless, its seedlings are able to survive and grow in waterlogged conditions. Flooding induces metabolic and morpho-anatomic responses. The immediate response is a change in the respiratory metabolism of the root system, but the long-term response also involves the development of hypertrophic lenticels and cortical aerenchyma in the shoot area just above water table level. This combination of responses results in an acceleration of glycolysis, to compensate for the low energy yield of the anaerobic metabolism, together with an improvement of the ventilation system so that oxygen diffuses down and the potentially toxic products, such as ethanol, can be readily removed.

35

Present status of the mangrove forests of Bangladesh. Ansarul Karim and Azim U. Mallik, Department of Chittagong, Bangledesh.

Although Bangladesh is invested with the world's largest mangrove forest, very little is known about the ecology of these forests. It is believed the *Heritiera fomes* is the dominant plant in the forests. Due to various demographic and allogenic factors, the dominance of the species is declining. Increasing pressure for fuel, timber, agriculture and industry is resulting in the destruction of these forests. On the other hand large areas of newly accreted land masses raised in the Bay of Bengal are being planted with mangrove plants with the objects of increasing the rate of accretion and consolidating newly accreted lands along the coastal belt.

The multiple use of the mangrove areas and the resulting environmental impact demands sound management and disposition of these natural resources. Little is known of the effects of natural and man-induced pressures on mangroves in Bangladesh. The research programme for determining environmental effects on mangrove habitats includes the study of the biological impact of various land uses, hydrodynamics, erosion, sedimentation rates, habitat alteration, rate of land accretion or subsidence and impact of pollutants. The studies may also include (1) Influence of various factors including plantation technique on the establishment of mangrove species plantations. (2) Storage and germination of selected mangrove species. (3) Ecophysiological studies on 'die-back' of *Heritiera fomes.*

A major problem confronting mangrove management is the lack of proper co-ordination between the various agencies of policy makers and between policy makers and mangrove researchers.

36

Source and fate of tree species in mixed dipterocarp forest East Kalimantan, Indonesia.
J. B. Kenworthy and S. Riswan, Department of Botany, University of Aberdeen, Scotland, U.K.

As part of a larger study, species of trees, saplings and seedlings in plots of primary (1·6 ha) and secondary (0·8 ha) forests were enumerated. The plots contained 209 and 121 canopy tree species respectively but the total number of tree species at all stages was 250 and 184. In the primary forest plot 25 species in the seedling stage are not present in the mature trees which suggests that they are invaders from the surrounding plot. The total number of species at tree, sapling and seedling levels are 209, 106 and 109 respectively containing 4, 5 and 6% secondary species. None of the secondary species in the tree canopy are present in the seedling or sapling stages. In the secondary forest the species at tree, sapling and seedling stages are 121, 58 and 77 respectively. Of these the secondary species represent 30, 24 and 17%. After 35 years there are 73 of the primary forest plot tree species found in the secondary forest. Results suggest that species diversity is very high even after 35 years recovery but the replacement of secondary by primary species has some way to develop even at the seedling stage.

37

Sex expression in an understorey Sterculia — *some observations under experimental conditions.* Kwiton Jong, Michael D. Swaine and Luong Tan Tuoc — Institute of South-East Asian Biology and Department of Botany, University of Aberdeen, Scotland, U.K.

Sterculia longifolia f. longifolia Vent. occurs in primary and secondary rain forests of Sumatra, Java and Kalimantan. Under tropical greenhouse conditions in Aberdeen University, plants flowered about four years from seed.

Observations based on three plants with respect to sex expression and floral longevity indicate that the flowers in an individual can initially be either predominantly male or bisexual (though functionally female) or a varible mixture of both types within the same inflorescence. Male flowers are shed 2–3 days after anthesis, while bisexual unpollinated ones generally remain longer on the inflorescence, 5–7 days. The ratio of male to bisexual flowers varies with successive flowering periods, but it is not yet clear whether this is related to intrinsic or environmental factors, or to their combined effects.

A striking difference in pollen quality between male and bisexual flowers has also been observed: the pollen of male flowers are fertile, the grains remaining discrete and germinate readily in a culture solution, whereas those of bisexual flowers are largely empty and distorted, occurring in clumps, and showing poor germination.

While the variability of sex expression observed in cultivated specimens of *S. longifolia* presents some difficulty with categorization of its sexuality, experimental pollinations indicate that the plants maybe self-incompatible and outbreeding.

Further observations are being undertaken, but ultimately a fuller understanding must come from field studies. *S. longifolia* (and possibly many other Sterculias) clearly deserves closer investigation in the study of sexual differentiation among tropical rain-forest angiosperms.

38

Occurrence and distribution of Syzygium sp. Andrew J. Lack, Department of Botany and Microbiology, University College, Swansea, U.K.

The tree, *Syzygium syzygioides* (Miq.) Merrill & Perry (Myrtaceae) is a common canopy and emergent species in lowland forests in eastern Sulawesi, Indonesia. In an area of alluvial forest all individuals of *S. syzygioides* over 1 m high were mapped in 100 metres square (one hectare). The circumference of each at breast height was measured. The resultant map included 527 individuals of which ten were large mature flowering trees. The great majority were seedlings and small saplings. They exhibited a significantly clumped distribution but with very few seedlings within 5 m of the adult trees, where most of the fruits fall. Most young trees occurred 10 m or more away from the adult trees. It is concluded that *S. syzygioides* is a shade tolerant species with limited dispersal powers, and is likely to increase in abundance if disturbance to the forest is kept to a minimum. It may not become dominant owing to lack of regeneration under the parent trees.

39

Conservation by domestication — the West African hardwood improvement project. R. R. B. Leakey and K. A. Longman, Institute of Terrestrial Ecology, Penicuik, Midlothian, Scotland, EH26 0QB, U.K.

Tropical forest is being destroyed at 50 ha. min^{-1}, so what will be the future for human populations and wildlife in the tropics? If, as proposed in the Man and Biosphere programme, 10% of tropical forest is conserved, what will happen to the remaining 90% of the land? Suggestions for mitigating the probably harsh consequences of these rapid trends must include collaboration by foresters and agriculturalists, with emphasis on the domestication of a wider range of species, particularly trees, with untapped economic potential. Thus a greater diversity of improved crop plants would underpin the agrisilvicultural systems currently being developed throughout the tropics. Domestication involves conserving genetic resources, propagating individual genotypes with desirable or promising qualities, inducing flowering and breeding or selecting for further improvements to yield, quality or pest tolerance. I.T.E., in collaboration with the Forestry Research Institute of Nigeria (funded by ODM), have carried out an eight-year project (W.A.H.I.P.) on *Triplochiton scleroxylon*, and it is currently proposed to extend research to include the mahoganies and other high-quality African timber trees. Preliminary tests have already shown that many species are amenable to vegetative propagation, and so trees producing many different forest products could be similarly domesticated. The growth of these, on a commercial basis, under different mixed-cropping regimes of varying intensity would considerably aid the maintenance of soil fertility and could assist in the conservation of much of the wildlife struggling to survive in areas where tropical forest has been replaced by ecosystems in which species diversity has been severely reduced for a variety of reasons. Here the 10% of conserved forests will be important for numerous studies of natural ecosystem functioning, for example on reproductive behaviour.

40

Seasonality and foliage phenology at Pinkwae, Ghana. Diana Lieberman and Milton Lieberman, Department of Biology, University of North Dakota, Grand Forks, ND 58202 U.S.A.

The forest studied, Pinkwae, is a 120 ha patch of undisturbed dry forest on the Accra Plains. Rainfall is low (1100 mm yr^{-1}) and highly seasonal in its distribution, with wet seasons in March–June and September–November.

Leaf phenology of 59 species in the forest and surrounding thicket were assessed every 10 days over a 28-month period. Leaf production occurred only in wet seasons, although not all species or individuals produced new flushes of leaves in each wet season.

Leaf fall occurred only in dry seasons; 19% of forest species and 55% of thicket species became fully leafless during the study period.

Major damage to leaves by herbivorous insects was generally restricted to newly flushed leaves. Approximately 13% of leaf cohorts produced were badly damaged by insects. The duration of flushing within a population influenced the probability of flush damage by insects; those which produced leaves over a long period had a greater chance of sustaining damage, while short flushing periods led to greater flush survivorship. Loss of flushes to insects was reduced in species with hairy leaves, and in species rich in presumptive secondary defence compounds.

41

Old world fruit bats as pollinators of tropical plants. Adrian G. Marshall, Institute of South-East Asian Biology, University of Aberdeen, Scotland, U.K.

The bats, Order Chiroptera, are divided into two suborders, the Megachiroptera and Microchiroptera, the first containing a single family, the Pteropodidae or Old World fruit bats, whose members are entirely frugivorous or nectarivorous. The majority of pteropodids (subfamily Pteropodinae) feed largely upon fruit but may sometimes visit flowers to take nectar and pollen; a minority (subfamily Macroglossinae) feed exclusively upon floral resources. Bats which visit flowers may effect pollination.

In West Malaysia there are twelve species of Pteropodinae and three of Macroglossinae. Of the latter, the two *Macroglossus* species roost singly in trees and fly short distances to feed upon trees which continually produce a few flowers throughout the year; in contrast *Eonycteris spelaea* roosts in huge colonies in caves, can fly at least 35 km from the cave to feed, and takes resources from many species of flowers which are widely scattered both in space and time. Malaysian Pteropodinae also visit flowers but we know little about this feeding strategy. In Ghana, we are largely ignorant about the feeding biology of the single Macroglossinae. *Megaloglossus woermanni*, a forest species, but we know a fair amount about the biology of some of the twelve species of Pteropodinae, which can be important pollinators of certain plants.

This poster displays some work undertaken in the last ten years, illustrates aspects of co-evolution between flowers and Old World fruit bats, and raises some questions which need answering.

42

An application of the point-centered quarter method in a phytosociological study of a semi-deciduous forest in the state of São Paulo, Brazil. F. R. Martins, Universidada Estadual de Campinas, Campinas, S.P., Brazil

The point-centred quarter method was used to study the floristic composition and the phytosociological structure of a forest area in the Vassununga State Park, in south-eastern Brazil (21° 43'S and 47° 35'W). One thousand trees were sampled, with 926 live trees, belonging to 33 families, 70 genera and 92 species. Thirty-two species accounted for 75% of the total IVI. The survey indicated that the structure of the semi-deciduous forests in the interior of the state of São Paulo is much more similar to that of tropical lowland forest than to that of temperate forests. This was in sharp contrast to the considerable floristic differences between this forest and the Amazonian lowland forests.

43

†‡Regeneration in French Guyana II: regrowth on a 25 ha experimental paper-clear-felling (ARBOCEL). Gema Maury-Lechon.

After logging (July–August 1976) 40% of the biomass remains on the parcel of which 10% surface had been compacted or overrun. In October two fires cross Arbocel: 15% of ground surface is strongly burnt and 20% covered by logs and crowns.

As early as June 1977 the main characteristic species of this region regrowth developed a mosaic pattern of scattered vegetation with apparent naked soil. They

disperse the *Cecropia* fruits over larger areas than bats do. Tanagers refuse most fruits during mandibulation of the piece and the phyllostomids destroy much fruit by thorough mastication of the pulp but on the whole, the latter agents ingest more fruits than the birds do. Seed germination success in experiments done with fruits obtained from faeces produced the following results: birds (32%), bats (78%), and controls (85%). Our results suggest that several behavioural features of foraging and actual feeding by the supposed dispersal agents should be observed to ascertain their efficiency to a plant population.

63

Floristic composition and structure in the Atlantic rain-forest of São Paulo State, Brazil. A. F. da Silva and H. F. Leitão, Universidade Estadual de Campinas, Campinas, S.P., Brazil.

A study was made of an area of seasonal rain-forest, on a mountain slope at 23° 27′S and 45° 04′W in municipality of Ubatuba, São Paulo state. The point-centred quarter method was used for the floristic survey and 640 trees with a minimum diameter of 10 cm were scored. Forty-one families, 87 genera and 123 species were sampled in the area, and the most important families were: Euphorbiaceae (96,7), Lauraceae (39,12), Leguminosae (36,10), Myrtaceae (33,16), Palmae (79,4), and Rubiaceae (98,16), the numbers in parenthesis showing the number of individuals and the number of species in each case. The diversity of the area is comparable with some areas of Amazonian 'terre firme' forest, but the floristic composition is quite different from the latter. Three rather ill-defined strata could be distinguished.

64

A comparison of floristic composition in various Brazilian forest types using cluster analysis. A. F. da Silva and G. J. Sheperd, Universidade Estadual de Campinas, Campinas, S.P., Brazil.

A numerical comparison of various Brazilian forest types, with special emphasis on the Atlantic Coastal Rain-forest, was made using cluster analysis. The comparison was made at generic level, using the Jaccard coefficient (Sj) and average linkage. Five areas of coastal rain-forest and composite samples to represent the Amazonian 'terra firme' forest and the South-east Brazilian 'planalto' forests were included. The results obtained suggest that the Brazilian Coastal rain-forest is very heterogeneous in composition and that some parts of this formation are more similar to other Brazilian forest types than to those of the Amazonian area. The higher altitude rain-forest of the mountainous areas near Rio de Janeiro appears to have a very distinct floristic composition in comparison with the lower altitude Atlantic rain-forest.

65

Floristic composition and structure in an upland semi-deciduous forest in south-east Brazil (Poços de Caldas, Minas Gerais). A. F. da Silva and G. J. Shepherd, Dept° de Morfologia e Sistemática Vegetais, Universidade Estadual de Campinas, Campinas, S.P., Brazil.

Floristic composition and community structure were studied in an area of upland semi-deciduous forest in a mountainous region of south-eastern Minas Gerais. The point-centred quarter method was used with one size class per point (DBH $\geq$ 5 cm) and 250 points with 1000 individuals included in the study. Floristically, this forest is rather different from those of the 'planalto' and the coastal rain-forest of the state of São Paulo. The family Lauraceae is well represented here, whereas very few Leguminosae were present. This is the reverse of the trend usually found in the semi-deciduous forests of the state of São Paulo. Structurally, the forest shows somewhat greater dominance than the lower elevation 'planalto' forests, but still falls within the high diversity syndrome of tropical rather than temperate forests.

66

Floristic composition and structure of a semi-deciduous forest in south-east Brazil, (Campinas, São Paulo). A. F. da Silva and G. J. Shepherd, Dept° de Morfologia e Sistēmática Vegetais, Universidade Estadual de Campinas, Campinas, S.P., Brazil.

Floristic composition and community structure were studied in a semi-deciduous forest of the 'planalto' region in south-eastern Brazil using the point-centred quarter method. Two size classes were sampled at each point (height $\geq$ 2 m and DBH < 10 cm : DBH $\geq$ 10 cm) and 180 points (8 individuals per point) were included in the study. Distributions of tree heights indicated a weakly-defined stratification and possibly three strata. Diversity indices and species/area relations show patterns similar to those found in Amazonian rain-forests, except that a somewhat greater degree of dominance was found in the present study. Floristic composition, however, was quite distinct from that found in Brazilian rain-forests.

67

Floristic composition and spatial structure of a riparian forest in south-east Brazil (Mogi Guaçu, São Paulo). W. H. Stubblebine[1], G. J. Shepherd[1] and P. E. Gibbs[2]; [1]Universidade Estadual de Campinas, Campinas, S.P., Brazil, and [2]University of St Andrews, Fife, Scotland, U.K.

Floristic composition and community structure were studied in a riparian forest in the interior of the state of São Paulo, Brazil. Within a 1·5-hectare plot, all trees with DBH 10 cm were mapped and identified. Ninety species were recorded in the plot. Floristic composition in this area was quite distinct from that found in nearby semi-deciduous forests. The map shows that several species present a highly clumped spatial distribution and that certain groups of species show a high degree of association. Diversity indices and species area relations show that the structure of the riparian forest is similar to that of the nearby semi-deciduous forests and much closer to the high diversity syndrome of the equatorial lowland rain-forests than to forest of temperate regions.

68

Leaf dynamics in tropical forest trees. M. D. Swaine[1], the late J. B. Hall[2] and Diana Liebermann[2]; [1]Institute of South-east Asian Biology and Departmental of Botany, University of Aberdeen, Scotland, U.K., and [2]Biology Department, University of North Dakota, U.S.A.

Leaf production, predation and mortality were studied in a species-poor dry forest under low rainfall in Ghana.

1. There were large differences in leaf longevity between species, varying between 1–2 months for the canopy liane *Grewia carpinifolia*, to probably three years or more in the understorey tree *Drypetes parvifolia*.

2. Understorey species, and shade leaves of canopy trees, retained their leaves for longer periods.

3. Leaf production and mortality were both correlated with moisture conditions in many species, especially those with short-lived leaves. Understorey (shade tolerant) species, especially *Drypetes*, were less responsive to changes in moisture conditions.

4. In all species, leaf damage (principally predation by lepidoptera larvae) was confined to the earliest stages in the life of a leaf, during flushing and before full maturation.

5. More heavily damaged leaves were more likely to be lost, and thus were generally shorter-lived.

The variation observed has close parallels with the *r–K* continuum: *Grewia* — fast-growing, shade intolerant, early flowering, responsive to moisture stress and with lightweight, short-lived leaves; *Drypetes* — slow-growing, shade tolerant, unresponsive to water stress, and with robust, long-lived leaves.

69

The management of mountain resorts in Malaysia. Noraini Mohd, Tamin, Unit Botani, Universiti Kebangsaan, Malaysia.

The montane environment of the tropical rain-forest is ecologically complex, supporting dynamic microhabitats and communities. The flora is acidophilic, hydrophilic and calcifuge. Plant communities on the forest floor are generally skiophytic and these are among the first to perish when a mountain resort is being developed.

There are four mountain resorts in Malaysia. Two of these, the Cameron Highlands, noted for its tea plantations, and the Kinabalu National Park, for its majestic mountain, are relatively well developed. These resorts are state properties and are fairly well managed. However, Genting Highlands, situated at the Pahang–Selangor border, in a water catchment zone, has been ecologically mismanaged. Extensive areas of montane forest near the summit have been cleared, resulting in severe soil erosion, pollution of rivers and disturbance of habitats and species composition. Incidentally this resort belongs to a private developer. Therefore it is evident that the government should undertake environmental impact studies before approving the development of mountain resorts. Once established strict checks should be carried out to ensure that the resorts are satisfactorily managed. This is to prevent the destruction of the montane ecosystem, which once destroyed, may activate chains of environmental pollution in habitats lower down the mountain.

70

*Tree fern demography**. E. V. J. Tanner, The Botany School, Downing Street, Cambridge, U.K.

I enumerated all the *Cyathea pubescens* in 1000 m² of Jamaican Upper Montane Rain-forest (130 in total) and I made a detailed study of the growth of 42 medium-sized individuals (mean height 188 cm).

The height stand table (numbers of individuals in height classes) show an approximately equal number in most size classes except the smallest which has large numbers. The total number of leaf scars on a trunk is well correlated with the total height of the trunk. The rate of leaf production in the group of 42 medium-sized tree ferns was 0·56 leaves per individual per 30 days (measured over 953 days) with higher rates of leaf production correlated with periods of increased rainfall.

From the data on the rate of leaf production and the number of leaf scars per individual an estimate of age, for that individual, can be calculated. The results suggest that a 1 m *C. pubescens* is *c.* 45 years old, a 4 m *C. pubescens c.* 120 years old and the tallest at *c.* 9 m are *c.* 240 years old.

Recruitment to the population seems to be approximately continuous because of the evenness of the size and age classes. The estimated mean age for a *C. pubescens* taller than 40 cm is *c.* 120 years old, a figure very similar to the turnover time of trees > 10 cm girth at breast height in the same site.

*see also *Bot J. Linn. Soc.* (1983), **87**, 213–227.

71

Floral biology and breeding system of Sterculia chicha *St Hil.* Neusa Taroda[1] and P. E. Gibbs[2]; [1]Departamento de Botanica, Unicamp, CxP 1170, Campinas 13.100 Brazil, and [2]Department of Botany, The University, St Andrews, Fife, KY16 9AL.

The neotropical, monoecious, forest species *Sterculia chicha* has been shown to have flowers which are adapted for pollination by Diptera, such as medium-sized species of the sapromyophilous genera *Acroglossa*, *Cochliomya*, *Gaemnochaetopsis*, *Ornidia* and *Parasarcophaga*. Controlled pollination experiments show that the species is self-incompatible. The fact that the pollen tubes grow to the ovules following both compatible and incompatible pollinations suggests that the incompatibility mechanism is based on the non-fusion of gametes in the embryo sac, as in the 'Theobroma-type', originally known only in the related *Theobroma cacao*.

72

Comments on the origin of secondary flora trees. C. Vazquez-Yanes and S. Guevara, Dept°. de Botanica, Institutade Biologia, U.N.A.M., Apartado 70–233 Deleg, Coyoacan C.U., Mexico.

A revision is made of existing knowledge on the ecology, distribution and origin of the fast growing, short living pioneer trees of Tropical Rain-forest. This group of plants is adapted to both natural and human disturbances.

73

Quantitative techniques for systematic sampling of the herpetofaunal community of a wet tropical rain-forest. Richard C. Vogt, Estación de Biologia 'Los Tuxtlas'. Instituto de Biologia, U.N.A.M., Apart. Post. 94, San Andres Tuxtla, Veracruz, Mexico.

Traditionally most herpetofaunal surveys in tropical areas depended on hand capture. Due to the differential abilities of the various species to elude their captors either by agility, crypsis, or living in areas difficult to sample — fossorial or arboreal habitats — often the relative abundances obtained are inaccurate and even the presence of some species goes unrecorded. Also the abilities of herpetologists are hard to standardize. Destructive sampling, removal of all the vegetation in an area, allows one to obtain accurate estimates of the species composition and population levels of those species, but has the obvious disadvantage of destroying the habitat you wish to study. An alternative method using terrestrial drift fences with a combination of pitfall traps and funnel traps provides a systematic means to compare the herpetofaunal composition in forests of different ages without the drawbacks of the other methods. Also 'aerial drift-fences' in conjunction with funnel traps allow one to sample the species composition at different levels in the canopy without having to pull the canopy down.

Species composition and population levels are compared for the herpetofauna of a virgin rain-forest, secondary growth, and recently cleared areas using drift fences, in southern Veracruz, Mexico.

74

The avifaunal component of a simplified tropical food web. Robert B. Waide, Center for Energy and Environment Research, Caparra Heights Station, San Juan, Puerto Rico, 00935, U.S.A.

Thirty-six species of birds are involved in the food web in a subtropical wet forest at 450 m elevation in Puerto Rico, and 10 of these are so rare as to be unimportant. The avifaunal component of this island food web is much reduced compared to the mainland New World tropics, with a disproportionate reduction in resident insectivores. Eight (47%) of the resident birds are frugivorous while only three (18%) are primarily insectivorous. There are two nectarivores, three predators on vertebrates, and a single species that preys on vertebrates and invertebrates about equally. Nine winter-resident parulid warblers are almost entirely insectivorous. The scarcity of resident insectivorous birds is correlated with high densities of insectivorous frogs (*Eleutherodactylus* spp.) and lizards (*Anolis* spp.), but a causal relationship has not been shown and awaits further study. An analysis of the structure of the food web shows that there are few components with complex interconnections.

75

Host-plant relationships of Panamanian psylloidea (Homoptera). I. M. White, N.C.C., 12, Hope Terrace, Edinburgh, Scotland, U.K.

Psyllids (Homoptera, Psylloidea) are usually oligophagous, with their restricted range of host-plants belonging to one genus or at most one family of dicotyledons. Furthermore, closely related species of most psyllid groups tend to live on closely related plants. On a recent visit to Panama, I. D. Hodkinson and I. M. White identified the host relationships of about 30 spp. (tabulated) out of almost 100 species so far discovered in that country. These host relationships were found to be very similar to those of related species known from other tropical areas. This sort of data is a prerequisite for detailed ecological research and will hopefully be of value to some current studies of rain-forest Homoptera in Panama. Several interesting forms of psyllid-plant attack were observed (illustrations) and the majority of psyllid species found were associated with leguminous trees and shrubs.

76

Tropical rain-forest in Sri Lanka. R. A. Wijewansa, 33, Athula Mawatha, Mount Lavinia, Sri Lanka.

The Sinharaja forest is situated in the south-western part of the Island of Sri Lanka and is the last of the country's primeval tropical rain-forests of any significant size. As it stands today it extends over about 9000 hectares. The elevation varies from about 150 to 300 m and the terrain is one of parallel strike ridges, in the valleys of which arise tributaries of two major river systems.

As is true for tropical rain-forest, Sinharaja is also very much an unknown quantity. In 1972 the axeman suddenly appeared — none other than the Government which wanted the timber extracted to feed a giant plywood complex then running under capacity.

A concerted effort by interested conservationists from different walks of life to prevent its destruction, saw success four years later after a part of the area had been logged.

This victory encouraged the commencement of a series of studies on different aspects of the ecology of the forest and has led scientists to very interesting findings. The research is being done by scientific personnel from the Universities of Peradeniya and Colombo and the entire forest has been set aside for posterity and now is a component under UNESCO's Man and Biosphere Programme.

SPECIES INDEX

See also the lists of species on pp. 28–9, 32–3, 34–5, 37, 39, 40, 49, 56–7, 61, 85–101, 120, 131–2, 158, 164